Praise for

CIRCLING THE SACRED MOUNTAIN

"THIS EXTRAORDINARY BOOK IS A DREAM COME TRUE. WHO WOULD NOT WISH TO BE TAKEN ON PILGRIMAGE TO THE HOLIEST MOUNTAIN IN THE WORLD BY A GOLDEN-TONGUED GIANT OF A TEACHER? IT IS NOT THE ALTITUDE THAT TAKES OUR BREATH AWAY AS WE READ, IT IS THE LIVING FORCE OF PROFESSOR THURMAN'S DHARMA. BY HIS OWN EXAMPLE, HE MAKES US SEE THAT IT IS INDEED POSSIBLE TO GO TO PIECES WITHOUT FALLING APART."
—Mark Epstein, M.D., author of *Going to Pieces Without Falling Apart*

"TIBETAN BUDDHISM HAS RECENTLY BECOME FASHIONABLE IN THE WEST . . . BUT THURMAN AND WISE GO BEYOND THE BUZZ TO DEMONSTRATE THAT IT IS ALSO A RELIGION RICH IN HISTORY AND TEACHING, COMPLEX IN MYTH AND STORY . . . THE TALE OF THIS PILGRIMAGE— PART HIGH ADVENTURE, PART BUDDHIST INSTRUCTION—IS CERTAIN TO EMPOWER AND INSPIRE READERS ON THEIR OWN SPIRITUAL ADVENTURES."
—*New Age*

"PILGRIMAGE IS A TIMELESS SPIRITUAL PRACTICE, A WAY TO TRANSFORM OURSELVES AND AWAKEN TO THE NATURAL HOLINESS OF LIFE. GO ON THIS SPIRITUAL ADVENTURE WITH ONE OF OUR PREEMINENT TIBETAN TOUR GUIDES, WISE BOB, AND HIS FRIEND AND FELLOW PILGRIM, TAD. TAKE UP THIS BOOK; CIRCUMAMBULATE THIS HOLY POWER PLACE. JOIN THE SACRED CIRCLE."
—Lama Surya Das, author of *Awakening the Buddha Within* and *Awakening to the Sacred*

D0004168

"FOR BELIEVERS OR THOSE WHO WANT TO DELVE DEEPLY INTO TIBETAN BUDDHISM, *CIRCLING THE SACRED MOUNTAIN* MAY BE A GODSEND."
—*The Washington Post Book World*

"ONLY THURMAN, WITH HIS DEEP UNDERSTANDING OF TIBETAN CULTURE AND SPIRITUALITY, CAN CONVEY TO WESTERNERS SUCH A RICH AND STRIKING VISION OF THE DHARMA THAT IS INSEPARABLE FROM THE LAND AND PEOPLE OF TIBET . . . THE READER GETS NOT ONLY AN EXCITING ACCOUNT OF TREKKING THROUGH A LONG-FORBIDDEN LAND, BUT A PRIMER ON TIBETAN BUDDHISM AND THE PATH TO ENLIGHTENMENT."
—*The Bloomsbury Review*

"THIS IS NO MERE TALE OF A TREK. DEEP BUDDHIST WISDOM, DRIVEN FROM THE HIMALAYAS BY BLIND ARROGANCE, HAS BEEN GIVEN NO CHOICE BUT TO SEARCH THE WORLD FOR NEW HEARTS AND HOMES. TO EMBRACE THIS BOOK, TO CIRCLE ITS RADIANT INNER MOUNTAIN, IS TO DEFY CHINESE OCCUPATION AND HARBOR TIBET'S EXILED, EVER-JOYOUS SOUL."
—David James Duncan, author of *The River Why* and *The Brothers K*

Circling the Sacred Mountain

A SPIRITUAL ADVENTURE
THROUGH THE HIMALAYAS

Robert Thurman
and Tad Wise

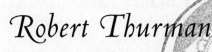

Bantam Books

NEW YORK TORONTO LONDON SYDNEY AUCKLAND

CIRCLING THE SACRED MOUNTAIN

PUBLISHING HISTORY
Bantam hardcover edition published March 1999
Bantam trade paperback edition / July 2000

Images appearing in photo section were provided by
Tad Wise unless otherwise noted.

Book design by Dana Leigh Treglia.
Map by Jeff Ward.

Cover photo copyright © 1999 by Jock Montgomery.
Cover type copyright © 1999 by Richard Rossiter.

Library of Congress Catalog Card Number: 98-41563.

ISBN 0-553-37850-3

Published simultaneously in the United States and Canada

Bantam Books are published by Bantam Books, a division of Random
House, Inc. Its trademark, consisting of the words "Bantam Books"
and the portrayal of a rooster, is Registered in U.S. Patent and
Trademark Office and in other countries. Marca Registrada. Bantam
Books, 1540 Broadway, New York,
New York 10036.

PRINTED IN THE UNITED STATES OF AMERICA

BVG   10 9 8 7 6 5 4 3

To Geshe Wangyal, once again, for introducing me to *The Blade Wheel of Mind Reform*, the innermost heart of the Dharma; to Lama Govinda, for showing the way to Kailash; to His Holiness the Dalai Lama, for opening the door to the palace of Demchock; and, in the spirit of Kailash, to all the generations of my whole family, especially my grandchildren, Dash, Caroline, Max, and the calm and beatific Maya Ray Nena!

R.A.F.T.

For my children, Sax, Riley, and Anna.

T.W.

Acknowledgments

My thanks to Buddha, Shiva, and Uma, and to all the pilgrims who preceded us to the holy mountain; to Tad Wise, for his spontaneous leap toward a culmination of aeons of self-overcoming and several years of hard work; to all my other Kailash brothers and sisters, may they thrive in blessings and happiness; to all the people of Geographic, for getting us there; to Brian Tart, for envisioning it and seeing it through; to Jisho Warner, for shining it up; to Ryan Stellabotte, for launching it; and to my constant friend Nena for the inspiration, her own brave journey, and her patient help with this one more task.

R.A.F.T.

My thanks to editors Brian Tart, Ryan Stellabotte, and Jisho Warner; to George Crane; and to Robert Thurman for taking me to the Holy Mountain.

T.W.

Contents

PART ONE *Going to the Mountain*

CHAPTER ONE	*Off the Deep End*	3
CHAPTER TWO	*Kathmandu*	21
CHAPTER THREE	*The Tibetan Border*	37
CHAPTER FOUR	*Acclimatizing*	51
CHAPTER FIVE	*Milarepa's Cave*	67
CHAPTER SIX	*On the Road*	83
CHAPTER SEVEN	*Reaching the Mountain*	103

PART TWO *Circling the Mountain*

CHAPTER EIGHT	*The Southern Gate of the Mandala Palace*	123
CHAPTER NINE	*The Great Freedom Pole*	137
CHAPTER TEN	*The Mansion of Hayagriva*	159

CHAPTER ELEVEN *The Female Yak Horn Cave* 181

CHAPTER TWELVE *The Cool Grove Charnel Ground* 203

CHAPTER THIRTEEN *Tara Pass* 217

CHAPTER FOURTEEN *The Dakini Secret Path* 231

CHAPTER FIFTEEN *Mila's Miracle Cave* 245

PART THREE *Returning from the Mountain*

CHAPTER SIXTEEN *The Holy Lake* 267

CHAPTER SEVENTEEN *The Border Bribe* 293

CHAPTER EIGHTEEN *Up and Over the Pass* 309

CHAPTER NINETEEN *The Eclipse* 323

CHAPTER TWENTY *Kathmandu* 343

Just to leave one's homeland is to
accomplish half the Dharma

—MILAREPA

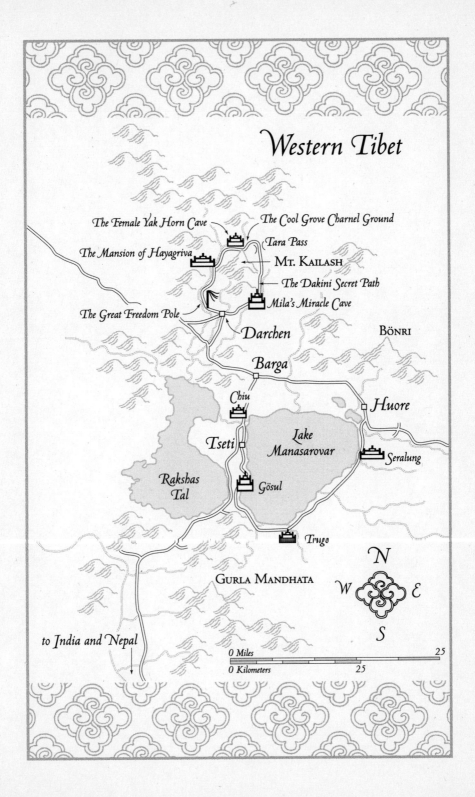

Western Tibet

The Female Yak Horn Cave

The Cool Grove Charnel Ground

Tara Pass

The Mansion of Hayagriva

MT. KAILASH

The Dakini Secret Path

Mila's Miracle Cave

The Great Freedom Pole

Darchen

BÖNRI

Barga

Huore

Chiu

Tseti

Lake Manasarovar

Seralung

Rakshas Tal

Gösul

Trugo

GURLA MANDHATA

N

W · E

S

to India and Nepal

0 Miles   25

0 Kilometers   25

PART ONE

Going to the Mountain

At the center of the earth, there stands a great mountain,
Lord of Snows, majestic, rooted in the sea,
its summit wreathed in clouds,
a measuring rod for all creation.

—KALIDASA (4TH CENTURY CE)

CHAPTER ONE

Off the Deep End

TENZIN

$\mathcal{M}$t. Kailash is the *axis mundi*, the cosmic pillar that upholds the vault of heaven. The sacred mountain had haunted my dreams since I was a young Tibetan Buddhist monk in my twenties. I had been initiated, in a complex ceremony that I've only recently begun to understand, into the sacred mandala of the visualized presence of the totally enlightened Archetype Buddha Paramasukha Chakrasamvara, a name that can be translated as Superbliss-Machine Embrace. The Chakrasamvara initiation ritual teaches that Mt. Kailash is the most magical site on earth, the abode of the father and mother of the world, the gods Shiva and Uma. For that reason, Shakyamuni Buddha, the founder of historical Buddhism, is said to have manifested himself there as the Superbliss-Machine Buddha. His mythic purpose was to turn all the divine energies away from violent passion and toward gentle bliss.

During my initiation into the mandala, I was told by His Holiness the Dalai Lama that the Superbliss Buddha's Mandala Palace, home to sixty-two Superbliss deities, is always present at Mt. Kailash. The palace doors are always open there and its radiance is always emanating. During the next couple of years, I often wondered about the mountain, but I eventually became preoccupied with other aspects of my life.

At the end of the sixties, having exchanged monastery for university, Mt. Kailash returned to my mind with my study at Harvard of the exquisite Sanskrit poem *The Birth of the Prince*, which was written by Kalidasa, the king of Indian poets. My wife Nena and I were beginning to host our children on this earth and when our daughter was born in 1970 we gave her the auspicious name Uma, for the gentle mother goddess whose heroism and cosmic beauty were described so vividly in Kalidasa's poem.

We first went to the Kailash area during my year of dissertation research in India, spending six idyllic months in the Himalayas in the exquisite hill town of Almora on the ancient route of pilgrimage to the mountain. Outside our window lay the exalting vista of Mt. Nandadevi, which looked like a woman lying on her side, and Trisul, like the trident after which it is named. These mountains also represented the father and mother of the gods. We were guests of Lama Govinda, the famous writer and Buddhist scholar, who had also once been a Buddhist monk. Long a friend of Nena's, he became a mentor to us both. He had made a pilgrimage to Mt. Kailash in the 1940s, going there with the true devotion of an initiate. He traveled on foot and by Tibetan pony with his Parsee wife, the artist Li Gotami, with a small caravan of yaks to carry their artists' gear and living supplies. His father was German, his mother Bolivian, and he had studied esoteric mysteries since his youth at the turn of the century. He had become a Buddhist monk in Sri Lanka in his late twenties, spending years in meditation and in scholarly study of Buddhist psychology. Visiting the Himalayan town of Darjeeling, he met Dromo Geshe Rinpoche, converted from Theravadin to Tibetan Buddhism and returned to lay life. He married an idealistic young woman, also a spiritual seeker, and the venerable and delightful couple ended up in the Almora ashram left them by W. Y. Evans-Wentz, the American editor of the first translation of the so-called *Tibetan Book of the Dead*.

One evening, on his eightieth birthday, Lama Govinda kept us up at his house well into the night with the tale of his circumambulation of Mt. Kailash. Pilgrims have always feared the frequent blizzards that suddenly materialize around the mountain. If caught in one in those days, travelers were stuck without any conceivable source of help, there being no radios, helicopters, or jeeps to send for assistance. The mountain was infamous for its dangerous changes of mood. Lama Govinda told us he had discovered an ultimate place of power on the north face of the mountain, a place where one could plant one's deepest wish for the world, and all the Buddhas and gods and dakini-angels would see to its accomplishment. Mt. Kailash could be that powerful. It was worth all the danger to try to get there. He looked at us meaningfully and then, murmuring, almost tearful, began to recount the horrors that were going on at that very moment all around the world. Having drawn our attention to the inconceivable anguish of the many suffering beings, he then fell silent. It was the summer of 1971, at the height of the Bangladesh atrocities. I had a momentary fantasy of a clandestine foray into Tibet to circle the mountain right then and there, but it was clearly unrealistic.

At night, I dreamt from time to time of Kailash as a great crystal energy source radiating infinite shades of blues and crimsons and greens and golds, sending these life-giving rays right through the intervening mountain ranges to light up our souls. A pilgrimage up beyond the snows was a tempting but daunting prospect, since the sacred mountain lay beyond the Indian border in Tibet, under the dominion of the troops of Communist China. No one, especially no friend of a free Tibet, would have access. In 1971 the Chinese invaders were still involved in the overt phase of their genocidal program against the Tibetans. The people of the

Land of Snows were starving, dying, struggling, and fleeing, and those safe in exile were trying to preserve their culture and the shreds of their lives; all were crying out to the unhearing world to stop the holocaust that they were suffering. In the midst of this horror that enveloped Tibet, Kailash just stood there like a roof-peak ornament, glowing and radiating its inexhaustible light and energy.

The inaccessibility of Mt. Kailash gradually came to represent to me the suppression of the power of human goodness that we need to make our dreams of peace come true.

Upon our return to New York from India, I met the eminent Hindu swami Satchidananda, who joked with me when he heard my Buddhist name, Tenzin, which I had received from His Holiness when I was ordained as a Tibetan monk in 1964. It means Upholder of the Teaching. Back in the householder's life, some of my friends still used it informally.

"Ah, Tenzin," said the swami, "you must be the one who climbed Mount Everest!" He smiled warmly, looked at me deeply, and shook my hand. A feeling lingered in me after that encounter that my journey into the Dharma was only working at half speed. Was I only "climbing" in books? Shouldn't interior achievement support external achievement as well? Maybe I could go to the mountains and change the world as well as change myself.

Getting up a mountain just to be at the top has never appealed to me, however. While the physical challenge is stimulating, it seems like a conceptual exercise to prove you can meet the challenge. But Kailash is not a climbing mountain; it is far too holy for human trespass. The great god Shiva lives there with his beloved Uma, while the Superbliss Buddha and his circle of artist deities dance there, keeping the gods happy. Humans get their blessings by circling the mountain in pilgrimage, not by scaling its strictly forbidden peak. Trapped as it was behind communist lines, it seemed to me that the mountain itself needed to be liberated, restored to its spiritual purpose. Because it is a mountain that amplifies prayers, I hoped that its liberation might help liberate the world.

In 1979 I was nearly forty and in India again, moving on from my years of philosophical studies to learn more deeply about the Unexcelled Yoga Tantra spiritual sciences and arts, the ultimate technologies developed in India and Tibet for mastering death and life. The situation then looked more hopeful for Tibet. Mao Zedong had died and the Gang of Four had been routed; so it was just possible that the new leaders Deng Xiaoping and Hu Yaobang would reverse Mao's genocidal policy in Tibet and let the Dalai Lama come to the aid of his long-suffering people. Several delegations from the Tibetan government-in-exile in Dharamsala, India, traveled to China and through Tibet, making the first survey of the degree of devastation wrought by almost three decades of communist class-struggle, intellectual oppression, and cultural revolution, carried on simultaneously with invasion, occupation, colonization, and economic exploitation. The Tibetans were horrified—by the intensity of the Tibetan people's outpouring to the delegates, agonized accounts of terror and torture, tears, hysterical demonstrations, and weeping prayers sent to the Dalai Lama; and by the total devastation of all material signs of the Tibetan Buddhist spiritual culture. Huge monasteries, temples, wayside monuments, even cliffside carvings were all reduced to rubble.

It was still out of the question for me to travel to Tibet, so I couldn't visit Mt. Kailash. My priority was to work hard to help the Dalai Lama come to America so he could tell the story of his nation's tragedy to the wider world.

His Holiness the Dalai Lama was finally permitted to come to the U.S. in 1979, giving talks arranged at Amherst College and Harvard University, teaching at my teacher's monastery in Washington, New Jersey, and visiting Congress and the national shrines in Washington, D.C. In 1981 in Wisconsin, he bestowed his beloved Kalachakra initiation for the first time outside of Tibet or India. During the elaborate ceremony I had a new vision and new encouragement about the old self-world, interior-exterior duality. The Kalachakra Tantra—the Time-Machine Spiritual Technology—has the exquisite arts and yogas of the Unexcelled Tantras, while also presenting an apocalyptic dimension that centers on the prophecy of Shambhala. It tells of a magic hidden country of highly evolved bodhisattvas (enlightened beings dedicated to serving others) who live up near the North Pole and practice the Time-Machine internal yogas; they cultivate hi-tech communication, defense, and life-supporting infrastructures. At some point, the world finally comes under the dominion of a single, tyrannical Big Brother and the force field over Shambhala dissolves, allowing everyone on the globe to find it. The tyrant invades and is welcomed by the Shambhalans, but then he turns on them and tries to annihilate them. The Shambhalans then fight back and use their hi-tech machinery to destroy the military power of the evil invaders. The whole world is liberated from tyranny and becomes a realm of goodness and happiness.

This prophecy moved me the first time I heard it. Birth and death and life and loss and pain are bad enough on the individual level. It seems completely gratuitous for bad leadership, self-destructive behavior, and sheer stupidity and malice to add to the difficulties. Buddhas are exalted beings—both human and divine—who have accomplished complete enlightenment. When a bodhisattva—heroic seeker of enlightenment—becomes a perfect blissful buddha, she does not bail out of the mess and leave living beings stuck behind. Shakyamuni as a buddha achieved a state of consciousness that ranges through time as freely as through space, enabling him to be present in all possible futures of all beings, to help them visibly and invisibly to optimize their own progress toward freedom. The Buddha as Time-Machine expresses artistically and spiritually this pervasive presence of enlightened compassion in every moment of time, making time into a machine for the optimal evolutionary development of beings. The amazingly peaceful, colorful, and cheerful feelings in any Kalachakra initiation come, I believe, from the subliminal awareness of this positivity immanent in time.

After the initiation I was sitting on a dock in the lake near Madison, my hand playing in the cool water. As the ripples flowed from my fingers out into the lake and out into the world, I suddenly saw gentle ripples of goodness flow toward Washington, into the mandala palace of the government—the White House, Washington Monument, Lincoln Memorial, Capitol building, out over the Potomac through the Jefferson Memorial, even into the

Pentagon—and then I saw the ripples continue around the world to Europe and Russia and Japan. This little vision made it seem for a moment that goodness had the power to triumph after all. Maybe I could come to see this in my lifetime. Maybe I could leave a world alive with this possibility to my beautiful children, instead of delivering them innocently to the violent wheel of demons we habitually see out there. I began to join His Holiness's efforts on the political level, to struggle for the freedom of Tibet and no longer write it off as a lost cause.

Life now seemed to have reached a kind of mature seriousness for me. I had to find further means to accomplish an integration of the outer and the inner. I had been slowly working changes in myself, seemingly endless changes, and yet always seeing more flaws to correct, more virtues to cultivate. My friends and family went through similar progressions, but the outer world seemed always to go intractably in the other direction. However close it got to solving its crises and turning to its potential goodness, yet another catastrophe would occur and things would get worse, heading off in the wrong direction once again. I wanted to find access to forces capable of transforming the world out there, not just myself. I kept coming back to Mt. Kailash, the magic gemstone, and to what Lama Govinda had said. Could it be the crystal key to initiate this shift?

Kailash might be the place where planting my deepest wish for this world would help make it come true, a place to pronounce my vow for the universe, the gateway for the apocalyptic emergence of this world as a living realm for beings to become buddhas. I had learned from Lama Govinda that the campsite on the north face, at Drirapuk, was like a spiritual megaphone. Whatever prayer you make there is automatically transmitted instantaneously throughout the planet and even beyond.

I made up my mind to go to Mt. Kailash and decided that I needed a team to go with me. By midsummer in 1995 there were eight people ready, pilgrims all at different points in the Buddhist path, and my trekking company wanted us to go that fall. And then I bumped into Tad Wise in a coffee shop in town. He was there with his new partner, showing off their baby girl. We wished them well and sat down for a coffee. To my amazement, when Tad heard I was taking a group to Mt. Kailash, he instantly wanted to go along himself.

Tad had been a student of mine at Amherst College in the seventies. We had a bit of a bond, because we were both from Woodstock in upstate New York, a more earthy and realistic place than Amherst. But Tad was a hard case. He was interested in the Dharma and in developing himself, but he had high literary ambitions, a well-entrenched Western personality, and a complex family background. In his college years, Tad bonded with our family as if he were another son, yet he resisted the spiritual vision of the aim of life, also rather like our own children.

At one time he stayed in our summer retreat house while writing a book. Like any son, he had problems that needed real help: alcohol, unstable relations with women, frustrated ambition. Once in a while, he would ask for a Dharma teaching. Then he would resist anything offered.

So I was surprised when he put himself forward to come to Kailash. I thought that he must desperately need Buddhist mind-reform methodology. I let him know that the teachings would be intensive once we got to Tibet. I planned to teach everyone—myself included—the full force of *The Blade Wheel of Mind Reform,* a powerful and poetic indictment of ignorance and self-centeredness, and an effective method for overcoming them. Normally you would not teach such a forceful Dharma method without first providing a strong foundation in Buddhist practice. New students need time to acclimatize to the Buddha Dharma, the teaching of the evolutionary lifestyle. If you put the self-addiction on the table right away, challenging basic narcissism at its root, people may react allergically and feel that their very personality is threatened. Their addictive self convinces them that the teaching is an assault, you the teacher are their enemy, and the habitual self is really still their best friend. So Buddhist teachers usually skirt the issues of self-habituation and self-preoccupation initially.

I wanted this trip to Kailash to be a no-holds-barred, leap-into-the-abyss kind of journey. We would not coddle ego-habits, self-promotion, or self-seeking. There would be no room for denial, no soft-pedaling to nudge people along. There is no time for that; we stand at the end of history, after centuries of genocides and atrocities beyond imagining, at a precipice of doom for all that lives on our fragile planetary surface. We must drop the pretenses and the self-deceptions, we must rise to a heroic level together. We have made all life vulnerable to the impact of our ignorant prejudice, greed, and hate. We must now take responsibility and turn it around as soon as possible.

You do not need a doctorate in philosophy or years of sitting at your guru's feet to experience the transcendent wisdom of *The Blade Wheel of Mind Reform.* You can do it at any time with the right understanding and the right effort. I have invested a lot in the belief that Kailash is the core of our global structure of life, the sacred heart of the joy that makes life worthwhile, or even plausible.

The group circling the sacred mountain will invite transcendent wisdom in its fiercest form, Yamantaka the Terminator of Death, to destroy our inner enemy of egotism. Each of us will have to face the deepest teachings, the most clear-cut reflections of the self and its habits. The *Blade Wheel* is designed to kill the ego to save our lives. We all need that. Tad needs it. The world needs it.

But most of all, I need it. I learned some time ago that a teacher is always teaching himself. As you think through things for your students, you deepen your own understanding. You can only explain effectively for others what you are willing to experience yourself. When I was a disciple of my first teacher, Geshe Wangyal, in my early twenties, he held up to me a bright mirror in which I was forced to see my negative personality features, misperceptions, and negative impulses. I never could have sustained such devastating clarity without him there with me as a live example, looking at himself, still working on himself even at sixty years of age, though he had every right to sit back and rest on his laurels of enlightenment accomplished. He even accepted my faults, committed himself unconditionally to my potential, leaving it to me to recognize how much better it would be to overcome this, to rise to that challenge, to reach for the deepest insight. And at the end of our intensive time together, after a year and a half or so, he brought out for me *The Blade Wheel of Mind Reform.* He entrusted it to me as the real thing, the grandest and deepest teaching, the root of both the good life and the bliss of supreme freedom. Ever since then the *Blade Wheel* has been humming there in the back of my mind, in the bond of memory between my late good friend Geshe Wangyal and me. I kept the text with me, wrapped in Tibetan cloth, and I read the book several times. I jotted down translations. But I knew there was a way to go deeper into and through it—with sincere companions at the center of the earth.

TAD

It's the end of May 1995, a week after my thirty-ninth birthday. I'm the proud father and Cynthia the proud mother of new-baby Anna on display at a Woodstock breakfast spot. We're gaily jabbering away, drinking far too much coffee, as beneath this "happy family" the ground rumbles. Cynthia wants out of Woodstock. As usual, I'm not sure what I want.

Through the screen door I hear high, imperious European tones, looking up I find Tenzin and Nena Thurman—that larger-than-life royal couple of Tibetan Buddhism—totally filling the door. I've known the Thurmans since I was seventeen, having been off and on friend, student, house sitter, stonemason, and jester to the court. But I haven't seen them in a year or two; they've never met Cynthia or, obviously, Anna. There are hugs, introductions, congratulations; pancakes are ordered, and more coffee.

Tenzin means simply Upholder of Teaching in Tibetan. That's what he was called when Nena met him, because that's what he was. He was the first American to be ordained as a Tibetan Buddhist monk, though his teacher, Geshe Wangyal, privately counseled him not to take full vows of celibacy, even while introducing him to His Holiness the fourteenth Dalai Lama. It was as if the old Mongolian lama knew this "white monk" would also be first to ask to be released from monastic vows. His Holiness was younger then, and gave Thurman whatever he requested, along with his religious name. Tenzin is what his friends and family still call him.

When we first met I didn't know what to call him. My stepfather introduced me to Bob Thurman, who'd built one of the domes featured in *Woodstock Handmade Houses.* Bob had tall, beautiful children with strange names, who looked like they'd been sculpted from marzipan. The entire family was other-worldly and proved a great comfort to me at uptight Amherst College, where Bob had become Professor Thurman. This really complicated matters, for though I was coming down with a clear case of hero worship, I still wondered what to call this glass-eyed giant, who had lost one eye in his youth, at the start of his road to wisdom.

Twenty years later this academic who cleared his own land, built his own house, and roughhoused three sons into manhood has become the American firebrand of Buddhism. Under thirty pounds of restaurant-food roll, he's solidly muscled and not in the least bit shy about putting you in a headlock to prove it. With a voice that pinches with a nasal insistence like Dudley Do-Right, then thunders like Richard Burton, Robert Tenzin Thurman is a combination of opposites: an apostle of peace who grapples in debate like the hockey player that he was when he played for Exeter in high school.

Our breakfast nook soon takes on the air of an Irish pub at last call, with gesture, laughter, and language lashed together in happy storm. Tenzin is pounding the tabletop, Nena howling like a tea kettle, Cynthia and Anna gurgling brooks of laughter. "Now tell us, Tenzin," I inquire, "are you going to Tibet again soon?"

"Absolutely!" he thunders. "Next fall in all likelihood. An expedition to Kailash, the holy mountain, the center of the universe. In October, I wish it could be sooner, I'm off to most remote Western Tibet—quite high up and an ordeal in itself just to get there. Incredibly powerful place. Really the most powerful place. I've been trying to get there for years!"

At the sound of the word "Kailash" a bell goes off in my head, and at the end of this speech I hear my own voice blurt back: "I'm coming with you." If I'm shocked, Cynthia must be reeling. A knowing glance is exchanged between Tenzin and Nena. As I would later learn, acquaintances were constantly asking for a place on the Kailash trip, then backing out again.

"Really? How interesting," Tenzin responds politely, his huge, handsome face glowing like a jack-o'-lantern, one eye following me, the other, glass, staying put. "Well, it's only nine thousand dollars to go. Come up with that and we'd love to have you along."

My mind doesn't register the cost. I'm somewhere else; swirling in snow and wind. Looking around the table I drink in the sight of Cynthia and Anna with a mixture of joy and grief. I'm leaving them. No one else realizes it yet, but I'm already ten thousand miles away. For some inexplicable reason, the instant I hear "Kailash" I know exactly where I'm bound.

Though impressed with my audacity, this incredibly over-scheduled scholar of Tibet is still a bit leery of my sudden Buddhist resolve. I've been a slapdash disciple, in and out of favor for years. The next weekend I drive up to the tumbledown Dharma castle to talk about the trip. Both Nena and Tenzin speak in high voices and peer at me through narrowed eyes; there is an air of audition to the visit. Unintimidated, I ask more about what will happen.

"I give Dharma talks on these trips," Tenzin says, seated at his rough-hewn desk-throne. "Really an A-to-Z primer on Tibetan Buddhism and the path to enlightenment. Between your personal odyssey, the mind-crunching altitude, and the unfamiliar terrain and climate, you'll be quite overwhelmed, I think. You'll be facing the throne of Shiva, the destroyer, confronting death every step of the way. No breaks for wine, women, and song."

"That's right, Tad," Nena chimes in from the next room, reclining, as usual, on the broken-down velvet couch with a view of the back side of Meads Mountain through a huge circular window. "This is a remarkable opportunity for you. To really get it — and not play the Artful Dodger yet again!"

"Because," Tenzin continues, grabbing back the verbal baton, "I'm going up there with a very clear purpose. I want to plant a specific prayer in the mind-stream of the planet, to get us beyond this moment of impending doom. For one reason or another I've been prevented from doing this earlier. Nena and I were close several times, but now it looks like the time is finally right for a pilgrimage, to make offerings and meditate upon a solution for a world that has very nearly blown it." He examines my face carefully before continuing. "These days the Chinese have been upgrading their equipment at the borders. If my passport number goes into a computer I may not get through at all. Or they could follow us . . . it could get a little rough and you could end up leading the expedition!" He laughs, muttering, "Heaven forbid."

"Heaven forbid is right," echoes Nena. Then, in a more conciliatory tone, she begins one of her favorite sentences: "I have a favor to ask of you, Tad."

Years ago I gave the Thurmans a capstone left over from one of my masonry jobs to serve as the hearth beneath a woodstove. The woodstove has since been removed and Nena now wants to use the stone as a bridge at the front of the property. I rouse the youngest son, Mipam, from his science-fiction novel for help. Together we carry out the monster and stand it up next to a huge, curvaceous wall I built five years ago. Mipam starts philosophizing, as Thurmans will, while I make a few preparations, and— singlehandedly—lay the stone across the gurgling brook. It's solid. The Thurmans are delighted. Inconsequential as this may sound, it is an extremely important moment for me, harking back to the complicated relationship between Tibet's most famous saint, Milarepa, and his guru, the translator Marpa.

The eleventh-century Milarepa was the son of a prosperous Tibetan whose early death reversed his family's fortunes. The executor of the will was the dead man's brother, Mila's uncle, who reduced the widow and two children to maids and stableboy in their own mansion. After suffering beatings and humiliations at the hands of his own relatives, Mila apprenticed himself to a local warlock of great power in pursuit of vengeance. Bringing a sorceror's curse upon the farm of the usurpers, Mila created a hailstorm that blew down their house, killing thirty-five people. With the locals up in arms, Mila fled.

Searching for a teacher and for atonement for this profound crime, Mila encounters Marpa the translator and his wise and loving wife, Damema.

Marpa drinks wine and treats Mila like a serf. Though Damema tries to intervene, the relationship deteriorates. Marpa tells Mila to build a huge stone tower of a certain shape, and Milarepa accomplishes this feat, only to hear that the tower must be dismantled and rebuilt in another shape. Uncomplainingly Mila resets every stone, but not without bruising himself. Marpa tells him to rebuild it again, and upon completing it, to rebuild it again, until it has been rebuilt a total of four times. By now Mila is a broken mass of blisters and bruises. Withdrawing into seclusion, running away, coming back, and finally resolving to commit suicide, he is at last summoned by Marpa, initiated, and made his adopted son. Armed with strong teachings, Milarepa is instructed by Marpa to search out a deserted cave, to give up associations with men and women and to dedicate his life to meditation for the good of all sentient beings. Overcoming numerous hardships both natural and supernatural, the spiritual progress of this onetime warlock is so momentous as to propel him into buddhahood in a single lifetime.

Like several other resonances in our relationship, my relocating the hearthstone recalls the Milarepa-Marpa archetype. To me it seems like an obvious joke.

"Good," Nena says, smiling approvingly at the new bridge. "You've become quite strong. If Tenzin has a heart attack, you can carry him off the mountain." Through much resulting laughter she insists: "You will, in fact, promise to do precisely this, if need be!"

There's no turning back. I'm committed, with only a few short weeks to prepare for the trip of a lifetime. I help Cynthia and the baby move to a charming apartment in Portland, Maine. I reassure my ten-year-old daughter, Riley, who lives with her mother in Woodstock, that I'll send postcards at every opportunity. I send a similar message to my son in London. I lay a few stone walls for a few bucks and read everything on Tibet and Mt. Kailash that Tenzin recommends.

The trek itself will take between twenty-five and twenty-eight days, depending on whether we fly to Lhasa from Kathmandu and drive west straight across the Tibetan Plateau, or if, road conditions permitting, we drive overland straight from Kathmandu north through the Himalayas, swerving east and then west to Kailash. In either case we'll be on the road four or five days. The trip around Kailash itself takes about the same. Then we'll visit holy Lake Manasarovar, drive south to the Tibetan border and hike out through the Nepali Himalayas to Simikot.

Day by day I work at making it happen. Passports, visas, reservations, money, physical conditioning, attempts at spiritual practice. I journey to the holy mountain predisposed to a Buddhist point of view but not made much happier by it. I falter on the central tenet of "selflessness" since, like many committed to the arts, I suffer from an enlarged sense of self-importance. Some might say I am not a Buddhist at all, simply a huge admirer of buddhas.

Once I begin to research Mt. Kailash I soon realize it is, indeed, the most astounding place. Prophecies are heard there and it is said to be protected even from nuclear war. The Hopis acknowledge it as the other end of the world backbone that sticks up as their Black Mesa. But Kailash, the eastern spine-tip, is better protected, sublimely worshiped, and the most divinely ornamented place on Earth. It is called Mt. Kailash by Europeans; Kang Rinpoche, or Snow Jewel, by Tibetans; Mt. Meru by Indians. It is the spiritual crown of the planet, atop the very northernmost sector of the Himalayas, in the most remote region of Tibet.

The first European to see it and live to tell was a mad Swedish explorer named Sven Hedin. Early this century he came back to the Swedish academy affirming the ancient myths that tell of an ice-encased, perfect four-sided pyramid, at whose foot nestles the highest lake in the world and the source of all the major rivers of Asia. He said Kailash is this jewel mountain, which pilgrims of the Hindu, Buddhist, and Jain faiths spend years journeying to, through all sorts of weather, in order to walk clockwise around the thing, never attempting the peak.

When people ask me about my impending journey to Tibet, I explode with all this. Heads nod and mouths mutter appreciations. Sometimes I feel the glow of good fortune, sometimes, a shadow of dread. I shouldn't talk about it anymore, I realize. There are hundreds of preparations to make. At the top of the list, a visit to my father's dying mother.

At ninety her heart has deteriorated, and she's been moved into a hospital for the aged on Cape Cod. Sitting by her bedside, waiting for her to awaken, I suddenly notice a Tibetan wisdom bell on her windowsill—an old, thick one I've never seen before. I sit up with a start because I'm always describing the words "Mt. Kailash" as sounding like a bell. And now, fulfilling a heartbreaking duty, what should confront me but an ancient Tibetan wisdom bell?

When Mimi finally awakens I ask her about this most mysterious object. She tells me it was a gift from her second husband, who traveled widely. After a few minutes she tires visibly and a nurse in the doorway taps the face of her wristwatch, signaling for me to end the visit. It's an awful moment that I simultaneously wish would never come and was already over. Taking a deep breath, I ask: "When the time comes, Mimi . . . may I have that bell?"

"Yes, of course!" she yells happily, some of her old power momentarily returned. She adds emphatically, "And that time will be soon!" With these words five gnarled fingers grab my hand; we weep, laughing. It's the last time I see her.

When my father hears of his mother's death he stops drinking on a dime. For a drinker of his proportions this is a dangerous move. At her funeral by the Atlantic his bellicose, belligerent self is transformed into a picture of mourning dignity. Hobbling to the ocean with a walker, kneeling at the water's edge, he splashes his neck and face with one of the two liquids considered by him holy, before scattering her ashes in the sea. The next day, helping him to his bedroom I put it as simply as I can: "When you drink everyone hates you. When you're sober everyone loves you. And I would rather love than hate you." With the word "hate" I break down, as does he. We embrace and he swears he'll stay off the booze. I've been off it, myself, for two years.

Just before I take off I'm camped out in a New York City apartment of my family's that has been a den of iniquity in the soap opera of my life. The most obvious consequence: three children by three mothers. Tonight, I call a roster of women: my mother, my daughter, two sisters, my first love, two others, and lastly Cynthia. When I put the phone down around midnight I'm ready to truly live, or to die. By some screwy logic that puts me soundly to sleep, it hardly seems to matter which.

CHAPTER TWO

Kathmandu

TAD

*T*here's a mountain sticking through the top of the clouds! My first glimpse of the Himalayas! A monstrous, capsized, barnacled keel lies just outside the window of this Royal Nepal four-prop preparing to land. It's green, jagged, and lethal-looking, slicing through whipped cream clouds so thick, I'm surprised the glass isn't splattered with milk.

I'm in Shangri-La class (second class was full) grateful for some stewardesses who aren't beautiful, pissed off at the four-star champagne and brandy I'm refusing, knowing none of this matters anymore. Because I have reached the other world. After twenty-three hours in the air, there is here. I'm arriving ahead of Tenzin

21

and the group to acclimatize to Asia, explore the city we depart from, and try to relax before the rigors of the journey.

Outside the window the clouds pull thin and a smattering of farms with glistening crops in corduroy fields yield to dusty roads dotted with cows and humans. The low-slung city suddenly explodes into sight. Sun-baked brick houses materialize, rooftops sagging with clotheslines, gardens, and garbage heaps nestled between. A lonely swimming pool surrounded by palm trees amidst an attempt at high-rises. A circle with a pinprick of a policeman directing traffic on wide, dusty, swirling boulevards teeming with bicycles, motorbikes, rickshaws; pedestrians pulsing through these arteries under a blue haze of smoke. Children rolling tires with sticks wave at the outskirts of the runway, as the plane embraces its ink-black shadow shimmering off the hot asphalt.

I grimace through the single awful instant the wheels strike tarmac, bounce, resettle, and hold the ground. We roar by a rusting Russian monster of an Aeroflot cargo plane parked before the terminal. Inside the airport windows bareheaded and turbaned faces are shading their eyes from the glare, laughing, pointing, waving at us; welcoming us into the city caught between the ages. A silver-toothed smile refracts panoramically from a Hindu grandmother's laugh. Her prayers have been answered. We're safe and sound at the gates of the carnival called Kathmandu.

Inside I buy a visa on the spot. Forty-two dollars for five weeks. Purpose of stay: tourist, business, or pilgrim? The middle will do. I grab a motorized rickshaw cabbie and establish a price to Boudha.

"Boudha? Two hundred rupees."

"One hundred rupees or I get other."

"OK, OK." Glazed eyes smile respectfully over a blue-black mustache. We rev up and sail down this wide, windy arc of a road without distinct lanes, traffic flying around in not just two, but four directions; vehicles jostling for position like horses in a race. Much noise and insane bumps. Drivers bluffing, swerving toward each other, then away, cutting each other off. The air is awful, hopelessly polluted. Breathing through a bandanna, I squint at the sprawling crowds lazily moving out of the way of our horn. Motorcycles with Hindu women riding sidesaddle behind nylon-jacketed swains. The older ones have children hanging off the rig, one kid, two, three. I eventually see a family of five on a motorcycle, the youngest on the proud father's handlebars.

Behind wide concrete sidewalks ancient architecture buttresses up against Coca-Cola-ad-clad shacks. Tee shirts sport images of Madonna, The Police, Kurt Cobain, and Michael Jackson. Their music is an aural pinup blaring from trashed transistor radios taped to bicycles and rickshaws. Like *Playboy* centerfolds staring out from a prison wall, they are the teasing promise of an always sexy, never hungry, never dirty, always American life plastered across the chest of Asia: dirty, hungry, ambitious, tired of being ignored, and willing to do anything.

Dropped off after ten miles at the front of the temple town of Boudhanath, I pass through the medieval gates and stare up at the huge indigo eye painted on the ceramic upside-down champagne glass of the Great Stupa. Buddhists and Hindus alike clap their hands over their heads and kneel, pressing to the ground. Hindus peel right and Buddhists peel left. Me? I stare at the eye for a moment, noticing that darkness is falling fast.

Five days later, still sniffing through a bandanna, I have to get away or I'll be physically ill. So I hike into the hills on the western edge of the city, contending with goats and monkeys. But Kathmandu is like a beautiful woman with bad breath and after a single hour of fresh air I can't wait to get back to the stench of her. This starts with gasoline fumes, adds charcoal smoke, roast goat and chicken, sandalwood, frankincense, to hashish and feces, and the resulting perfume is Kathmandu. Truly, this is the air of samsara, the round of rebirths caused by desire and its inevitable misery.

The Vishnumati River is a huge garbage heap. Above it, to the west towers Swayambhunath—commonly known as the Monkey Temple. Indiana Jones never escaped from anything as dramatic. Three hundred sixty-five stairs of cut stone proceeding steeply up past beggars, pushers, German tourists, and—yes—monkeys, all after something. At the top, enlightenment seems little more than a photo opportunity. But, fulfilling a promise for a friend, I make a circuit of the huge, bronze prayer wheels. I've even learned to put my forehead to the feet of the sacred statues.

It's twelve miles back to Boudhanath, where my room in the Kailash Guest House costs less per night than a cappuccino stateside. I'm making the hike on Durga, the Hindu Christmas, when instead of opening presents, they cut throats. Everybody is dressed in their best with festive bloodspores on foreheads, doorways, cars, motorcycles. Blood is running from the temples. The heads of the dead animals are lying around like empty Moët bottles after a yuppie wedding. I round a corner and encounter a naked young woman sitting in a roadside pile of smoldering garbage. She is beautiful—but for the contorted grimace on her face. I am attracted, disgusted, intrigued, ashamed. I continue, well past curfew, to hike back to the guest house, climbing over the spear-pointed gates shortly before dawn.

Most mornings I'm awakened by chanting and trumpets from a half-dozen monasteries beehived into Boudha. The locals seem distracted, walking quickly, semiconscious, not looking at one another but not getting in each other's way. Like New Yorkers hustling to work, but with one difference: Only porta-phoners, taxi drivers, and crazy people talk out loud in New York. Here every one is mumbling aloud, counting off their prayer beads, circling this towering white and gold, indigo-eyed mound, which Chokyi Nyima, a local, much-revered rinpoche, says represents the mind of the Buddha.

At the Yak and Yeti—150 dollars a night—I meet the group poolside. Tenzin introduces me first to Jock Montgomery, trek leader of medium height; early thirties, darkly bearded, catlike, with confident clear eyes, and a handshake that neither advertises nor denies a lean strength. He is a serious high-altitude hiker and white-water kayak master, who lives in Bangkok and takes good photographs. He seems a bit uncertain about the Dharma part, but maybe that's good—he'll stay in contact with the practical realities of the trip.

There are Leopoldo and Valerie, he a Mexican-American psychologist and she a Euro-American health professional, a lovely adventurous couple with no children; they have a sense of a special spiritual quest in which their deep relationship is grounded.

There is James, our most elderly, a clearly WASP writer and bon vivant, who is entering the sannyasin stage of wandering world-renouncer as he prepares for the final stages of life. His spiritual sensibility seems primed, though protected by an incisive intelligence.

There is Richard, the painter and sculptor, who has sacrificed everything to come, and is positively glowing with the sense of accomplishment of having made it this far. He seems deeply attracted to the mountain, with or without the teaching.

There is Wolfgang, a first-generation German-American, ostensibly here to research background for a book, but with a deep longing for some higher purpose or fulfillment of being itself.

The trip roster also includes a name identical to that of a kid I went to junior high school with, who was then a fourteen-year-old Maoist with a large vocabulary and a low tolerance to alcohol and drugs. In trouble at home, he fled to Amsterdam at just fifteen. I hadn't seen him in over twenty years. I'd come to think of him as one of the casualties. Now, hearing the words "Sorry, I'm late," I glance up to realize Jay has not only survived, he has prevailed. A swarthy, handsome, humorous face lights up at the sight of me, and the first icebreaker of the trip becomes our powerful, if clumsy, embrace.

I am deeply impressed by each of these individuals and by their incredible dedication to the pilgrimage. Not one of them seems to be sure why they chose to come, yet each has made impressive sacrifices to come, not only in money, but also in time, training, and intellectual preparation. There is a sense of synchronicity, of fatedness, about the group.

Everyone accounted for, Jock consults his clipboard and gets down to business: One, drink water. Lots of it. The first preventative against altitude sickness is upward of four or five quarts a day. Two, the habitual response of "I'm OK," is not OK. Altitude sickness, Jock explains, is one of the mysteries of hard-core adventuring. Different people react in vastly different ways, and no one person necessarily reacts the same way twice. He points out that Sir Edmund Hillary, the first man to climb Everest, can no longer tolerate trekking above twelve thousand feet.

Tenzin adds a cautionary tale: On his last trip through a different part of Tibet, a celebrity trekker remained stoically reticent about her discomfort until she was suddenly in a fight for her life, a fight won only with oxygen, a pressurized bag, the help of several seasoned Sherpas, the light of a full moon, and a healthy dose of luck. Jock nods in agreement. "The rule is," he summarizes, "complete and thorough self-monitoring and say what you feel when you feel it."

During this minilecture I size up the group, trying not to stare at James, who is a cheerful, balding, white-haired gentleman with the kind of all-but-extinct aristocratic New York accent (seasoned with just a touch of Ha'vad Ya'd) still heard at the bar during the intermission at the Metropolitan Opera, but whose tenacity atop the Himalayas I cannot help but question. As if to nip my superiority in the bud, Tenzin adds, smiling slyly: "It's usually the gung ho, pumped-up health freaks who get into the most trouble, pushing themselves until they're in over their heads. Don't push yourself, the mountain will do the pushing for you. Just take it easy and everything will go just fine."

Here is his go-with-the-flow attitude, which is but one facet of Tenzin's highly complicated character. Five minutes before, as we stretched out poolside on some chaise longues, he begged some sun cream from me, complaining, "I can't believe it! I left this great hat, a perfect Australian bushman-sun-here-I-come hat that Nena specifically bought for the trip, on the kitchen table. Just rushed back from this world-religion-and-environment convention in Greece and left the hat on the table!" An absent-minded professor who can take you apart like F. Lee Bailey one moment, and completely disarm you with oafish sincerity the next, Tenzin is like the ocean. When the sun is shining he glows, happiness rolling off him in waves. No one is more fun, and the "fun ones" crowd around, drawn by the lure of humor-laced intelligence. But when the clouds scud across his face and the wind of his voice starts to howl like a gale, his glass eye glows ominously and the real one glows more dangerously still—then a regular Ahab takes shape at the helm. And he will always be in command on this trip since there are but two beings Tenzin will bow to—and only one for sure; these being his wife, Nena, and ultimately his guru, the Dalai Lama. Fortunately, I know this going in. And the good times are all the more magical. And the bad times? These, too, shall pass. I've been surrounded by just this sort of character my whole life, and actually, I enjoy the challenge.

Jock is wrapping up preliminaries: "Any extra baggage not completely necessary to the trek—specifically sleeping pads— should be left behind. Geo Expeditions has supplied each of you with a sleeping pad. Tuxedoes, hairdryers, and toilet-seat warmers should also be checked here where the hotel will hold them for you at no extra charge." The group smiles at the well-timed joke, trying not to seem nervous or overly curious of each other since we are both.

"So clean up and meet for dinner at six in the hotel restaurant. The food is excellent. At seven we've been invited to a cocktail party in our honor."

There's an accelerated path in Buddhism called Tantra. If the accelerated telling of a life story could be called Tantric recall, that is what Jay and I partake of as I make piles of my clothes in my Yak and Yeti suite. The doorman in full uniform including a short sword salutes when we go out, and the ten of us divide into two vans bound for the private home of Jim Edwards.

His stationery declares "Tiger Mountain" to be "the pioneers of Himalayan treks, jungle lodges, and wildlife camps." Maybe his prodigious hospitality is good for business. Maybe he wants to tell stories of his elephant polo championship to a new group of strangers. I'm told he's no one to get on the wrong side of, but I never found the wrong side of Jim Edwards, our generous host.

Various Dharma writers and photographers are present, talking and soaking up the free booze and waiter-dispensed canapes. I'm well into my fourth club soda with fresh lemon juice when I have the good fortune to engage one of Tiger Mountain's higher-ups in polite conversation. Uttara Crees, a small, elegant, circumspectly charming Hindu woman of anywhere between twenty-five and forty years of age, tells me of her Kailash experience in the most beautiful English I've ever heard.

"My grandmother in India used to dream of making a pilgrimage to Kailash. She never did, but she awoke in me this tremendous curiosity. So when I was offered a chance to go, I said, 'Yes!'

"Of course, this was also the first invitation to individuals outside the Chinese regime in nearly two generations. Tiger Mountain was the experiment, you might say, being among the first and most civilized of the trekking outfits.

"Our host was the director of Chinese tourism, and our cook was Chinese, the rest were a mixture of nationalities who hadn't done any commercial trekking in recent memory. No one had. It soon became obvious that the officials were just as inexperienced as their guests.

"We began about this time of year, in October. Gathering at the border town of Zhangmu we drove onto the Tibetan Plateau at Gutso, at about fourteen thousand feet, where we waited for our petrol and food to arrive. At the start of the journey westward, two people—myself included—lost some skin helping to set up tents. The temperatures were already fifteen to twenty degrees below freezing and the metal tent poles burned our palms painfully.

"On our first day across the plateau westward, our Chinese driver—who dismantled and reassembled his revolver to calm his nerves, I think, at every rest stop—shot a yellow sheep. Our first bad omen. And I must mention our most interesting crossing of the Tsangpo River on the ferry at Saga. We were grating and crunching through the icy river when I found that we were not carrying ice axes or shovels and so could not lend one to the ferry operator. Luckily, we found and purchased an ice pick at Saga.

"At Zhongba, the last outpost, it started to snow. Then we started climbing up into a wilderness of white that quickly proceeded to get worse. We were driving in jeeps but couldn't see the roads very well and got stuck often.

"But what an incredible experience to wake up at five in the morning, freezing, with icicles hanging from our mouths—as through the campsite charged a bellowing herd of wild asses!

Maybe they were some unheeded warning. For not a day later we were snowed in just short of Mayum La, a pass just shy of seventeen thousand feet. We could neither go back nor go forward. Here two in the party got sick, and one person started hallucinating.

"Our host now decided that he and a guide would climb the thousand feet to the top of the ridge in hopes of discovering some means of rescue from the other side. They didn't return until dark. The director of tourism had himself succumbed to altitude sickness, but his companion was worse. The guide was bleeding from his nose and mouth, and had been half carried the last three miles, barely making it back to camp.

"I knew he wouldn't last if we stayed there. I stayed up all night knowing something had to happen. By now the temperature was five below zero. There was a sharp wind which, I felt, would slice our ears and noses off! We had no water. And how awful to lick snow all day when you're freezing cold already.

"So there I was, half lying in my sleeping bag, in the jeep, because we could not pitch tents in the deep soft snow. I was cold, numb, and frightened, and kept repeating over and over to myself: 'Tomorrow we have got to get out of here,' when, in the early hours of the morning, I finally dozed off and had a strange dream. I dreamt of a monk. A Buddhist monk. With first light I got up to find him. It's difficult to explain, difficult even for me to understand now, but I knew that somehow I had to find this monk or people would commence dying.

"I had only gotten a short way from the jeep when I saw a light down the mountain. I didn't know if I was hallucinating or half crazy, so I turned back and woke up a driver, and dragged him to the exact spot. 'There,' I said, pointing, 'do you see that light?'

"He agreed that he did, that it might be ice reflecting from a lake, or it could be a human encampment. Concluding that it was, nevertheless, our only chance and that the two of us were as ablebodied as any in the party, we struck out for the beacon, not arriving at our destination until early afternoon.

"The light did, in fact, turn out to be of human origin. It was a truck stuck in the snow, and in the truck were nine Buddhist monks. They were headed for Thugo Gompa on Lake Manasarovar. One monk seemed to be chosen by the others to speak with me. So between my broken Tibetan, my Nepali, his broken Nepali and the driver's somewhat better Tibetan, communication, of a sort, transpired. After an hour's negotiations and much Tibetan tea (the monks had industriously collected yak dung all along their journey and this is what allowed them to make a fire) we agreed that we would give them all our food and pressure-cooking equipment in exchange for all their fuel and the monk chosen to talk with us to escort us back to civilization.

"All nine monks helped us dig the snow and push the jeeps out of snowdrifts for as many hours as they could, still allowing sufficient time to get back to their truck . . . then down we started. At the banks of the Tsangpo River we chained the jeeps together, as we always did, so that if one vehicle got stuck the other might tow it clear.

"The first jeep got through all right, but the second ran aground on something and then the chain broke. Naturally, I was in the second jeep. What a terrifying moment! Not knowing when some ice chunk would melt or shift and we'd be rolled over into this mushy, half-frozen water and swept who-knows-how-far downstream. The river was clunking at the bottoms of the doors, like an icy death politely knocking.

"Luckily, the monk was with us and we were able to open the front window of the jeep. He carried all of us—carried, one by one, and our tent, and whatever food we had—back and forth through that freezing water to a little island in the river.

"We just crashed in this one tent and went to sleep. Hoping to wake up tomorrow and still be in this world. Thankful that the two sick people, so close to death in the last few days, were in the first jeep, which (as it turned out) just drove and drove and drove until it reached medical attention.

"The next afternoon trucks appeared on the shore, and we were rescued, although the traction of the towing mechanism against the river's ice completely destroyed the jeep. We arrived in darkness at Zhongba, a town transformed into something of a circus by our appearance in the middle of the annual Yak Festival. It was quite an arrival. I remember we set up our tents in the field and fell into them. I was so tired I just unrolled my sleeping bag and climbed into it without even taking off my boots. There I was, falling asleep with all these nomad faces looking in through the tent door. We could not zip the flap as the nomads kept unzipping it out of curiosity. It wasn't until the next day that I discovered my toes were blue and I'd suffered a case of frostbite."

Uttara smiles at an elderly lady walking by and concludes. "Yes, that was my first attempt at Kailash. Unsuccessful, of course. Except that it taught me to survive by trusting my intuition. Now I'm supposed to be circulating among the guests, you know. Socializing is, after all, a very real part of my job, Tad."

Dazed, I thank Uttara profusely and return to the bar for a fifth lemon soda, feeling both lucky and frightened. Over the last few months I've paid great lip service to the perils of a Kailash sojourn. The night before the overland journey begins I finally realize this trip may actually prove dangerous. Just to the side of the bar Tenzin and Jim Edwards are admiring a satellite photograph of the Himalayas. Kailash is quite recognizable, looking pristinely straight, white, and very, very cold.

In the morning, with the last real coffee we'll taste in a month growling in our stomachs, we sit in a corner of the luxurious lobby. It's 6:40 A.M. Bob Thurman clears his throat and the voice of Tenzin speaks to the group for the first time.

TENZIN

Meeting The Blade Wheel of Mind Reform

Well then, fellow pilgrims! We all have come to circle the sacred mountain. If all goes well our preparations will bring us to a most magical place, together with the opportunity to become more enlightened beings. For a thousand years, Kailash has been a magnet for Tantric practice, the special, accelerated path designed for the extremists of the Dharma. I've been working on a translation of the incredible—and radical—ancient teaching, *The Blade Wheel of Mind Reform.* Don't worry, it is quite accessible for anyone, even someone fairly new to Buddhism. Once we first acclimatize to the path of the Buddha's teachings—the Buddha Dharma—the *Blade Wheel* will be my special gift to you. But you must be brave and concentrated, and first master the basic structure of the path. On our way to the mountain, we will work on meditation themes from the Tibetan Lamrim tradition, the Systematic Path of Enlightenment, developed by the eleventh-century Bengali master Atisha, who came to Tibet late in his life and was a tremendous force in Tibetan Buddhism. The Systematic Path was further refined by later masters, including the great lama Tsong Khapa (1357–1419) and then the Dalai Lamas. When we get to the mountain, we will turn to the *Blade Wheel.* We will also perform a fire-offering ceremony at the heart of the mountain, dedicating all our merit and virtue to the transformation of the whole world for the sake of all beings. If all goes well, after the mountain, we will touch the wheel of bliss.

My trips in the Himalayas are always Dharma trips—we travel through our inner landscape as well as through the countryside. I always teach the Dharma to travelers on several levels. First, you want to visit Tibet, so we visit empathetically the inner Tibet, the interior of the Tibetan mind, which was long ago reborn through the gate of the Buddha Dharma. Second, you want to know your world, so you need to know yourself—for this the Dharma is still unmatched as a guide. Third, you may now or later decide that this life is an opportunity for you to take charge of your own evolutionary process—and the Dharma is the art for doing this effectively.

Our little band of nine people on this special trip has special luck, since we're taking the hardest of pilgrimages. Indians and Tibetans feel it takes a special destiny for pilgrims even to reach Mt. Kailash. If they get round it they are empowered at a new level for the rest of their lives, the sins of lifetimes washed away. They circle it in three ways. First, they use the suffering and hardship to purify their negative karma, the dangerous evolutionary gravity of past actions. Then, they employ all their wisdom like a diamond drill to cut themselves free of the vicious cycle of samsara and ignorance, and to reach an exact understanding of reality. Third, if all goes well, they use the power of compassion to turn the wheel of great bliss to transform the universe into a realm of liberative art for all others. We will definitely go through the first level. We will reach strenuously for the second. And I hope we will be blessed enough to catch a glimpse of the third.

This morning, I will read through the opening verses of the *Blade Wheel* as a good omen at the outset of our trip. I will not comment much, nor will I return to it until we reach the mountain.

> Peacocks range the poison-plant jungle,
> Never drawn to the medicine-flower bed,
> Since they thrive on the essence of poison.

> The elegant spiritual heroes
> Likewise range the jungle of the life-cycle;
> Not fond of the sweet gardens of pleasure,
> They thrive in the jungle of sufferings.

> Our lives controlled by our inner coward,
> Obsessed with pleasure, we drown in suffering.
> Empowered by courage, willing to suffer,
> The spiritual hero is always happy!

> Here now in this apocalyptic life,
> Passions are like the poison-plant jungle,
> Where hero peacocks always flourish,
> And coward crows destroy themselves.

> Rigidly selfish and self-preoccupied,
> How could crows digest the toxic passions?
> Hopelessly hooked on the powerful addictions,
> They'd lose their lives of being free.

> Spiritual heroes are just like peacocks,
> Roaming the life-cycle jungle to transmute

The addictive poison-plant passions,
To change all poison to elixir.

Helplessly wandering the life-cycle,
Pushed by self-habits, slaves of the devil
Self-fascination, seeking ego-pleasure —
Stop! I volunteer to suffer for others' sake!

The many sufferings of all those beings
Who are just like me, addicted to passions
And unconsciously driven by evolution,
Pile them all up on my pleasure-seeking self!

Ever driven by the pull of selfish desire,
May I resist and satisfy others instead!
Even when friends turn against me,
I'll take the blame, saying, "My mistake."

When my body succumbs to disease,
My bad-action blade wheel comes full circle,
Since I caused so much harm to others' bodies —
Now may I take all sickness on myself!

When suffering overtakes my mind,
My bad-action blade wheel comes full circle;
I must have often disturbed others' hearts —
Now let me volunteer for all sufferings!

When I am tortured by hunger and thirst,
My bad-action blade wheel comes full circle;
I tricked many others, I robbed and hoarded —
Now let me embrace all hunger and thirst!

This is a heavy teaching, worthy of great Kailash. All of us here, I'm sure, are peacocks — aiming to transmute the poison of addictions into the elixir of wisdom energy — not crows. Remember these verses out on the rough and bumpy trail; let them inspire you when you feel discouraged. During the next week of covering territory and acclimatizing on the way, we will work up to the yoga of the peacock a bit more gently. I will give you experiential teachings on the stages of the Systematic Path, which organizes the entire Buddhist teaching into practical steps for inner development. We begin with our relationship to the spiritual path, and to the spiritual teacher and the tradition. Then we will go on to the themes crucial to the cultivation of a genuine self-appreciation and a sound self-esteem, along with detachment from the various kinds of bondage people get into when they don't appreciate themselves. From this we will move to the themes essential to developing compassion and genuine altruism. We end with the profound psychology of selflessness and voidness, the ways of developing transcendent wisdom of the precise nature of reality. We need this for release and liberation. This may seem like a lot, but our task is to master these themes experientially, getting the essential points and learning how to make them vivid in our meditations so they become second nature to us. And then we will be ready for the mountain—and for the *Blade Wheel*.

Now onward, to Tibet.

CHAPTER THREE

The Tibetan Border

TAD

*T*rue to plan we load into a minibus on October 5 at 8:10 in the morning. Driving through the last neatly pleated hills of Nepal we get down to cameo biographies. Wolfgang is researching a crucial scene in a novel about Tibet that he's abandoned a more practical life to write; Leopoldo is a prison psychologist grateful to be cleansed by the huge vistas, reminiscent to him of parts of his native Mexico. Richard is madly in love with his girlfriend and her two kids, but Kailash appeared and who of us could refuse the call?

Behind us, in a van of their own, follows a cast of porters and Sherpas. Our drivers are the men our lives will depend on for more hours and days than I can, at present, imagine. Before day one is done we'll know why drivers are paid better than doctors in Tibet. Every moment you continue your earthly life in their cars is a small miracle. We have three drivers on the trek (a fourth driving the truck.) One guy I love, one guy I like, and one guy I fear. The last looks like a heavy drinker and he drives too fast.

First stop: Bonepa, just to relieve the kidneys and stretch our legs, and for me to play harmonica for kids. Getting them trustful, rambunctious. Once the playful dynamic is established, I wheedle a high note and chase little ones into their mother's skirts. Now, straying off the main road, I walk past sheet-iron shacks built on stilts and stumble on a primitive roulette game played with ancient rupee notes by half-naked children. Here I get my first wish.

Everywhere I go kids ask for money. With harmonica at my lips I say, "No, no! You pay me! Musica rupee!" Well, here in Bonepa, one little beggar takes a rupee from his pile of winnings, and, in a wonderful role reversal, throws it at the rich American. My first earnings as a musician in Asia! Of course, I bet it immediately on the game, and—much to the crowd's delight—win. A few adults peer out of the storklike tin-can cabins, smiling with keen curiosity. I bet the pile again and lose—which delights the crowd even more. With a mock-mournful rendition of "Waltzing Matilda," I head back to the van.

A few hours later, in Kodari, we hit the first Chinese checkpoint. The officials are little more than boys in uniform playing tough, smoking cigarettes, and striking macho poses. They take their time looking over our papers, and finally decide all baggage must be removed from the vehicles. It's a bluff. There is no thorough search, only time for me to play a few tunes for some more children, two of whom are about to kill a giant spider. Tenzin prevents the assassination and places the bug a safe distance away. No such deus ex machina intervened on the behalf of the occupants of a bus we find freshly hauled up from the gorge eight hundred feet below. For them, the beyond was a lot closer than any hospital.

We actually set foot in Tibet upon crossing the Bhote Kosi River, on both sides of which trees, shrubs, and moss cling to every perilously steep bit of earth and rock that hasn't plummeted to the white water several hundred feet below. The vans are a thing of the past, so we hoof it a quarter of a mile over an impressive bridge. Up the notch is the "ledge-town" of Kodari, cheap, fast-built concrete structures peering down on us from bulldozed terraces. A hotel sign blinks with only a portion of its bulbs functioning. Armed sentries stand at both sides of the bridge. A memory from my reading swims to the surface: "Is this . . .?"

"Friendship Bridge?" Jock—oozing irony from every syllable—finishes my question. "What's wrong, Tad? Don't these guys just give you that warm-all-over-feeling?"

"Sure. Right. Friendship Bridge," I whisper, glancing over the stone eyes of the guards; remembering the testimonies of Ama Adhe, Freedom Momma, and Tenpa Sopa. She—whose husband and father were covertly poisoned, who became a member of a woman-only underground, who was interrogated, tortured, imprisoned, then beaten, raped, starved, and worked for twenty years. He, part of the Dalai Lama's escape team who, having successfully fled, was sent back into the firestorm of Norbulinka with a letter of explanation to the Tibetan people. There Tenpa picked up the forbidden gun, fought the Chinese, was wounded, and, too weak to commit suicide, captured. Then he too was interrogated, tortured, starved, and worked to skeletal thinness for twenty-seven years. Eventually each of them—along with a few other lucky Tibetans—walked this very bridge to liberation. Finally reaching Dharamsala, India, each was granted an audience with His Holiness, but neither could speak at first, for the tears clogging their eyes, mouths, and hearts.

The lucky get out this way. But we're going in. Are we stupid? Is this ill-advised?

"Indeed," I think to myself, "be very friendly, Robert Thurman. This name on your passport could alert these petty officials to just who you are: intimate of the Dalai Lama. Notorious China critic. Yes, that's right, Tenzin, stoop and smile, scrape and bow. We need you on this trip."

Above Kodari we're transferred into blue, canopied cargo vehicles that start with a crank and die with a whimper. The truck in front of us is picking up army personnel. More toy soldiers trying to disguise their curiosity with an air of nonchalant superiority. Ahead, the Chinese are dynamiting new sections of road, which doesn't do much for the old ones. Tight turns have become "squeak-bys." Outside, tires are less than a foot from the edge too much of the time. I'm clammy with sweat, even if I'm cold in a sweater. Jock is sitting elephant-rider-style on the cab of the truck in a tee shirt. We bump along a short distance, then the truck in front of us stops. Wolfgang, Tenzin, and I are gathered just behind Jock, keeping an eye out for rocks shaking loose from the ledges above. The soldiers get out and start smoking. It seems we'll be here a while.

Tenzin returns to his mutterings, as he will the whole trip long. This time, however, the linguist chooses to share.

"I am reciting the mantra of Superbliss Buddha Chakrasamvara as a female Buddha, the Vajrayogini. It goes: *Om om om sarva buddha dakiniye vajra varnaniye vajra vairochaniye hum hum hum pai pai pai svaha.* I have done informal retreats on this deity. I've also had the initiations of the male forms of the deity. This whole pilgrimage for me is like a retreat. I myself am going to recite this mantra. Try to get it going in your mind. It doesn't mean that you can't talk or interact, it's just you try to do this during breaks, you know, to get through a few thousand repetitions during this month, using whichever mantra you choose.

"The purpose of saying the mantra—it's called the seed of the deity—is to bring the deity close to you. By reciting it you get a sense of familiarity with the deity. By the time we get to the mountain, we'll have developed that closeness more strongly. Then we'll recite it at the mountain.

"If it's too long, you can always fall back on *Om mani padme hum,* which is the very simplest one—wisdom and compassion in union: 'the jewel and the lotus together.' Another good one to recite is *Om tare tuttare ture svaha,* which is a mantra of Tara, the female form of Avalokiteshvara."

One by one we climb out of the truck. Tenzin is teaching a mantra as three Tibetan nomads draw near. His glass eye seems to be scrutinizing them when, in fact, he is unaware of their approach until they're only two feet away. They are, without trying to be rude, practically in his face before he sees them. A loud Tibetan greeting results and their faces light up like long-jawed lanterns. Now, conversely, they become bashful, covering their faces in shy surprise. The most courageous of them discourses at length about the dynamiting ahead, explaining that it probably caused the landslide farther up the line.

Other Tibetans in ill-fitting suit jackets and battered dress pants converge to hear the blond giant speak fluent Tibetan. A truck driver explains that he has been stuck on this side of the avalanche for two months. Unable to abandon his vehicle, he's made a little money transporting people and supplies to the edge of the landslide and back. He finishes a can of Pabst Blue Ribbon (the Marlboro of beers, here) and tosses it resignedly into the gorge below.

Not long after Tenzin retires to the truck for a nap, a Chinese soldier-boy climbs over the hood and, in a strange mixture of arrogance and friendliness, tries to engage him in conversation. Tenzin feigns no Chinese, playing the uninformed tourist.

With the truck ahead finally filled and the two-hour delay over, we start. The front-running truck is the guinea pig, hitting all the trouble spots first. Through a mudslide they fantail around, then we fantail around. They go over a huge bump, we go over a huge bump. They trounce their kidneys over a minefield of potholes, we do the same. The circuit is broken only when they get stuck. At this we back up, and our driver gets out to assist.

Soldiers pour out of the truck, shovels and crowbars in hand. Much yelling, pushing, and grumbling, and finally the truck lumbers out of its trap. This follow-the-leader roller coaster proceeds hour after hour, while I keep one eye on the drop, ready to claw my way out from under the tarpaulin and leap free of the falling truck.

We bump and thump on. At one eroded hairpin turn, the driver stops maybe ten inches from the edge, yanks up the emergency brake, opens his door out over the abyss, skitters from the cab and views our quandary from a couple of angles. The problem, we can plainly see, is that the road rises in a prodigious hump on the uphill side, exactly where the turn is tightest. Now, having monitored dozens of possibilities in an instant, he leaps back behind the wheel, disengages the brake, revs the engine, and we lunge forward, hearts in mouths, prayer beads in hands, as—sure enough—the hump unweights our traction and we churn sideways toward the edge. Wolfgang and I are hanging out on the wrong side, staring bug-eyed at The Long Goodbye, our mouths agape, when the wheels catch with a lurch. We lose no time in communicating the true recklessness of the driver's courage: the edge had eroded a good foot and a half under the road we've just maneuvered.

Finally we arrive at the official border town of Zhangmu, at eight o'clock Chinese time. As my feet hit the hard dirt that surrounds the town, an awful irony rolls over me. I haven't had a drop of liquor in eighteen months. I'm on the spiritual quest of a lifetime. But like it or not—I'm drunk. Not a little, no. More like a three-martini reel. At my feet is a playing card with a Chinese girl in bra and panties. Naturally. All the addictions rearing up at once. I pick up the card and stuff it in my pocket.

"It's bad karma," comes Wolfgang's Teutonic protest.

I think to tell him off, but I'm legless. Philosophically and literally. With ridiculous regret I pull the card out of my pocket and return it to the dirt.

At the border office, Tenzin is talking with a little officer of fifty or so, who has three stars on his shoulder. Suddenly our leader with "little or no" Chinese is jabbering away a mile a minute and once again proffering a smile. The officer wades in closer until he's a mere three feet from the babbling giant. He must be asking where Tenzin is from. With the word "American" the Chinese officer unconsciously takes a single step back. With "New York," another step back, as the smile tightens to a squint of begrudging respect. I'm carrying five books, two tape players, an entire case of batteries and ten blank one-hour tapes. Wolfgang has several pictures of the Dalai Lama stashed on his person, which is a crime in Tibet, but Tenzin is clean. He isn't even carrying a camera, and so the lie comes quite naturally to his lips. Books, tapes, pictures, magazines? "None. A few maps is all we have."

I've propped my back up against a wall, trying to steady myself sufficiently to fill out a visitor's permit. Jock is telling us that the only numbers we need to get right are the dates and passports. I'm smiling. This guy has dealt with altitude drunks before.

Approaching the flimsy gate that is raised and lowered as a symbol of power, I start to laugh.

"No laughter," Jock advises quietly, "don't even smile. They'll think you're showing contempt."

"They'd be right," I slur, vaguely shocked with the rebelliousness wafting off me like the stench of gin.

"It's too late to be officially admitted," Tenzin is explaining, "but since we're carrying no books we can stay the night and come back in the morning."

Once inside the Zhangmu Hotel I stare through cross-rigged drapes and grimy windows at the grey peaks across the valley, practicing a clumsy mantra, wishing I knew what it meant. After a while, I'm called to dinner. I stumble out and rush up the stairs, only to realize it's freezing. Returning to my room to find a parka, I rush up the stairs again, ink blotches spill over my eyes, my chest heaving like a badly loaded washing machine.

"Hey, slow down fella. It's called acclimatization because that's what you're supposed to do. Acclimatize." It's Jock, cool, calm, and collected.

On a bluff overlooking the narrow, steep street a large blinking neon light advertises karaoke at the rear windows of the rival hotel. The smaller buildings' roll-down metal doors are locked tight. From shacks and lean-tos constructed on the street itself, sitting atop crates and leering from brick-lined darkness, wide, shadowy faces peer in hostile curiosity. Who is Chinese and who Tibetan? I don't know.

Jay is leading us. He was here a few years ago, on his way to Lhasa, and remembers a remote restaurant worth sniffing out. Up a flight of stairs and over a bridge-like parapet, we enter a large, sprawling room. We're seated around the circular table and greeted by a Tibetan waitress wearing the traditional striped apron that announces a married woman. She is very pleased to see us. Soon we're feasting on plate after plate of what I will too late realize is the best food I'll get in the next three weeks in Tibet. A combination of Chinese and local cuisine: soups, noodles, rice, chicken and rice, yak and rice; sprouts, tofu and cabbage; *momo*s (Tibetan dumplings), puri, dal, and tea. Some drink beer despite Jock's warning that altitude problems are exaggerated with alcohol.

After dinner Jay goes off to karaoke night to continue drinking and to dance with the wives of smiling, drink-buying men. He dances with men, too. Very Klondike-esque. I won't hear of this until the following day when I realize that much of my old life will be relived for me through this witness of my youth.

Breakfast is in the basement. And to be fair they've tried very hard to scramble eggs, cook bacon, toast bread, and boil water. I stick to the bean sprouts, onions, and glutinous cellophane noodles, with a double strong dose of Nescafé washing down a couple of Alleve to battle the pain in my temples. I also dispense a ration of acidophilus, echinacea, goldenseal, vitamin C, and a garlic pill to myself and to Tenzin. Nena made me promise to keep him dosed with these supplements.

Jay and I are discussing traveling incognito. There is a long tradition of this in Tibet. For centuries any European wishing to travel unmolested would do so in disguise. Even then they took their chances, like any other, since the *dacoits*, or bandits, particularly prevalent in the Kailash region were not picky about their prey.

I've spent the early hours reading Lama Govinda, learning a new mantra, making a few notes. Now we're all at breakfast and Tenzin declares that he will give his first formal Dharma talk. I whip out my tape recorder and place it, sidewise in front of him, on the Nescafé jar. I've used a section of cloth that is precious to me to wipe the untrusty water droplets from an otherwise clean cup. I spread the cloth on my lap. We're not sitting in lotus position, there's no incense smoldering on an altar, and yet we're being watched by the help as if we were setting forth on the teachings of a forbidden religion. I'm now able to distinguish between the Tibetans with their bigger cheekbones and the narrow-faced, less robust Chinese. The dozen or so Asians in the cafeteria make no effort to disguise the fact that they are watching our every move.

Tenzin is up-beat, energized, smiling broadly; everything about the man says *this is what I live to do.* "The first theme," he insists, "is the relationship to the spiritual teacher. It's crucial to have a personal relationship with an enlightened person, if possible. That, in itself, is another whole discussion, but in a way it's central to Tibetan Buddhism."

Of course this is the first issue, I think to myself. And it is a huge one for me, as interior questions shout themselves aloud: Is Tenzin an enlightened person? Has he accepted me as a student? Have I asked him to be my teacher? As his good eye cordially brushes by mine, Tenzin explains:

"The relationship to the teacher in Buddhism is not a big deal, in contrast to Hinduism. Buddhists challenge the heavy guru idea; they call the mentor 'spiritual teacher,' and 'spiritual friend,' as a close friend, not an absolute authority. This emphasizes how you have to free yourself, develop your own enlightenment. No one else can do it for you. But in Tantra the sort of transference relation to the teacher is very important. You spend twelve years to investigate such a central figure. You don't jump into receiving teachings from the first teacher. Not initiatory teaching."

Twelve? Today it's been twenty—as Tenzin begins again to speak the Dharma.

TENZIN

Here we are in Tibet, at last. I'll now admit that I was afraid I'd be denied entry, rejected as too good a friend of the Dalai Lama and sent back to Nepal. But it didn't happen. I'm so glad we're on our way to Kailash. I can tell you that I am hoping there will be a magical key there to open the heart of the world, beginning with the hearts of the Chinese leaders to get them to relent on Tibet and let her people go. If only they realized how magnificent it would be to free Tibet and release her people. They could again fire up the furnaces of their monastic factories of positive evolutionary energy and pour pure spiritual energy into the vision of the positive evolution of the planet.

Tibet is hard to understand. After thirty-plus years, I just begin to see how its form of society has no parallel on the planet. We have no categories for it. Tibetan civilization is a living model of an alternative modernity, a viable lifestyle that is modern in good ways but not destructively materialistic. Once free of this modern materialistic occupation, Tibet will serve as a beacon for a joyous postmodern lifestyle.

But later for Tibet. We came here on pilgrimage, to perform the Dharma, and we should confidently feel a sense of destiny.

The Systematic Path

The first meditation theme in this path is the relationship to the spiritual teacher. Once you actually start the path, it is crucial to have a relationship with an individual who you genuinely feel represents the living teaching. You might presume that because you're a modern person and Buddha lived long ago, you'll never attain enlightenment. That's why a living mentor is of the first importance—as it is in Zen. We begin by imagining the teacher as the Buddha, concentrating on finding the Buddha alive for us through the icon of the teacher.

Once you're actually working on the path, you take up the preciousness of human life. Usually people think of religious practice as beginning with putting oneself down—"I'm so ignorant" and "I'm so sinful." But to contemplate the preciousness of human life is to focus on the tremendous achievement of having become a human being—thinking back karmically, evolutionarily, over just how much it took to get to be a human being.

In Carl Sagan's *Cosmos* series, one program went all the way up from the Precambrian slime. He walked along a cosmic calendar in which biological evolution takes place over a month of many hundred-million-year days. Finally, on the last day of the month, in the four-billionth year, Homo sapiens shows up, the inheritor of this incredible journey up from primeval ooze.

The Buddhist feeling about evolution is even more cosmic than that, except it's not only a genetic or material process on the part of some genes or species. The focus is on the incredible journey of the individual: We ourselves were worms. We had to evolve through the chain of life-forms, until finally reaching this human-lifetime window. Through it we realize instincts are optional. We can reprogram ourselves not to grab the thing in front of us immediately, as a crocodile does. Not to run away from something that seems a little worrisome. Humans can become like rats in a cage, overpopulate, become self-destructive. Or we can become buddhas; completely self-creative. The choice is before us constantly.

We have all evolved not only up but down the ladder of life-forms many times. Once you have the human life-form, if you waste it just making money or building up the ego, if you die having no control over your unconscious, never having become aware of your full potential, it's a tremendous waste. You may be dragged by subconscious impulses into lower life-forms for a very long period of time.

Tibetans are steeped in this vision of evolution, cherishing human birth as the only realm for attaining enlightenment. So your aim in life is to develop yourself at least to the point where you'll have a shot at another, even better human life, and, in the best case, full enlightenment. The full unfolding is possible only for a human who's totally dedicated, with the best facilities, faculties, and health.

Buddha told a parable for this. He said that there's an old blind turtle who lives in the bottom of the seven oceans and who surfaces once every century for air, and there's a golden yoke floating randomly around the seas. As often as the blind turtle at the bottom of the ocean happens to raise his head through the neck hole of the yoke when he comes up for his centenary breath, that's how often you can get back to the human life-form from being in the involuntary life-forms of the lower states of existence. You really should appreciate what you have right now. This human prize! Look at your thumb. We don't have to see this thumb as coming merely from being a successful aggressor. Rather it comes from being playful, experimental, gentle, and generous. If we were going to be more successful as an aggressor, why have a hand like this, with wimpy fingernails that break on the slightest scratch? These monkeylike fingers are playful, even erotic; they're not naturally aggressive.

The saber-toothed tiger is aggressive. He could bite your head right off. But nothing forced him to vary his instinctual programming, he just jumped and ate whatever was in front of him. Humans have to think about it, to learn to empathize with each other, to talk to each other. That's where the flexibility of our form came from, from arriving at the boundary between self and other. Sociality is the specially human virtue and the source of language. You never develop language if you just eat everybody you meet!

There are of course many different types of human lives. The most advantageous form of human life, which many Westerners enjoy, is endowed with the eight liberties and the ten opportunities. The eight liberties are liberty from hell, the ghost realms, animal forms, god forms, titan forms, human slave societies, and human lives without functional senses or intelligence. The ten opportunities involve having access to education, being in a world where a buddha has visited, being in a central country where the teaching of freedom is available, and so forth. We're now visiting what was once a central country, meaning a nation where liberative, self-transformative teachings and practices are embedded in the core of the culture. Today it's buried under communist indoctrination, but it's still alive in people's hearts, even though most of them don't articulate it. It gives them a certain tolerance and cheerfulness even under tremendous duress.

In many societies there's no notion of liberation or self-illumination or education, merely training for life as a hunter or a warrior or a computer programmer. The real teaching of freedom is very rare. The materialistic mode, in both its Western liberal form and its communist form, offers no possibility of real liberation. We have ideas like the pursuit of happiness, the fight for freedom, and the land of liberty, but nobody has any idea of what liberty is.

Real existential and experiential liberty, where you can completely control your entire environment, choose your embodiment, and freely travel through time and space, is completely inconceivable to us.

Real freedom was not taught even by the religions in Buddha's India. You had to worship gods and then they might save you from suffering and put you on a nice shelf, eventually, if you were lucky. But that still left you under their control completely. God can put you on the angel shelf instead of in the roasting pan, but you still don't have freedom. He has freedom. You attribute it to God, but you don't have it.

That's why the most important of the famous noble truths taught by the Buddha was the noble truth of freedom, which is the truth of nirvana. Contemplation of this noble truth of nirvana opens people up to the very idea that there is such a thing as freedom. Once you can imagine it, you feel a different sense about the meaning of your life. That you could be reliably, calmly, blissfully free, with absolutely nothing to compel you. No problems or suffering. This is unimaginable at first. Coming from a Protestant background if I even start to think about being free and happy, I unconsciously feel anxious, expecting someone to hit me or step on me. That's how we've been conditioned.

Awareness of freedom is part of Tibet's special legacy. So is the rare preciousness of human life. Enjoy this contemplation of your potential. Count your blessings carefully. Be honestly proud of yourself. Karmically, you all made great efforts and did great things to get to be such beautiful human beings, to be here at this time. After this talk, we will move into discussions of death, impermanence, and suffering. You can get depressed by focusing too intently on those themes. You might feel too negative about yourself. You must master this first theme of the value of human life in order to develop a more intense level of appreciation for yourself and for the fabulous opportunity you have.

CHAPTER FOUR

Acclimatizing

TAD

At the border we hear about a landslide further up the line. I stow this information, uneasily. Then a couple of mountains roll by, another town or two—and here's the landslide. Where the road used to be is now a freshly formed flank of earth swarming with nearly a hundred porters hurrying toward us with work permits in one hand and work ropes in the other.

Our head Sherpa (called the sirdar) Lobsang, is choosing porters as we lumber forward stiffly, some of us giving our day packs to the porters, who appear out of nowhere caroling us with, "I carry, sir. I help. Very dangerous, sir. I help!" Their wide smiles and confident hands are both comforting and disconcerting. I shrug them off and hurry to catch up with Tenzin.

"Everyone be careful here. Be quite careful!" he booms out. Under his breath he informs me that a western trekker recently lost his life on this slide. Is he watching me for a reaction? I do my best to appear unafraid.

Getting around the boulders is easy until the half-dozen routes converge onto one convex rim about eleven inches across. This is all that remains of the trail. Sherpas in rotting sneakers are bottlenecking at both ends, impatient to double up, yet resorting to single file. Under their feet glistens a lip of packed mud overlooking a two-hundred-foot drop to a thundering gorge. I'm thinking: "How embarrassing to die on the very first maneuver."

I hesitate. Take a picture, tie a shoe, watch the porters take turns. But there's Tenzin already over, so clearly I can do this. Just don't look down and don't look up. I feel watched, as if the grim reaper is glancing up from a nap. Then I'm over. I've done it. Trying not to advertise my profound relief, I turn to watch our senior member gear up for the pass. He traverses it without incident.

Above the landslide several of our group are perched on rocks, nodding out in the sun. Low pines and bush partially obscure a very familiar-looking spike-leafed plant. I catch Jay's eye and point with my chin. He smiles, conspiratorially.

Leopoldo asks if he might borrow my copy of Tenzin's translation of *The Tibetan Book of the Dead*. I'm feeling useful at last. I have also loaned an extra set of sunglasses and a sink stopper to Richard, who "plain out forgot" the stopper in Zhangmu, which endears him to me.

Backing down the road come three nauseating-green Toyota Landcruisers, with several joking, smiling men in each. Our kitchen staff and porters are introduced. I fall on my knees before the cook, Pawan, and start prostrating. Everyone laughs, especially Pawan.

We put in a long day's journey in a few short hours, climbing an additional thirty-five hundred feet by midafternoon. In Nyalam I fall out of the car and sense laughter in the eyes of the locals. Happy, not hostile laughter. It's another dusty, gray road town, with roll-down doors open for business. Feels like the wild, wild west — except on a severe slant.

In a two-table restaurant decorated with a beaded curtain doorway and a cheesy poster of the Alps, Tenzin reviews his first talk, explaining that, ideally, questions about one teaching should be addressed before the next is presented. Richard, the painter, takes one look at the poster of the Alps and explodes with hysterical laughter. "Maybe we'd better acclimatize another few hours," Tenzin concedes, shaking his head at Richard in good-humored disbelief.

"I have a question," volunteers Wolfgang, who takes off his Australian bushman hat, and places it on his lap.

"Oh good," smiles Tenzin, "someone is holding on to their wits!" Wolfgang's sparse gray hair and reserved spectacles give him a serious demeanor, yet when he laughs his face lights up with youthful vigor. "Zee preciousness of human life is totally familiar to me," he states proudly. "But what came up for me was this: I happen to have been brought up in another belief system. Namely a Christian one, in which our souls were created as such, and we didn't have to go through a period in the past when we weren't human, and so on."

"That's quite correct," Tenzin says, nodding slowly. "It brings up a basic point that is very important. In order to develop a strong sense of the preciousness of human life, it must connect to one's belief system. The belief system doesn't necessarily have to be the Buddhist karmic belief system, but it has to be one that is critically aware of the uniqueness and special opportunities of this life-form.

"Most of us are brought up in the modern world believing that we are material entities and that the brain is the source of the mind, and that when the brain ceases to function that's the end of it. That is the underlying modernist belief. Very few people live by a sense that they will have a future existence. And very few really believe that they had a former existence. This is really very rare, and so is the theme of the extreme preciousness of human life."

Wolfgang is smiling and holds his hand open at his chest, like a surgeon waiting for gloves, "I'm not a materialist — that's not where I am. I know several of my past lives, I know all this. But still, I never discovered a past life as a dog."

Laughter accompanies this remark.

"I'm not saying that's where you are," Tenzin affably qualifies his argument. "I'm coming back to where you are. I'm saying that the basic ground on which our society works reduces us to an illusory subjectivity that is completely destroyed in an instant by death. Even if we, personally, have developed something different, this is still what's considered rational in society. It's 'feed the physical body, because that's all there is.' Our medical system prolongs the life of the physical body, even in a coma, because death is the absolute end of the whole thing.

"The other secret tenet of the Western materialist mind-set is that the rational thing to do is to have the most pleasant physical circumstances for this life. Never mind what happens after that. Because 'I'm not going to be around. And I wasn't here before. I didn't have any hand in creating the situation that I'm in.' There's no sense of eternal pain or terrifying hell realms. There's no goal except immediate self-gratification and so the license to waste other individuals is great."

Tenzin is geared up, the group's shared silence acknowledges we are here to listen. "So that's the background. Even if we have elaborated another theory, we're living what the Tibetans call 'life for the purpose of this life.' We're identifying with the self as this body and these appetites and impulses, and living to satisfy those.

"Buddhism teaches infinite consequentiality, meaning an infinite past consequentiality, and an infinite future consequentiality. The great thing about the horizon of that infinity is that there is no limit to how amazing you can become. You can go far beyond God and become anything you want. But the danger that goes along with infinite positive potential, of course, is that you can let yourself go into infinite negative states as well. Further, the human mind fears infinity, for the same reason it fears the dark. Limitlessness is scary. What you can do, in the meditation on the rarity and preciousness of human existence, is look at your own ideology and try to analyze it: 'What is my worldview? Why do I feel I'm contained within such and such a setting?' When you look carefully and find something that seems to be a solid wall or a boundary, look critically at that. Ask: 'Is that really so? What is the scripture from which it comes? Did God say so? Did the scientists find this out? Can they prove it?'

"When you start looking critically like that, you begin to find that all the ideas you have about the world start to dissolve, especially the materialist view, which can't account for any of it. Because the notion of nothing is just . . . nothing!" Tenzin explodes into nonsensical laughter, then recovers and bolts on.

"It's the irrational way our minds work that we despair over nothing. For example, Miguel de Unamuno, the great existentialist, said he was afraid of nothingness—*La Nada!* He made a big fuss about it. But that's ridiculous, nobody's afraid of *la nada. Nada* is *nada!* It's nothing to be afraid of—it's nothing! You can't become it."

Remembering one of Hemingway's best soliloquies on *la nada,* I can't resist joining in. "But nothingness is an insult to a creative being. An artist spends a lifetime filling sandbags to keep nothingness at bay. For an egomaniac, it's terrifying."

Tenzin looks at me blankly. "No, it isn't," he says impatiently. "Lots of egomaniacs shoot up heroin without hesitation. They ask the dentist for sodium pentathol imploringly; they're not at all terrified of it. And whether it's permanent or not, they don't care. Absolutely not. Modern egomaniacs feel 'nothing' is sitting there, waiting for them. It's like falling into a deep sleep. Perhaps they might have some thought of 'Maybe I'll be back.' But they don't care as long as everything is obliterated."

Like an annoying fly, I have been batted out of the way, as Tenzin finds his place again in the book of his mind. "The point is: When Miguel de Unamuno said he was afraid of *la nada,* he was fooling himself about the real deal here, which is the idea of infinite consequentiality.

"Today's meditation is the appreciation of one's own life—its amazingness, its majesty, its opportunity—and the danger of losing it while still being un-self-controlled, un-self-aware. This meditation is an opening of one's self, which is a gradual process. Not like 'Ah! I see it, brother. I believe!' Not just adopting some slogan. It's a critical peeling away of those layers of boundary that are put in by all different cultures. They're trainer wheels, our myths. They're comforting in a delusory way because they lull us into coasting along, wasting our opportunity. We think that God will take us to heaven as long as we repeat the right slogans. If people don't like the slogan, blow them away, the ultimate way of dismissing another person. As in Bosnia. Or on the Los Angeles freeways.

"But where do they go when you kill them? And what happens to your karma now that you're a murderer? 'No, no, don't worry about all that,' say the false authorities, who claim to shield you from killer karma, but cannot.

"Now, in the idea of infinite consequentiality everyone has been in your face infinitely, already. All of us have been each other's parents, we've been each other's lovers, we've been each other's arch-enemies, we have killed each other, we have saved each other, we have eaten each other, we have fed ourselves to each other. We've done every conceivable thing to and for each other, already, many times. So now why do you think this guy—some mysteriously awful and angry guy—is in your face? And ready to kill you? Well, could it be you blew him away last time? Suddenly everything you do reverberates infinitely back to you."

Behind his hand Thurman whispers loudly: "That's the preview of *The Blade Wheel of Mind Reform*. Now, back to today's feature!

"Once you attain the idea that you made your body through your own acts, you will resist those fools who tell you to go out and kill and be killed over a few acres. Their prayers have little impact on your destiny—even their gods don't have the power to raise you up into the happy hunting ground. In fact, if you've died and been reborn driven by the fear and rage of battle, you may have become a crocodile, slimily slithering around in the river! You're going to be one ticked-off crocodile.

"Before you let that happen you start saying: 'Wait a minute. You don't control my life! You—king—don't own my life. My parents—you don't own my life either. My soul is my own spiritual gene carrying the code of all my past actions, and right now

it's carrying my code of being human because of all my past generosity, justice and morality, tolerance, effort, concentration, and
intelligence. I'm not going to throw all that away for some lousy
four acres!'

"So individualism gets incredibly strong. The insight into the
preciousness of the human life endowed with liberty and opportunity is based on this idea of infinite consequentiality coming from
the past and going on to the future.

"And then there is this scary side. We really don't like the
sound of hell. We completely rebel against it. Still, when we open
up to the possibility that we could infinitely evolve into a positive
state, we become aware that there is also the danger of devolving
into infinite negativity. To enjoy the positive fruition, we must face
that the negative side is also there. We can always backslide and
chance getting squashed. But because there's an infinite positive
potential, we can become completely enlightened if we really take
advantage of this human embodiment of leisure and opportunity.
Right, Richard?"

Something snaps in Richard. His insane laugh sounds like a
space ship lifting off, as up, up, up the pitch floats into the lunatic
range.

We go for dinner to a different yak-butter-and-beer hole,
where the greasy food is terrible. A four-man mountain-climbing
team of mad Frenchmen barges in, soon filling a table with beer
liters, wine bottles, and smoldering ashtrays. Tenzin engages them
in French and their tale bubbles forth. We're looking at victors.
Two of the four men made it to the top of some mountain or
another just shy of twenty-four thousand feet.

"With oxygen?" I ask Tenzin, who asks the Frenchmen, who
explode in pride of accomplishment. "No, no! *No oxygène!*"

I lead the applause, while the climbers refill their glasses and
point them at us in brief detours leading back to their mouths.
There is something in their eyes I haven't seen before. Or rather,
something that isn't in their eyes, that I usually see. Sanity. These
men have opium-eaters' eyes. Insane eyes.

They smack each other across the head and pound their own
chests, reveling in primordial machismo, the only Westerners we'll

encounter who are completely uninterested in the Dharma. But these mountain-climbing lunatics seem to recognize something familiar in our leader, an explorer's courage, and impatience with those who can't find a similar courage.

In our rooms upstairs I accept an herbal laxative from Wolfgang. He suggests two pills, I take three. "So this is what impotence must be like," I think wandering down another dim hall to another dead mattress, "fear of failure being half the problem." The next day I start giving away toilet paper, hoping reverse psychology might have an effect.

I wake up to big pain, a nasty, two-bottles-of-Spanish-champagne-with-a-Christian-Brothers-Brandy-float pain. It's dark outside. With a flashlight I find painkillers and water, and force them down. Jay is lightly snoring in the next bed so that fearless-leader Jock can have his own room. I want to cry. I miss my daughters — little and big. That's righteous love. I also miss Cynthia. That's righteous, too. I also miss another woman, which is decidedly not righteous, and it all makes my head bang.

The dawn is coming up over gray mountains and even grayer buildings as I stumble to the edge of town, to Nyalam's claim to fame: a gigantic boulder glittering with broken glass and, maybe, some legitimate mica. There's a loudspeaker perched on the back of it. I wonder what they say over it. "This big Tibetan rock is no longer a Tibetan rock, it's a Chinese rock, which is most fitting, since China is bigger than Tibet, and bigger still for the addition of this big rock."

All around me tower naked giants. Hairless. Treeless. Only spots of green, specks of cranberry, cairn stones, and prayer-flagged towers dot the horizon of horsetail clouds — these turning mango and salmon over the cold, stone mountains.

I return and after breakfast we are all invited into Tenzin's room for the Dharma talk. Jay sits down cross-legged on the carpet-covered concrete. Jock and the others follow, all but Richard, who falls back into a desk chair, and me, sitting upright on the bed across from Tenzin. As Tenzin pulls his feet into a half lotus on the bed, the room is expectantly silent.

TENZIN

Spiritual Friends and Impermanence

If everyone would now leave the discursive and go into the meditative mode, we want to go back to the very source of the path. Which is the focus on the teacher, reliance on the spiritual friend.

As you listen try to half close your eyes. Settle into a meditation state, because I'm going to give you some visualizations. Calm yourself by focusing on your breath. Just breathe—count ten inhalations. Once you're calm, begin to visualize. Imagine a field of vision up above your forehead, which you see with your mind's eye, your third eye, rather than with your normal eyes—a kind of space and light, a boundless sky. In that sky is your greatest mentor. It doesn't have to be the Buddha. It certainly doesn't need to be me. It could be Christ, if you have a strong relationship with him. Or Mother Mary. Or Moses, if you have a relationship with him. It could be Rudolf Steiner, Gurdjieff, or some great teacher you had in school, a parent, or a grandparent, the Dalai Lama, or Thomas Merton. Whoever the person is, whatever the religion, it doesn't matter; the race, gender, and era don't matter. Choose him or her to embody the state of being that you aspire to—enlightenment, the total knowledge of everything worth knowing.

Visualize that person present there before and above you as a body made of light. Now the being looks at you, and you see the face—it's hard to visualize whoever it is, at first. It's just a flash, because your mind is unsteady. You see that being up there above you—I'll just use Buddha because that works for me—right here, not dead a thousand years ago, and he's happy that you're going to meditate now. He's looking down at you, smiling because you are concentrating on opening your mind, and from his smile light rays flow down. Like streams of medicine, they flow into you and make you feel more light. You begin to feel blissful and buoyant, as though a spotlight is shining on you, lifting you up in this spiritual limelight that makes you glow with bliss. It drives away smoky, dark doubts, negative attitudes, and worry. Visualize that you're being bathed in this radiant aura emanating from a being of total omniscience. It takes a lot of imagining. Don't forget to breathe— you must breathe to imagine. At least in the beginning.

It is crucial to develop this positive setting before meditating on anything. A luminous setting is the key to lifting ourselves out of our habitual ruminative thoughts, our sense of self-identity, our self-world. We need to enter into the space of saints and sages and gods and goddesses and create a new space of possibility for ourselves. We don't just say: "Well, I'm going to do something, but it's going to be the same me that does it." This goes along with the presupposition that after I finish it'll still be the same "me" who just spent time meditating. Instead we start meditation by creating an ideal space, and then we enter that space and everything opens and becomes possible. This is a path of becoming aware of and then shifting our sense of orientation, substituting a more positive view.

This space where we take refuge when we meditate is known as the refuge field. It is a kind of portable shrine we learn to live with, as we make our lives more and more spiritually positive.

Now fill the field around you on your level with a great crowd of beings below the luminous presence. These beings cannot see the enlightened beings above, since they are not consciously seeking refuge, but they can see us. In the front ranks of this crowd are all those we know closely—our lovers, our mates, our children— looking to us because they sense that we've entered a different field. They perceive the light that suffuses us from the mentor-being as our own new glow. For this reason they're smiling too. Their pleasure manifests in more light and energy flowing back to us in turn as more empowerment, more energy and en-couragement.

From the mentor-being to us, to the other beings, back to us, and back to the mentor, a figure-eight circuit flows. We sit at the central point of the figure eight. We're not just developing in isola-tion, we're beginning a conscious evolution in relationship with all those around us.

When you get a little more stable in this meditation, you try to include people you don't care about, and then even people you dislike. But don't try that right away or it'll put you in a bad mood. Instead work on creating this figure eight of light and love. Cultivate this field of bliss, which you have earned through much evolutionary struggle. Sense the incredible preciousness of this accomplishment. Feel pleased with yourself, soberly impressed with what you have achieved. You don't need to adopt a completely different belief system as long as your old one allows you to feel that you are precious. So hold that thought. Proud, pleased, and happy, glowing with energy.

Without leaving the refuge field, we turn to our next theme, impermanence. Right away we address death, reflecting upon how transitory life is. We know very well that some of our plans may not come to pass. We have no idea at what time we actually will die. Sure, we're going to die. All beings die. Even gods die. Therefore, we meditate upon what are called the three roots of immediacy.

The first root is the certainty of death. Death is instantaneous when it happens. It's the withdrawal of your awareness from your senses and your body; your consciousness shoots out into a dreamlike state. Developing a strong certainty that we are going to die liberates us from unfocused practice. It dawns on us that this body and mind and these five senses will cease to be.

The second root is the uncertainty about when we will die. Often children die before their parents, well people die before sick ones, a person in safety dies before one in danger. There is no certainty. The causes of life are few and they are fragile, the causes of death are many. We habitually go along secure with the idea that there's going to be some time later when we're going to die, "when you are old and full of sleep," but there is no knowing when.

The third root is the certainty that when we do die the core of our being is what we will take with us: The Dharma is the only thing that will help us. Our bank account will not help us at that time; our muscles, our nerves, our skin will not help us at that time; our organs, liver, heart, none of that will help us at that time; our eyes, ears will not help us at that time; our friends and relatives will not help us at that time; our coarse beliefs, our factual knowledge will not help us at that time. The one thing that will help us at that time will be how much of the Dharma we have integrated into the core of our being: our openness, fearlessness, tolerance, generosity, intelligence, calm. That's what helps us confront death. It's all we can take with us.

If we neglect the deep core of our being, it shrivels. If we are intolerant, clutching, not generous, with no concentration, then we're going to be in trouble when we die. The only thing that will help us is what we have invested within.

While meditating on this third root, take an inventory of your life. Realize that you're spending ninety-five percent of your time strengthening the body and making it healthy, spending money on medicine, earning money to pay for clothing, medicine, food, face lifts, cosmetics, vitamins. You pamper the body of this life although after death it will turn into garbage. You make huge investments in possessions and property, none of which will belong to you in the future. Someone else will be signing the checks. The government will be taking its inheritance tax. The kids will be blowing it on this and that. And yet we spend ninety-five percent of our time on these things we can't take with us. What a waste!

From the three roots grows our awareness of impermanence, of the immediacy of death. We come to feel that there is no time at all. We become alert to the moment, making the moment as full as possible, because we're not investing it in some other thing. We don't know what could be happening next, so we concentrate on what is happening now. This kind of awareness, held in creative tension with the preciousness of human life, is extremely liberating.

Concluding, look up again into the spiritual sky above you. Your mentor or mentors, he or she or they, are delighted that you're reflecting on these deep themes. Their pleasure at your understanding flows toward you as a cascade of nectar. The mentors themselves actually dissolve into light, flow down, and come to rest in the center of your heart. Their own life stream merges with yours.

Before we break the meditation we cherish a last taste of this nectar. Their luminous energy has filled our hearts; we are re-

newed and refreshed. We must also remember gratefully to dedicate the merit of this practice for the sake of all beings—all those
we have gathered around us and all the others behind them.
Whenever you do something good, you should never leave it just
by appropriating it to yourself. That would lessen the positive
impact. You should right away invest the positive achievement—
the merit—in the larger good of the world. This multiplies the
good immeasurably. So in order to dedicate whatever merit we
have created here today, we resolve to become perfectly enlightened buddhas so that we truly can become a mentor for all beings,
to help them reach their own full potential, their ultimate freedom
and happiness.

TAD

When Tenzin is finished and the spell is broken, we all look the
way we used to when hallucinogens plied the punch. At this moment every one of us is ready to climb the mountain. I throw my
Milarepa books in my day pack along with a sweater and poncho
and ever-ready-never-used umbrella. Up and out we go for an
acclimatizing local hike.

There's a breast-level countertop at the bottom of the stairs,
serving as the hotel's front desk. In the two days we'll spend here
I'll never see it used. The team in charge is always holed up in a
cubicle across the hall watching Chinese TV. They look up just
long enough to ascertain there is no complaint.

Outside, pebbles are frozen to the ground, as is shattered glass
to the pavement. Up an alley onto a street skirting the huge boulder, we pass the best house in town. Beams set between stone
walls are brightly painted, yak skulls hang from corner posts, a
lonely flower box bursts with small blue and yellow blossoms. The
stonework is drywall and of better quality than its neighbors. In
the Himalayas, as in the Catskills, mortar is usually the sign of
inferior work glued together.

The glass-strewn concrete road soon stubbles into weed,
flower, shrub. Wild grass sets in with a forgiveness. Broken pieces

of mani stones—flat-faced boulders carved with *Om mani padme hum*—line the track leading to a small chapel. Inside is a gigantic brass prayer wheel and nothing else. The chapel isn't locked, although equipped to be. Surrounding it, like huge playing cards set into the ground, are large fragments of destroyed mani stones.

"Dynamited," Thurman growls. "By the thousands. The Chinese blew them to pieces along with the monasteries. They forced the Tibetans to build roads out of the dynamited mani stones, forced them to make toilets from them, forced them to defile these perfect folk shrines, these simple, blessed, outpourings of love for the Buddha. But it didn't work!" he trumpets, humor routing rage, "Did it, *Eisenschlanger*?!"

"Apparently not!" Wolfgang returns, taking a picture of a newer, whole carving of the great mantra *Om mani padme hum*.

Eisenschlanger means "iron snake" in German. The iron snake is the mythical creature associated with persons born in 1941 and other years at sixty-year intervals, according to Tibetan and Chinese astrology. This includes both Tenzin's and Wolfgang's birthdays. From this discovery forward they call each other Eisenschlanger at their friendliest.

We hike for an hour. I'm talking to myself, falling behind, passing back and forth between euphoria and paranoia, not at all confident that things are working out well.

I come up behind Tenzin conversing with Valerie and Leopoldo. "The trick is to get that infinite bliss and be totally present here in all this concreteness! That's the real trick, that's buddhahood."

It's a user-friendly thought. The kind I, for one, could use against all this airlessness. But Tenzin isn't satisfied. He's honed an edge, now he must use it.

"No separation. There's no difference between buddhahood and blade-of-grass-on-the-Tibetan-desert-plain-hood. None whatsoever. So your reflex to be totally present to the suffering of any being—even if you know that suffering isn't really real, but they only think it's real—that's the compassion of the buddhas. In the Mahayana Buddhist vision, this moment is not an empty void, buddhas are right here with us. They're really aware of all we're aware of. Every grain of sand. The whole. We're surrounded by the love of buddhas."

He takes a deep breath. All around us on this walk, oblivious to Tenzin's teachings, the earth crust thrusts up and gnaws down. Unending miles of milled rock and sand tumble from higher to lower in effluvial fans of debris. The variegated patterns of these spills form triangles, like the bottom portion of an hourglass. Over distance these become like snakeskin. Look at one too long and you'll see it move. All of us see such strangenesses, I'm pretty certain, it's not only me. We've all come to be changed by strangeness.

That night I got really sick. Something I ate, or the altitude, or my constipation. Jay came in with some soup once, during the first wave of flulike symptoms—nausea, headache, fever, and acute time travel. Illness is the first mind-expanding experience many of us know, and the last.

I'm trying to surf the sickness, ride it out like a storm or an avalanche of images from an over-worked mind, when the cavalry arrives. They shouldn't come in. They'll get sick. And I'm not up to it. It's like having more than one lover in a bed, it's too much. There's no knowing what could happen. I'm sick, I'm nuts, I feel awful. I may tell you that your face is an ulcer with a beard growing on it. Or ask why there isn't a beautiful, unmarried woman on the trip.

But I surrender and in they come, like silly monsters crashing Mila's cave. Tenzin has a weird look on his face and says: "We've come to make you better." Yeah, really. I'm in a sleeping bag, clothed in two sets of long underwear, with my parka, jacket, and this sort of buffalo-robe blanket stretched over me—a Tibetan blanket filled with sand so it doesn't blow away. My teeth are chattering, however, as Wolfgang places a charcoal lump in an ashtray and lights it. Richard is kneeling at the foot of the bed. Through all these layers he's grabbed my big toes, and he's blowing over them, as if cooling hot porridge. Tenzin is standing to my left grinning, and out of the grin come Tibetan chants, prayers, invocations, deals with dragons, pit-perambulations, bell-bongings, sky-scrapings; I mean the weirdest, strangest-sounding stuff, yet familiar, like the muffled bangs and groans of a radiator in an old house in a blizzard. Wolfgang lights herbs on his charcoal and wafts them to the four points of the compass. Richard seeks out and pinches my little toes. As he exhales Wolfgang says: "Don't open your eyes." I feel a slight burning and a lovely, frankin- censep jolt. And now there are other slice-me-to-the-quick smells, as Tenzin's chanting swells, and I feel them to both sides of me and at my feet. Richard is blowing over the tops of my feet and pinch- ing the top of my head while only touching my feet, and someone's saying: "He'll sleep now."

CHAPTER FIVE

Milarepa's Cave

TAD

I wake up and assess the damage. It's minimal, which is remarkable. I can't say that I'm cured, however. It's like knowing at the first moment of consciousness that you drank too much but you don't feel the hangover. Still, it could be a creeper, a time bomb. I get up gently, my head like a fishbowl mounted on a gyroscope. In Kathmandu-purchased flip-flops, I walk carefully around sizeable puddles of standing water in the bathroom. The urinals have brooms standing in them and chairs in front of them, with string passed over the flush handle and through the rung of a chair. Language not necessary. I get the idea. No pee here.

67

I wash my face, trying not to breathe, and head the old fish bowl back to the room, greeting greeters a little shyly. "Much better, thanks."

Jock's head appears in the door, instantly relieved at the sight of me. "Welcome back, Mr. Spaceman! Guess who bought you a present?" And with a sort of summer-camp-counselor hokum, he whips forward a hand holding a four-foot bamboo pole, maybe two and one-half inches in diameter, green but dried and frail looking. "The walking stick you've been looking for! It was a mop handle in a previous life in a grocery store, but we lost the mop, and the store."

It still looks like a mop handle to me, too domesticated, and so—as with many things I have come to love—I don't like it at first. Maybe it's too much like me, light, thin, and long. It looks like it will split on a rock somewhere. But I thank Jock and ease the gyroscopic fishbowl down the stairs.

In a dirt-floored tearoom next door, some brave soul is questioning away about "the mind of immediacy," and despite a few greenish-gray and solemn faces, Buddha-Bob, as we used to call Tenzin at Amherst, answers: "The mind of immediacy is not a morbid mind. It is a liberated mind. All that's inconsequential drops away, you see? But you have to really reflect on your own death, that that'll be it for this life of hopes and dreams. You get all tortured about the great novel you're going to write and all this. Then you're going to be done. The novel is going to be dust! The libraries are going to burn down. It doesn't mean you might not still write the novel, but you relate to it in a very different way. You become more immediate about the process of writing.

"It's like haiku," he goes on. "One word could be the great thing. That would be enough. That would be it."

I should leave it here. But sorry, Tolstoy didn't write haiku.

"Right. But this collection of molecules is only going to exist for a short period of relative time." I'm asking for relative reality, please. An acknowledgment that there is at least the reality of the illusion of reality.

"No. This collection of molecules ultimately doesn't exist at all. It's a total illusion. You know, every molecule in your body changes in what, seventeen seconds or something? Every cell is changed every seven years. There's no permanence in anything. The continuity, though—your continuity—will go on, certainly. And you will print more molecules."

Frankly, I'm confused. First it's all illusion, then it's not, then it is again. The picture of a river winding through a trail of boulders goes off in my head, and I say: "And so maybe the why is really the how. And instead of searching for one gigantic explanation I should be content with many tiny explanations."

"A little too deep for me, but it has promise," Tenzin concedes, allowing me to escape into poetics like Br'er Rabbit into the briars.

It's a thought I've been playing with, like a scab, for years. That the why is actually the how. Now, on the chessboard of Dharma talks the idea has survived an introduction. I know from experience that merely surviving in debate with Tenzin is a victory.

We pack up the jeeps and momentarily tempt the hostel-keepers away from their television with a pile of money. Then we're off again with a stop just beyond the town at a famous monastery built in front of a cave where Milarepa stayed in the twelfth century.

Half an hour up a less-hazard-strewn road, we pile out and trundle down a maze of shadow-alleys, leading to a windblown brick terrace presiding over the gorgeous train wreck of earth called the Himalayas. Between us and these treeless wonders stretches a valley that looks like a roughly sewn patchwork of fur and tanned hides. The brush growing in hollows stitches the seams. The whole of it is high in the middle, as if the quilt had been shaken out and was billowed at the center, just about to land. But the separate pieces of hide hang at different angles to one another, like the angular curve of a soccer ball. The wind helps support this airborne impression, as mottled cloud shadows fly at high speed over the whole. In the distance two small bleached houses stand amidst a crude line of stones denoting a garden.

Turning back to the alleys, these, too, throw shadows and then, as a cloud briefly darkens the sun, cease to. The flickering quality feels like a speeded-up movie. We surprise children in novice robes at every turn. They smile, signaling furtively for pens and candy. The robes sublimate begging for money into begging for things. A cheerful abbot appears, shooing the novices away with a tolerant smile and welcoming us into the white-washed adobe monastery built around one of Milarepa's meditation caves. Squinting for a minute in the main teaching chamber, our readjusting eyes make out the low student benches in the middle, as gaily painted walls depict Tibetan deities all around. Tenzin and—to an impressive degree—Jay run through the characters and situations. As storyboards these frescoes do their job. As works of art, they fall short. This presents a philosophical as well as an aesthetic problem.

Every monastery we see on this trip is a rebuilt one. While some portable relics were spirited off and hidden before the destroyers did their work, a great quantity of new murals, sculptures, and *tangkas* now hope to replace the lost masterpieces, but they cannot. Why? Imagine for a moment that a majority of George Balanchine's dancers were tortured, raped, and killed. That the scenery and props to his ballets were all burned, along with the theaters in which they were originally performed. The master, himself, is dead. Those of his disciples who do survive are greatly diminished in powers, and publicly humiliated at every turn. Now try to mount *Jewels* without weeping. Do we call this performance a failure or a triumph?

The tangka masters are gone and what survives of their work is rarely seen in its intended place; still, it's the toast of the art world. So it is very likely that, like a white British Eric Clapton continuing a black American tradition, the tangka, too, will survive and evolve, but not, it would seem, in Tibet.

I'm distracted, saddened by this. I turn around and it's talk time again. Tenzin is already seated on a raised box, my companions sit cross-legged on lower boxes. The abbot and an assistant stand against the wall, impressed and amused. I stumble onto the box beside Tenzin, the cord holding my sunglasses to my neck is tangled with the earphone cords connected to the cassette player. I finally get myself straightened out and start recording. When I look up, there's a sweet-faced young boy holding a cup of Tibetan tea for me. I accept the cup, but even the faintest hint of the smell has me on the edge of vomiting. I place it beside me and suddenly realize where I've taken rest: in the trumpeter's seat, with two six-foot-long horns pointing their mouthpieces toward me.

Jay, sitting in a full lotus across the aisle, is smiling, blissfully. I hate sitting like this, my long legs are stiff and don't fold up and I have no ass to speak of—it's bone to wood. Could Jay be smiling at just how unheraldlike I feel sitting in front of trumpets?

The boy is offering Tenzin tea, but in midmeditation the good eye is all but closed. The boy, looking hopefully at the glass eye, is confused. I sneak out the camera and squeeze off a picture; now one of Jock and Wolfgang and James; swing around and there are Richard and Jay, twilight zoned.

TENZIN

Examining Suffering

It's amazing how luminous the clouds seem up here. The altitude must fluff them up into these towering shapes—animals and castles and faces and plumes. I love to look up at them from our little ant's view from the surface of the earth. Acclimatizing to this altitude takes time. Facing the fragility of the body is good for meditating on suffering. Getting sick is one way to remember the immediacy of death. Transformation often works through sickness.

You have all heard of the great Tibetan yogi Milarepa, who lived and achieved buddhahood in the twelfth century. He spent his whole life up here and higher, floating with the clouds as his meditations made him more and more luminous in his own right. Tad identifies with Milarepa, makes me out to be a kind of Marpa, rough and tough and not giving him the higher teachings. But our Tad is known for artfully resisting the teachings, while I've always thrown them his way. I'm no Marpa, and Tad's no Milarepa. Still, since we're making a pilgrimage in his haunts, simulating the teaching and learning of the very highest practice, the Milarepa inspiration is appropriate.

Returning to the Systematic Path, begin with the visualization of your mentors in the sky above you. Begin every meditation session in this way, invoking and drawing inspiration from your enlightened spiritual friends. Luminous and smiling, they put a spotlight on you, filling you with the light of their understanding, lifting you up out of your usual patterns of mind. The elixir of light flows down on you, honeylike and warm, making you cheerful and calm and filling you with light. Darkness and worry fade away.

Fill the field around you with the many beings you know and love, and with all the others who touch your life. See them look toward you as the mentors' light reflects from you to them. See their faces brighten. Remember your last meditation on the preciousness of human life. How fortunate we are to get to this embodiment endowed with liberty and opportunity. Think about how you would like to use this rare chance. How few others have it. Feel pleased, proud, and appreciative of yourself.

Now recall the three roots, finding the points that make the most sense to you: that death is a certainty; that the time of death is completely unpredictable; and that nothing of this life will translate into the next except what enlightened qualities you have attained. Give up all of your mental and physical possessions, the body that you identify with as your self. Your soul will proceed into new forms, guided by imprints of generosity and morality, tolerance, enterprise, concentration, and intelligence—the opposite of stinginess and fear and paranoia. Forget about the peripheral things. You will go forth with your luminous soul, your sea of infinite bliss, your buddha-nature, so build up that subtle deepest part of yourself.

Your immediate ambitions and anxieties about what's going to happen are less important. Stop worrying about them. Stop nagging yourselves. Concentrate on the real nature of our existence.

We come now to the Buddha's first noble truth, the noble truth of suffering. People first hear of this theme and think it's the morbid invention of a killjoy. But it's not gloomy; it's merely realistic, a method of evaluating "what is our actual experience?" First we notice how difficult it is to even steady the mind to make such an inquiry, for our internal monologue is constantly demanding, "How can I feel better?" Constantly thinking: "When I get there, then I'll feel good." "When I wake up tomorrow I'll feel good." "When I have this food, that thing, that relationship—then everything will be all right."

We're constantly in a state of vain hope, hoping to get someplace where we'll finally be happy. We're always seeking happiness, but we very rarely experience it. We usually have a little pain over here, a little strain over there, we're miserable when the temperature is a little off. Some internal or external thing is constantly agitating us. As we get older, particularly, the organs and joints don't work as well, and we don't look as good in the mirror anymore. Sometimes we have the experience that we remember some past time as having been good, but then if we really look back carefully we realize that we were still trying, anxiously, even then, to get to some other place. So our actual daily existence is unsatisfactory.

We've all had many experiences of hoping to reach some goal, like graduating from school, wanting to make friends with someone, wanting to own something. Once we got it, it broke. The friend became a pain in the neck; upon graduating from high school, we had to worry about college, and after that hurdle, we had to worry about a job, and then we wanted a higher position. Nothing ever seems to work out if you really think about it. We are dependent for our well-being on all kinds of factors beyond our control, and life is always frustrating. Our own reactions are not under our control either. We can't accept hardship with equanimity. We can't stay cheerful when we're ill. On top of being in pain, we get mad that we have the illness. This is a small corner of the endless round of suffering called samsara.

Gradually, it becomes clear that internally we're victims of emotions and desires that constantly nag us, and externally we're the victims of environment and circumstance. No wonder we want to attain nirvana! We want to get away somewhere—to Tibet! Or to some beach we're constantly thinking about. Or even—at the end of sixteen hours of this kind of irritating existence—we just want to be asleep on our pillow, to be unconscious.

But why is life so unsatisfactory? A second ago we were so grateful for this precious human embodiment. What happened?

It's this: The world is not treating us right. Our own body treats us abominably! Time is terrible; gravity is worse; our emotions are toxic. Still, we feel we have a right to be happy. We feel we have a right to be calm and cool and to feel bliss, even ecstasy. But the world is not bustling to provide our ecstasy. So there's a struggle between our expectation and what is.

Just as an experiment, give up the pretension that you constantly maintain to the world and even to yourself, that just over the next hill all will be well. Stop saying: "If I can just get to the next level, I'll be happy. If I can just get back home. Or if I can just get away from home, move to another state, it'll be OK." Realize that's a delusion; that every time you get one of these goodies, it proves unsatisfactory. You immediately want the next thing, and then another, better one. Right?

Begin to feel sympathy for yourself in this very difficult predicament. This is what the noble truth of suffering means: We're habitually out of balance, and all of our experience will inevitably be frustrating and unsatisfactory. We have to acknowledge this and accept the fact that we're off balance. We're simply not going to find happiness, the way we're facing our situation, feeling ourselves alone and struggling in an alien world, trying to get the better of it. Once we're set apart in this way, in the battle of self versus the world, the self has got to lose. The world is bigger and stronger; it's inexhaustible, while we get tired so easily.

This is called a noble truth because it only seems true to a noble or holy person, a person who has found a different way of relating to the world, no longer habitually self-centered. That person is no longer pitted against the world. That person has come to see the process of self-preoccupation itself as suffering, so our whole lives look like suffering to them. Even what we think of as temporary relief, a noble person sees as suffering: Our temporary states of happiness seem pretty good to us in relation to the immediately preceding irritation, but they soon turn into new irritation, and therefore are called the suffering of change. The conditions we normally perceive as suffering are called the suffering of suffering. And our overall cosmic situation is called the suffering of creation.

When you meditate on this carefully and thoughtfully, you

begin to feel genuine sympathy for yourself, you begin to excuse yourself from chasing your illusions. You begin to turn that hope-for-happiness in a more practical direction by shifting the situation from you-versus-the-world.

Whatever your fantasy is: to become a billionaire, a yogi, a president, or a king, a movie star, a famous writer, these are the ambitions of this life. But look at people who have the things you think you want. Look at the president of the United States. You begin to realize the guy has got a permanent headache. Look at a movie star, you see many of them in complete misery. Look at famous writers, many are alcoholics. Realize that none of these goals are truly satisfying.

Now meditate on the dark areas of life. Think over the many varieties of suffering. Don't avoid it, thinking these are old wives' tales meant to frighten you into being religious. Facing suffering realistically has to do with frightening yourself, developing a healthy prudence and a concern to avoid future misery. Review the animal kingdom, think of its prevalent misery, which Tibetans call one eating another. As an animal you live in constant fear of being eaten by another, while your hunger drives you to devour whatever comes before you. Imagine the misery of the *pretan*s, creatures worse off than animals with horrible lives of hunger and thirst. Finally, open up to the miseries of the hells; they are so vividly described, they can keep you awake at night, even if you don't believe them. Actually you should be careful with your imagination.

Turning to the second noble truth, the noble truth of causation, you begin to analyze the self-versus-the-world structure itself, since it's clearly the cause of all the suffering. Anything you get in a normal, egocentric human life—any goal—will not be satisfactory. Once you're in opposition to the universe, since it is infinite and you are not, it is bound to crush you in the end. Ignorance, which is the fundamental self-construction, or better, misknowledge, the habitual assumption of being a separate, independent self, this is the root cause of all suffering, according to the insight of the Buddha. Once you assume yourself as really there, apart from everything else, you feel a craving to connect with things, you want to increase the odds of winning against the universe by incorporating as much of it within yourself as you can. This is the first primal reaction of the alienated self—desire, greed, and attachment. When the world won't give itself over to you, when it even comes to take things away from you, then you feel fear, anger, and hostility—the second primal reaction of the alienated self.

Slowly open your boundary by reflecting on the preciousness of human life. Open to the infinite connectedness and consequentiality of all life, your being beginninglessly involved with all beings, and your responsibility for your own states of existence in an infinite future. If you let yourself get caught in evolutionarily negative forms of living, that will produce endlessly negative fields of experience for you. The key insight here is that everything is limitlessly interconnected, there is no independent part of evolution, no separate person disconnectedly involved who can ignore consequences. Knowing that the causal pattern of evolution is inexorable on the relative level helps you avoid both the irresponsibility of reckless activity and the hopelessness that arises from the fear of losing the positive results of good activity. This is crucially important.

One of the great causes of our suffering is hatred, and all of its variations: resentment, anger, bitterness, dislike, irritation, aggressiveness, hostility. Hate is very powerful. When we're gripped by hatred we go into a rage and become completely out of control. We smash up our own beloved body and commit suicide. We smash up people whom we love, wives, husbands, children, parents. Rage can turn us into a complete maniac or demon—temporarily. It's one of the most dangerous kinds of energies, very difficult to control. Any force we can marshal within ourselves to prevent and forestall the explosive moment of rage is really beneficial. So let's look at rage.

The key thing that lets rage explode is precisely the sense of disconnection from the world—when we've "had enough," something just "pressed our button," someone just "crossed the line." It erupts from nowhere, coming from deep inside, yet seems independent of everything, and promises to sweep away all the undesirables around us: the behavior of other people, the circumstances, the way society is.

We think that things will be better, after we've blown it all away, but cruelly and sadly, we discover that we've simply destroyed things around us, creating reverberations that will come back to us horribly. Our bruised beloved, for example. Our own bruised body. Property we destroy. When we cool off we always face a worsened situation. This is not far-fetched. I could come up to one of you and smash you on the foot with a stone and you'd immediately explode. And I'd do the same if you did it to me. Which means that we are not really very far from being the victim of this kind of energy.

And this is why we make a point of visualizing in vivid detail extreme states of violence, misery, and suffering. By meditating upon them, we can begin to feel a healthy fear of the possible negative consequences of our violent actions. We begin to see and to hold back our extreme emotional reactions.

The great Milarepa, whose cave is in this monastery, was unjustly treated by an uncle. He, his mother, and his sister were enslaved, and the long bitterness and hatred from that led him finally to study black magic and to retaliate by killing his uncle's whole family. Later he became remorseful, realizing the awful negative consequences of letting himself go like that and harming so many innocent people. He was so grateful for that vision being opened to him that he began to welcome the fear of what he could become if he went on being a killer. Using that energy, he developed the power to overcome his inner negative impulses. He went into these high mountains for years of deep meditation. He turned that rage into the inner fire, which is called *tummo,* meaning furor. It takes the energy of fury and turns it into a kindling-of-inner-ignorance melting into a state of bliss. He kept warm with the internal heating system of the tummo furor-fire, even in these freezing Himalayan mountains where he was living. His second name, Repa, comes from the fact that he wore only a cotton cloth draped over his naked body, even in the dead of winter at eighteen thousand feet. He himself attributed his buddhahood to his gaining a profound vision of the suffering of the egocentric life-cycle.

Facing suffering gave Milarepa the power to find freedom from suffering and to achieve real happiness.

When you realize the noble truth of suffering, you develop not just disgust with the world, but a realistic sense of sympathy for yourselves. You make a decision, thinking, "Why should I allow myself to go on being pushed around by these winds of emotion and the arbitrary actions of others? Why should I remain a hostage like this? I must free myself from this imprisonment." And when you understand the second noble truth of causation, you develop a creative insight into how you are trapped in suffering by your misconception of yourself and you feel enthusiasm about seeing through this primal delusion about your self and your fundamental alienation from the world.

This is where we leave it today, with a slightly more realistic assessment of our state. Perhaps you'll notice that even acknowledging suffering makes us a little more tolerant of everything. We get a little relief just from beginning to face it.

Now our mentors in the sky above us smile happily, looking down upon us: "Ahah!" they say, "you're beginning to get a little true compassion for yourself. A little bit of awareness of the noble truth of suffering and a hint about the noble truth of causation." The light of their pleasure flows toward us and we brighten up and shine that light back out to the beings around us. We think back about how this insight into suffering fits together with the immediacy of death and with the preciousness of the human life. They all fit together, they're not contradicting each other. We see how the three themes—preciousness of life, immediacy of death, and suffering of egocentric unenlightened living—combine to open new understandings.

We then dedicate whatever merit we've generated, whatever new insight we've gotten, for the benefit of all sentient beings, so that we may become fully enlightened and achieve freedom from suffering, in order to share that real happiness with others. As we make that dedication, the mentor in the sky above us melts into light and dissolves into us. We feel renewed and restored and we can then break off the session of meditation.

TAD

At this point Tenzin begins to repeat a mantra in a rapid, low-pitched mutter, *"Gewa diyi nyurdu dag . . . jetsun jamyang drub gyur nay . . . drowa kun kyang malupa . . . deyi sa la goeu par sho!"* Neither whispered nor spoken, but somewhere between the two, it's elaborate, exotic, gorgeous. The enigmatic smile on his face is an entreaty to abandon the American dream, among others. As if sensing both our collective fear and an eagerness to defeat that fear, he reels out of a half trance back into English. Laughing at something encountered in his mind, his eyes still closed, he shouts, "samsaric journey!" before re-engaging the clutch and slipping back into a higher gear.

We open our eyes, it feels, at the same time. Locals have gathered around this bright room. Parents of novices perhaps. Tenzin converses with the abbot, as local Tibetans gawk. I don't quite realize it yet, but we're a contradiction in terms. China is the only modern thing known. China equals progress equals anti-Buddhism. But here we are in fancy jeeps with cameras and tape recorders—the trappings of wealth attributed only to Tibetans in exile, who are vilified and forbidden reentrance. We come to exhume and glorify traditions the Chinese abhor, yet they allow it. This American Buddhist speaking fluent Tibetan, praising the abbot for his patience in raising this most-rare crop of novice monks—how is such a thing sanctioned?

The locals can't get over us. And while they are impressed and, it seems, heartened by our presence, there is no show of respect. Richard sums it up neatly, "We're television for them." He demonstrates, smiling at a family that does not acknowledge him except to gossip among themselves about him. "Not 'on' television," he continues, enjoying his high-profile invisibility. "No, we're the ghost in the machine itself."

Out of the hall and off to the side is the spiritual magnet that brought us here in the first place: Milarepa's cave. A most strange room has been built in front of and around it. Concrete buttresses and concrete slabs link the cave with so much of what the hermit

79

radically refused. To the side is the altar covered with photos, money, candles, and incense. The chest-high cave has a shed door at the front, with painted rough idols carved in relief. Mila, green as the nettle stew he ate for years, has one hand cocked to his ear, the other half-covering the withered parsnip of his penis.

The masonry floor gives way to wood, and finally, in back, to the womblike bedrock itself. My flashlight scours the ceiling. Here it is: the pockmark of Mila's holy handprint. My palm fits into it, but nothing registers. I feel like I'm in the Museum of Natural History on Central Park West copping a feel on the sarcophagus of a great king whose spirit has fled.

My camera flashes—a journalistic souvenir of proof traded for the buzz of true belief. Outside, Jay and James are doing prostrations. I can't help myself—they look foolish to me. This is it! I tell myself. The cave of a warlock-murderer whose single-mindedness of purpose accomplished buddhahood in one lifetime! What's more, I believe this to be true. I even identify with the man myself, as I identify Tenzin as my Marpa, putting me through ordeals and not giving me the real teaching. But what have I done, where are my murders to deserve that kind of punishment?

Guiltily, I crawl out and place a bill on the altar, then take a picture from my hip of a young monk counting a fistful of money. Outside the sight of me makes a novice happy. He points at my breast pocket stuffed with pens.

"No pens. I need them. I need them all."

He senses my weakness and motions me into a temple anteroom, like a drug dealer anxious for a score. He is certain of some gift, and his confidence is oddly irresistible. He's motioning for candy.

"Tell you what, this is a Power Bar. Not exactly chocolate truffles, but sweet—and I'll split it with you, OK?"

Yes, yes. He's glad of that; glad of the chocolate. Even if it's only a bite. I've strategically eaten only half of my half. The novice smiles, blinking, knowing the score. He puts a hand on my arm, beaming, hopeful, without quite begging, sensing somehow that even if it's for the wrong reason, his happiness has buoyed my flagging spirit, and so there is a fair deal made here. I make the transfer into his waiting hand. He squeezes my shoulder, pops the bar in his mouth, placing a finger to his lips with a smile that is pure conspiracy.

"No tell, I know, one picture though." The camera flashes in his gleaming face—a picture of devilish delight. "At least he knows what he wants," I think, but then, "No, he only thinks he knows. For this is the suffering of change. Will he remember me and my chocolate and smile? Or will he be angry at me for giving so little and leaving so abruptly? How do you walk out of a bar after one drink and walk out happy? How do you end an affair without feeling angry and disgusted? It's all the suffering of change. The first bite, the first drink, the first kiss."

CHAPTER SIX

On the Road

TAD

We saddle up, me in the coveted spot directly behind Tenzin, who rides in front beside the driver. Others take turns riding in the Dharma-mobile in which Tenzin rides, but I always ride there directly behind him, so I can hear him talk.

Tenzin is in a fine mood still, and I am anxious for it to rub off. "A good man, the monk in charge, a very good man. He told me a funny story. That Nyalam was named by Milarepa himself, who had been invited to visit the place and refused, calling it the Road to Hell. He knew a shit hole when he smelled one!"

It's good for a chuckle, but not much more. Our driver soon

83

passes the jeep in front of us on a spot where the road splits for a moment. They eat our dust. Tenzin comments in Tibetan, the driver comments back. He's the surly one. Richard is beside me. Soon we've pulled well ahead and my insides are taking a pounding, which is quickly bringing back the bad stuff from last night. I'm meditating on samsara, all right. Every pothole hurts. At first I smile at the pain, because, in a way, it's amusing. Maybe there's some wince to it, but really it's an attempt at a smile—trying to find humor in suffering which, for me, is the essence of manhood. But the road gets ridiculous, our driver is pushing the jeep as fast as he can, and the pain gets worse. Soon the smile is gone and the wince is complete. I'm grabbing hold of the strap above the door with both hands, hoisting myself off the seat slightly, lifting and sliding into sleep wherein the ache recedes.

The jeeps stop at a high mountain pass: the preeminent brown gully crowning a system of brown gullies chasing each other down to a gray plain. At the end of the plain I can see white-topped peaks. Hardly a chain. These eye-stinging stunners seem to begin a land consisting solely of mountains. The pass is marked with cairn stones and prayer flags and heaps of rags drenched by rain and baked by sun until the specificity of blouse or pants or shoe starts to fade. It's a sad, confusing place to me, marked with sad, confusing reminders of pilgrims who have come and gone, awash in a Dharma that is dry as a bone for me right now. I'm beginning to wonder why I came. Images from the civil war flash in my mind—vintage photos of the piles and piles of clothes belonging to the dead. And today, if I dare add an article to this death pile, it feels like I'm somehow hastening my own inevitable death. I don't feel up to it at present. Yet the Tibetan pilgrims gave up their rags here, at this wire; surrendered cast-off clothes to their gods. In their sky these saviors were shining. It's only my sky that has been robbed of gods, its rainbows scientifically explained, its thunderbolts bled of sorcery. I don't believe what I believed only a day ago. But why?

Partially it's because Tenzin is challenging the bedrock again. Time and space and life and death, self and selflessness. It's an intellectual game that I can follow for only so long before the threads that weave the world together start to come apart in my hands. I hear Shelley's admonition: "Lift not the painted veil which those who live call life." And I remember the experiences that are what I know of madness. I remember the voices advising that I kill myself quickly, before it gets worse, because of course, it will. But I'm past all that youthful crap, right? I'm not going to do anything stupid. I'm a father and a son—ye olde time-honored blackmail.

It's just that Tenzin's annihilative, apocalyptic approach is making me realize I don't quite believe in fullness or emptiness, but that the likelihood of either proposition robs me of any satisfaction with its opposite. I feel like Casey at the bat. I don't like any of the pitches. Not materialism, bled of mystery, and not emptiness reeking of nihilism; and the middle way? What middle way? Tenzin isn't talking middle way with me—no, he's pushing the bone-crusher stuff with me, and always has. Fine. But sometimes I miss a gentler way. Too much bone crusher and I get adversarial.

An hour up the road we drive by a family of nomads recognizable to Tenzin by their dress. They're from a region famous for beautiful singing, five of them mounted on ponies with cheerfully colored saddles, a three-stringed instrument half-sticking out of a shoulder sack. Yesterday I would have whipped out my camera and gotten at least one picture off. Today I feel like a Bowery bum looking up from the gutter, without a drink and without a prayer. I sigh, which can't be heard over the pounding of the jeep. But I hate that sigh, because it's my father's Irish, poor-me sigh, which I hear all the time coming from my own mouth. But worse, now I have children of my own who will hate it sounding from me until they hear it from their own mouths and learn to hate it there as well.

Strangely, I start to thirst for the Dharma again. Not because it represents the truth, or the light, or the joy—no, it's more medicinal. Dharma, I am starting to believe, is the only antidote to misery.

We pull over again. No dust kicked up behind us but our own. No little thunder cloud of distant friends. This means one of two things, we took a wrong turn or somebody broke down. People pile out. "What time is it?" somebody asks. I consult my watch. "Jesus Christ, it's only twelve—this day will never end!"

Richard smiles from under a cowboy brim, "It's High Noon in Tibet."

We've stopped at the edge of a ravine that falls away into a gravel pit. Above us are sharp gray-and-black cliffs cutting off the sight of vaster cliffs, the next tier up, which cut off the sight of yet another set like rows of sharks' teeth. Somewhere below I can hear water licking at a mountain's roots, or is that wind? No, it's too steady to be wind, too low-pitched. It's the growling belly of the earth's own nausea.

We wait a long time for the other jeeps. Seemingly immune to the dread I feel creeping over me, Richard smiles in my face. He is a strong, stocky fellow from Jim Harrison country, the north woods of Minnesota, with always-amused eyes beneath a receding hairline. Richard carries a few extra pounds of booze weight with such puckish grace that the sight of him never fails to cheer me.

Roadside, gray-and-black slate mixes with the peroxide blondness of mica. The rubble dotted with humps of moss and grass doesn't provide much of a place to flop down and relax. Tenzin seems to be doing all right in a half lotus down in the boulders and the dust, a mustard-colored scarf wrapped around his head and his boysenberry-colored wick-away-yer-sweat top. Now just as these wind-blown islands of grass remind me of drawings by Dr. Seuss, and cheerfulness attempts a comeback, I realize we've passed our last tree and I missed it.

The driver squats off by himself and smokes a cigarette. I don't know quite how, but no matter where I go I seem to be downwind of him, and even out in the open the smell makes me nauseated, and adds just a little more clang to my headache.

A jeep appears with bad news. The third one has broken down. Shit! I walk off and perch on a rock, believing my interior sludge has finally managed to leak out into the world and wreck an engine.

Finally two jeeps and lots of dust appear winding up the mountain road below, which means we've got to start driving again. Loading up I hear in my head: *If your pilgrimage is to come away with nothing, you cannot fail at it.*

But to think anyone could transcend the ego and still live in this world! That's what galls me about this selflessness stuff. It's the ultimate ego trip! With every crash of the jeep, corresponding stabbings of pain explode in full color behind my eyes. Now and again my wish is granted: sleep. Until BOOM! I'm awake and in pain as we stop again.

"How ya' feeling?"

It's Jock questioning me as I climb out of the jeep at a lunch stop in a barren field. "Ceaseless jokes at my expense," I laugh, "another picnic in the Himalayas."

The group is crashed out between boulders in a gravel field, with lunch on a tarp: tins of tea and coffee and sugar, chapatis, peanut butter, jam, the hot chocolate mix, and fish tins. There's a plate of Smiling Cow cheese wedges. There's a hot sauce and a really hot sauce. There's the big water jug we fill our little water jugs from. There's the tea water. I look it all over and go back to the jeep. From here I can see the dish coming, the lid lifted by the smiling kitchen boy: yellow cabbage and yak strips with rice. A made-up enthusiasm of voices greets it, everybody half laughing, half groaning. Now everyone is looking at me, making a noise like cows mooing English. Suddenly they're getting up from lunch mooing my name. Jock, James, Wolfgang, Jay, and Tenzin, with Leopoldo helping his Valerie with her windbreaker.

"Are you taking Diamox?"

They all want to know. Tenzin is looking like I should already be on it.

"But I've only got ten."

"Ten is enough!" Tenzin barks, as Jock takes over.

"At two a day that's five days' worth," Jock says, "at which time we should be over Drolma La, the highest point on the trip. After that you'll be far better acclimatized. Take one and see how it goes. Yo! everybody!" Jock yells, "not a bad time to try a Diamox and see how you react. Tingling fingers and toes are expected, light-headedness, dizziness maybe. Some people don't like it, some people do." There is laughter. Folks compare notes in clusters.

"How do you react?"

"Have you taken it before?"

"I thought I'd wait a little longer."

Jock is called by the drivers and runs off. After I've dug out the pill and swallowed it with water, he returns laughing and mumbling to himself. "Well, they've stripped down the jeep pretty good and rebuilt it on the spot."

"Great guys!" Tenzin yells and stalks off to congratulate the drivers.

"And don't worry about running out of Diamox, fella," Jock says sotto voce, "that's one thing we're not understocked with." "Oh yeah!" he yells again, "for those of you with refried beans for brains, we're going down to fifteen hundred feet or so for a first camp." Then quietly again, "But Tad, take the Diamox anyway."

With all three engines roaring and an order to stay within sight of one another, Jay and I mount up behind Tenzin, and the Dharma-mobile falls out. I watch a mustard cloud from the first jeep cake up on its rear window and get shaken off by a bad bump, like the screen of an Etch-a-Sketch being cleared. On the promise of lower altitudes and slower driving, I resolve to be more cheerful.

"Okay, guys!" Tenzin yells over the motor, "how about ten thousand mantras before nightfall?"

"I like the female form of Avalokiteshvana," I say, "you know, with all the dakinis—angels the colors of shining diamonds."

Jay starts it off, I join in. *"Hum hum hum pai pai pai svaha. Om om om sarva buddha dakiniyl vajra varnaniye, vajra vairochaniye."* Tenzin listens for a moment, and corrects a pronunciation, "Vai-ro-cha-nee-ya."

We repeat slowly. He joins in for a few bars, then corrects another, subtler point. Soon the clumsy clay of nonsense whirls smoother and smoother still.

"Faster!" Tenzin barks between breaths.

Now he starts rocking back and forth in his seat like the monks seated before the great stupa at Boudhanath, trancing out on the mantra. "But not too fast!" he cautions, as Jay and I smile at each other and start rocking slowly back and forth, showering the words like sparks from a skyrocket. For a second I wonder what the driver must think of this, but only for a second. For what he thinks is none of my business. My business is the mantra, and the business of losing the mind-business, just going with the mouth-music and the ear-juice. Jay is smiling, his mouth doing almost exactly as mine does. One little part of the song I do differently, and I find a lower harmony sometimes. That really drills it home. But then I get too interested in the way it sounds, so I go back to a simple monotone and just run with it.

A short way northwest a small lake winks at us in the bright midafternoon sun, just at the beginning of a huge, flat, golden-grassed plain. Behind us, to the south, the legends rise up.

We gather in an amazed cluster staring south back the way we came, at the ridge dividing Nepal from Tibet. The highest land bridge on the planet. Atop ever-rising brown mounds, streaked black with shadows and stream beds, the snows pool so bright that this line of demarcation seems to vibrate. Deep vertical shadows vein the steep walls, as along the tops splotches of light explode, more intense even than the slowly shifting white of the clouds. Somewhere Everest should be preeminent, surprisingly she's not. Jay points her out on the east: the sharp, off-kilter pyramid, Goddess Mother of the World, or Chomolungma to Tibetans. Bathed in shadow, her 29,028-foot-high fang seems less impressive than Cho Oyu, which is straight before us, massive at 26,899 feet and enveloping Gyachung Kang—a spike on the vast ridge at 26,082 feet, between the other two. Perspective robs the monarch of mountains of her mantle. The ridge itself seems the true wonder. It's about thirty miles away, dipping after Cho Oyu into the Nangpa La gap, then back up to Menlungtse, ending with the holiest mountain of Nepal, Gaurishankar.

Lobsang has joined us and is lovingly rattling off the names of the mountains, like a hunter identifying hard-won trophies. He's climbed them all, save Everest. Sherpa and head Sherpa on several unsuccessful attempts—the last one fatal to many climbers—he's finally heeded the pleas of his wife, giving up the big mountains forever. Yet looking into his leathery, tanned-near-black face, into eyes politely framed behind spectacles, I catch a glimpse of the wildness still, in this sweet and soft-spoken man. I look from his face to the ridge and back, and taste it for a moment: the climber's lust that takes hold and grants no reprieve. Not long ago, a bit late perhaps, his wife bore him a son who needs a father.

And so today the father goes on trekking expeditions only. Ours pays well, and he will lead cheerfully and confidently throughout. Still I won't soon forget the look in those eyes scanning the ridge leading to Everest, and I'd bet my last dime that Lobsang's boy, too, will devote his life to climbing mountains.

The next morning we get only five minutes down the road and the first jeep pulls over, stalled, as the puffy-eyed driver grinds the battery down, futilely attempting to restart it. So much for Tibetan mechanics! The other jeeps and the truck pull over, and after some debate, Tenzin leads us up a hillside overlooking a sod-roof cabin with a dog chained up outside. Beyond rolls the first collection of grass I've seen since we left Nepal that might actually be termed meadow. Not a New England meadow, but greenish, waving in the wind, and in all but a few places growing thick enough to obscure the sandy loam.

In the distance the meadow edges up to a bush-covered pile of boulders that have fallen from an outcropping, gnarled with brown-and-red cliffs.

We spread out on the sandy edge of a knoll, Jay in his full lotus, Valerie, Leopoldo, and James seated with their knees tucked up under their chins. Jock is sitting on a small boulder, Richard is lying flat on his back with a rock for a pillow. I'm sprawled with legs to the side holding the tape recorder, into which wind roars though there is no force to the wind. Tenzin clears his throat, leading us onward along the Systematic Path.

TENZIN

Some of you, especially Tad, are experiencing the high-altitude headache. It's a really awful feeling, even worse with the pounding on the road and the dust and the discomfort. But isn't it a relief to be out of those border towns and on the road through the mountains? The people in those towns sit there nursing the scars and bruises of the Chinese occupation, numb and shattered, like abused children. When they look up at you they seem to expect the worst. When something pleasant happens, they look around with suspicion. They have very little left of their natural human feeling, much less the characteristic Tibetan openness and transcendent dedication.

Out here, the landscapes are awe inspiring. The air is so clear and dry, the heights so extreme, the blue of the sky so deep you can't decide if it's a pale or a dark blue, against the mountains jutting up cragged and snowcapped. This was all sea bottom once, the great sea of Tethys, a swampish sea that stood between India, Africa, and Asia until the Indian tectonic plate rammed itself under Asia. If you look closely, you can see the parade of fossils along the cliff sides.

Every time I go through this land, I feel the spirits. They are haunted and dire, dreadful in every sense. No wonder the Chinese feel afraid here, quickly turning to drunkenness and then to violence. They cannot understand how the Tibetans can live happily within this starkness. And no wonder the Tibetans love bright colors and vivid paradisal landscapes in their paintings and visions. If the essence of the human life-form is its liminality, its location at the nexus of pleasure and pain, power and vulnerability, intelligence and instinct, then this landscape of Tibet is a physical reminder. Here we are high up between heaven and earth. We are forced to turn within to find resources, a source of happiness that can turn anything positive. No wonder the Buddha's teaching found such willing and grateful supporters up here in the land of snowy mountains.

The Loving Spirit of Enlightenment

Shifting into meditative mode, visualize the mentor field, the refuge field where you are present in an open field with all your loved ones, acquaintances, and opponents around you, creating the positive circuit of insight and energy for the sake of all beings.

The themes we have already learned comprise the first part of the path and are the foundation of the parts to come. With these— the preciousness of human life endowed with liberty and opportunity, the immediacy of death, the inevitability of evolutionary causality, and the suffering of the egocentric life-cycle—we develop the mind of transcendent renunciation, caused by our initial genuine compassion for ourselves. Once we feel compassion for ourselves we can allow ourselves to abandon compulsive pursuits. The immense relief we get from that abandon enables us for the first time to look at others and begin to feel real compassion for them.

To develop this compassion, it is first necessary to realize that we don't now feel real compassion for others. This can be a bitter pill, but when we examine ourselves we soon encounter a being so caught up in thinking about itself, in wanting happiness and not wanting any suffering, that not much attention is paid to others. We don't really care deeply about others, except in rare instances when we are in love or in some other exceptional state. Being habitually preoccupied with ourselves, we don't easily put another's life-pulse ahead of our own.

It's important to recognize that our habitual narrow self-obsession hasn't gotten us anywhere. It's a form of bondage, a form of misery. The best way to make ourselves unhappy is to be obsessed with ourselves. The more we evaluate—"How am I feeling now? What do I have? How good is it?"—the worse it seems. To break this obsession many methods have been employed, from hair shirts to heroin. In Buddhism, it's not simply that the enlightened teachings tell us: "You should be concerned with others. You should attain enlightenment in order to benefit other beings." Rather, we can find it true in our personal experience that we are happier when we care for others first.

One of the most famous techniques for the attainment of compassion is called the Sevenfold Causal Precepts. It descends via the great master Asanga, who lived in the fourth century of the common era. He received it in a vision from the future Buddha, Maitreya, who currently lives in a heaven above Mt. Kailash. Asanga meditated for twelve years, praying to visit that Buddha, and one trophy of his success is the following teaching.

Starting in the refuge field we have already set up, we add to the mentor host the future Buddha Maitreya and the great master Asanga and their unbroken lineage of spiritual descent through the great masters of India and Tibet and down to us today.

We then think about all the beings around us in the field and we set up the foundation of this teaching, which is called the ground of impartiality. We look carefully at all the people in the field around us—friends, neutrals, and enemies—and we wonder: "Is it true, really, that the one I love is so great? And is it true, really, that my enemy is so bad?" And we begin to look at the one that we love in a slightly critical way, and we say: "Well, I do think they're great. They look great to me, but, after all, they are nice to me. They have been kind to me. And they continue to be kind, in fact, and that reinforces my liking them." But we're old enough now to realize that if this very same person whom I love so much today were suddenly to betray me or hurt me, they would begin to look very unpleasant. I would really start to dislike them.

Similarly, the ones that I can't stand, who have done so much harm to me and have given me such headaches, if they started to be really nice to me, and do everything I want, and surprise me with all kinds of nice things and act in a very pleasant way to me, then I would begin to like them. Realizing this, we soon discern that the source of the like and the dislike is not something intrinsically objective in the person. It's actually in my reaction to their pleasing or displeasing me. The person whom I love and the person whom I hate are not really different as persons. They're both people, they both want to be happy. It's just that one has been kind to me and one has been unkind. So I invest each person with the aura of being really lovable or really hateable, but all beings are potentially lovable to me. Once we gain this insight, we look carefully at the lovable one and at the hateable one and begin to see the other side of each of them until we develop what is called impartiality.

Now I've had people say, "I absolutely cannot practice this teaching! I cannot develop impartiality, because I must hate such-and-such a person." Hitler is the usual one. But even the most evil person who ever lived was merely crazed and confused. There was somebody they were nice to, who liked them, and under different circumstances they could become nice. And even the most lovable person could become a maniac. It's very important to recognize this.

We have to extend our will for the happiness of other beings to all other beings, not just the ones we're fond of. This impartiality is the basis for the universal compassion of the bodhisattva. When we begin to get an inkling of it we then say, "Wouldn't it be nice to have a universal impartial sense of love toward all beings? For aren't all beings equally deserving of my love and compassion?" As we develop that mind, we get a little burst of energy, the mentors smile upon us. They are delighted, since a bodhisattva is someone who loves everyone impartially—so there's hope for us.

Once we have impartiality as a foundation, we can begin with the first of the Sevenfold Causal Precepts, known as mother recognition. This meditation is premised on the infinite past lives of ourselves and others. We reflect back, and even though we may not have a strong sense of our infinite past lives, we can nevertheless think: "If I was reborn an infinite number of times, then there's no type of body I did not at some time inhabit. I was reborn male; I was reborn female. I was reborn human; I was reborn animal. I've had infinite life-forms. Furthermore, all other beings around me have all been infinitely reborn. They also have been reborn into all possible situations and conditions of life. Thus no being exists who was not, at some time, my mother."

Motherhood in the mammalian life-form is an archetypal embodiment of altruism. Never mind the psychology of growing up; some of us may have had trouble with our mothers. Our mothers may have been confused in some way, and may have been unpleasant to us at some stage of our life. We may even very much dislike them. But this is deeper than that. Our mother took us into her body. She shared her bloodstream with us. We were a little parasitic formation that evolved from a tiny little seed into an embryo. She eventually delivered us with great labor and pain. Then she cared for us, suckled us, gave us a bottle. She woke up at all hours of the night to feed us. Without her protection and care at that time we would never have survived to today.

We can expand this to a primal, mammalian level of seeing all beings as our mother. And this is the first of the seven precepts. Each and every being was my mother at some time. I took rebirth in their womb. They gave birth to me, they nurtured me, they brought me up. I also was their mother, but this is not what I'm focusing on now. I'm focusing on the fact that each one was my mother. Even a person you might hate now was once your mother. Once you meditate on this you'll begin to develop a remarkable sense of familiarity with all beings. People start to look familiar, no longer strange. This mother-recognizing vision is so powerful, it can overcome racism, tribalism, nationalism, sexism—every lethal prejudice. It is a marvelous teaching, utterly magical. It comes from the heart of the future buddha, from an era beyond racism. It also lies at the heart of the Tibetan culture.

After we recognize all beings as our mothers, the second precept is the meditation of gratitude. We think of our mother in this life. We regress back to our infantile stage when we were just a helpless infant going "ga ga ga" and whining for milk and being cleaned and being held, and her smiling face going "goo-goo" to us, and she putting us to her breast, changing our diapers, bathing us, and holding us, looking at us proudly and lovingly. Almost every mother did that in some way. We have to find those memories, find the feeling of the child being held, and the love that it feels for that mother. We realize what a great effort she made to care for us. She lost her sleep and practically wanted to die when we were sick. She really did live for us, every mother does.

When we meditate on this we should reach the point where we feel so moved by the love of our mother that we become tearful. Then we take that strong emotion for the mother of this life and transfer it to all beings, saying to ourselves: "I really feel this way only about my mother of this life, but actually I should feel this way about all beings. Because all beings did these mother deeds for me at some time. And therefore all beings are my mother. And I have the same sense of warmth and oneness with them as when they gave of themselves so selflessly to me."

The third precept is called repaying that kindness. It's the second phase of gratitude, where we want to repay our mother's kindness. We look at the actual condition today of our mother of this life, and we look at all the living mothers and we wonder how they are feeling. We soon see they don't feel very good most of the time. Maybe they are getting old or are soon to die. Maybe they're sick with this, or maybe they're dissatisfied with that, or they're in a culture where they don't know about their own liberty. Or maybe they're already dead, wandering in the between—the state between death and rebirth—or they've been reborn in another life. Observing them we say, "Now how can I leave them in that condition of needless suffering, life after life?" We feel pity for them and form a strong wish to repay the kindness that they showed to us as mothers. Just as we feel a natural desire to care for our old mother of this life, we develop a powerful motive to care for all mother beings.

The fourth precept is love. The first thing we can do for all our mother beings is to really love them. What does it mean that we love them? It means that we can see the beauty in them. We can see where they could be happy and perfect. We don't get caught up in their theater of pain and misery. Or if they're already dead, we don't get caught up in their old dissatisfactions. We see how beautiful they were and are. We love them by seeing their loveliness. Everyone has moments of loveliness, when they feel released and peaceful and happy. We strongly meditate on that until all beings look lovely to us. Even the ones we now hate, who look ugly and horrible to us, even they can look lovely to us when we meditate in this way.

The fifth precept is compassion, in which we look at the actual state of all our mother beings in a clinical way and evaluate how close their lives are to their potential blissful, blossomed, liberated self. We realize that for the most part they are constantly batting their heads against various walls, doing the opposite of what would make them really happy. They're addicted to various emotions, delusions, bad habits—life in, life out. Further we see they can die in the grip of such drives, descending to even more miserable states. We connect this with our previous meditation on the vast suffering of the samsaric, self-centered life-cycles and we picture them falling into hells, ghost and animal realms—our mothers being devoured by lions. Finally it becomes unbearable that they should suffer so, and we vow: "I will do what I can, I will devote my life to relieving them of that suffering." This, at last, is the superhuman quality of universal compassion.

Then we go to the sixth causal precept. Remember to keep

each of the previous five going: mother recognition, gratitude, repayment of kindness, love, and compassion. The sixth precept is universal responsibility. Here we pull ourselves together and say: "I want them all to be free of all that suffering. But who is the one who is going to free them? I can't say God will do it, I can't say Buddha or Shiva will do it. They may be great, but they don't seem to have done it yet. Therefore I must do it. I must take responsibility for all these beings, all my mothers." This resolve becomes our messianic responsibility. We decide that we're going to devote all our future lives and all our energies to seeing that all our mother beings are completely and totally free of suffering. This wild resolution to do the impossible is the actual spark that kindles the spirit of enlightenment, the spirit that makes a being a bodhisattva.

In the modern worldview of one single lifetime, saving the universe is an insane goal. But in our meditation, our vow to liberate all beings from suffering is calm and rational. For from the Buddhist point of view, we have infinite lives infinitely entwined with other beings, so we must free every single one if we want to free ourselves. It becomes the natural thing to do. Even so, when we succeed in this meditation of universal responsibility, we feel slightly mad, wanting to embrace lepers or to feed our bodies to beasts. We become wild with compassion, unstoppable dynamos.

When Asanga gave this teaching, he cautioned disciples not to get carried away. "Don't feed yourself to the first tiger that comes by, because it will be hungry again tomorrow, but you the eaten disciple will be seriously delayed in your meditation! Don't destroy yourself impractically. Don't give your wealth away to the first beggar that you meet. Create the resolution to do it but guard yourself against hasty actions, because you owe it to your mothers to be practical and effective."

The seventh precept is the fruition of the previous six. The messianic resolution actually becomes part of your being. You give birth to a new messianic soul that is resolved to place the needs of others above the needs of self and to exchange preoccupation with your own happiness for a preoccupation with others' happiness. You reflect, "Wait a minute. I'm having this mad resolution to save all beings and to make them all happy, but I see that I can't actually get it all done. It's impossible. As I am now I'm not even able to make myself really happy. I've just had a little glimpse of renunciation and transcendence, and I feel a little happier, myself, and I feel more loving toward other beings, but there's not much I can really do for them. Who can do something for them? Well, I've learned that given infinite time I can develop into a being called a buddha, one who has the actual physical power to overcome misery in a really effective way. I aim to evolve into a being like that, so I can really reach out to all my mothers and show them how each of them can independently experience their own bliss." That seventh precept—the spirit of enlightenment of universal love and compassion for all beings—is a tremendous quantum leap in the evolution of a being. When you accomplish this, you have made your whole life magnificently meaningful. When you genuinely begin to work your way toward a vision of universal bliss, you have re-created yourself, have been reborn into the bodhisattva family, and have become exalted in the spirit of enlightenment.

Now run back through the themes, rehearse them to remember them contemplatively: We've reached the spirit of enlightenment of love and compassion by resolving to recognize all beings as our mothers and to forge a positive happiness connection with them. We did that through our understanding of universal or messianic responsibility, universal compassion, universal love, the wish to repay the kindness of all our mothers, remembering that kindness, and recognizing all beings as our mothers. We were moved to do this because we sought the relief of transcendent renunciation, having reflected how the egocentric way of living is unsatisfactory, how evolution is inexorable, how death is immediate, and how our human life is infinitely precious. These themes are themselves the path. Keep them in your minds and reflect on them little by little as we go along. Now you've had an inkling of the turning-inside-out, the explosion of positive energy that comes about from giving birth to the precious jewel-mind known as the spirit of enlightenment that leads to perfect buddhahood for the sake of all beings.

Once we've generated the seed of this resolve, our mentors in

the imagined field above us smile radiantly. Delighted at our revelation, they melt into light, flow down in a cascade of jewel-elixir
and fill us up, until our hearts feel one with them. We then dedicate the merit of our meditation to the happiness of all the mother-
beings around us, who in turn cheer us on toward buddhahood.
We close down the meditation field, feeling a fellowship with all of
the millions of beings on this planet and on many planets who have
gone through this and have had this inspiration to change from
being self-obsessed to being other-concerned. We feel their concern for us as one of their others, and we realize that this kind of
positive energy has been projected by millions and millions of beings of all types throughout the universe, so that we are joining a
great wave of positive energy that is everywhere. We feel happy
and buoyant.

Break your meditation, and let's head on down the road.

TAD

Quite a meditation. I can see tears in Jay's eyes. His mother died
long ago when he was a little boy and I can see that little boy in
him still. He loves Tenzin for speaking so beautifully about mothers, on this my own mother's birthday. I mean it when I say "wonderful talk" to Jay who grabs my hand with an astonishing force.
Loving the student who loves the teacher is my backward route
today.

"Happy birthday, Mom," I whisper, getting up and brush-
ing the sand from my pants. I see her sad yet still handsome
face. "You spoil me now—you should have spoiled me then. But
you do your best, I love you, and for this strange life of mine,
thanks."

We walk back to the cars and for two days we drive six to a
vehicle, with Jock riding in the truck with Sherpas and kitchen
staff. We leave my least favorite driver in the broken-down jeep.
My feelings about this veer from relief and a nasty that's-what-
you-get satisfaction to what, for lack of a better word, I'll call
compassion. Sitting in a broken jeep? Not allowed to leave it for

fear it will be stolen or ransacked? Stuck out there in the blazing heat all day, and the freezing cold all night? Alone? Not a pleasant thought. Strangely, over the next few days I'll think of this guy often, until I'm hoping, practically praying, he gets rescued, though by whom or what I'm not sure.

The terrifying and uncomfortable driving is long over now. Almost as if to cheer me up, the countryside starts showing off. A huge dune sits totally unexplained in a field of rye. A herd of wild mustangs emerges from around its crescent, defiantly throwing their manes. Behind the dune a strip of green meadow kicks in, behind that a stone and gravel moraine. Then the triangular washes of brownish-black sand at the start of the mountains, then cliffs out of the American west. Four distinct geographic types all crowded into a stretch of twenty visible miles.

Out on the plain again I spy a single blue sheep on a hillside. Jock, who shares the backseat of the Dharma-mobile with me, insists we stop to photograph it. "A blue sheep is a rare sight," he says, "and a good omen." I think of Uttara Crees, whose driver shot such a good omen, like the Ancient Mariner. We shoot this one with cameras and, without insulting anyone or anything, drive on.

Another hour up the forever-road and the mountains to the east have been ground down to bits. They're brown, treeless, all but grassless hills that once were snow-clad giants. Their steep majestic flanks are now dust under our wheels.

That night we camp around a boggy, hump-backed stream that looks like Cape Cod to me, complete with trash and beer cans all over the place. Old-fashioned beer cans you have to open with a church key that remind me of the arguments I used to have with my father when we went sailing on Cape Cod Bay. He would fill his Schlitz cans with water and sink them. "That's not pollution! Who sees 'em down there?" Right. Who sees 'em in Tibet?

There's a cairn draped with prayer flags at the base of a cliff in the distance, and I take a walk over to it before dinner.

It is what it seems. No bones or trace of buried treasure, no genie bottle or magic buddha waiting. Just a bunch of tattered, sun-bleached rags anchored in a stone pile in the shadow of a red crag, waving in the breeze at sunset. Even so I feel less alone standing by it. I don't feel angry or depressed by this show of faith—and that's progress of a sort, I guess, though my mood is slightly glum. Still I wish I could pitch my tent over here tonight, like some punk Achilles dropping out of the Dharma war. Where are you, Kailash? I wonder. How long until I see you? Will you fill the hole in my soul?

CHAPTER SEVEN

Reaching the Mountain

TAD

*T*he following morning we break camp by eight-thirty and head northwest across the Tingri Plain, picking up the southern road to Kailash, which turns due west at the Brahmaputra River. Through noon we dodge in and out of sight of it and after lunch we finally cross the Lion-Mouthed River ten miles shy of Saga, where we'll camp for the night.

The double-pontooned ferry runs along a cable fixed in the crotch of two crossed timbers on either side of the Brahmaputra. As we arrive, the craft is in midstream, returning over the milky glacial blue-green water.

The ferry is piloted and docked by two handsome, hearty

young Tibetan women in work clothes. They are both happy-go-lucky and efficient. Chatting with Tenzin, they habitually cover smiles with their hands, even though their mouths are already hidden with dust masks. Putting their backs into steadying the arm through which the cable runs, they catch docking lines, winching these by hand against stanchions welded onto the deck. Theirs are the best jobs in town, even if this boat is merely a barge hurtling back and forth across a five-hundred-yard stretch of water, water so fast-moving and clouded that the bottom is never once glimpsed at either shore.

A cargo of yaks, loudly and roughly unloaded by nomads with red strings running through their long, thick, black hair, leaves a place for two of our three jeeps. Also on board is a local bicyclist, very proud of his black, Taiwan-made three-speed.

"The geniality of Tibetans!" Tenzin yells into the river wind, smiling broadly at the girls. "Not that they can't be a pain in the neck, too, of course. But as a whole, people usually like Tibetans. They gravitate to them, and it has to do with the fact that for more than a thousand years the Tibetans have lived in a constant awareness of being related to all beings. Since the whole culture is so steeped in it and so many people use it to transform their tribalism and prejudices, they have all developed a sense of other beings being familiar to them, like family. They got out of the rut of 'me and my ancestors, my lineage, my mother, my father, my grandfather, my great-grandfather—we're the great lineage, and other families are all sort of alien,' which cultures that emphasize the ancestor-worship thing get into. So even in the midst of genocide the children of the Dharma are still cheerful."

As we land, parents unsuccessfully discourage their children from begging. I toss the remains of a loaf of rye bread bought in Kathmandu. The children catch it, sample it quickly, and are mystified. Now the parents taste it, and, as they disappear into the dust thrown up by our jeeps, I imagine they are explaining that such useless alms are a fitting reward for bad children who beg.

Throughout the sprawling settlement of brick, block, stone, and rusting corrugated steel, ragtag children look up from their mud games and run toward our dust-deviled jeeps, halloo-ing us as visiting royalty while we approach, then shooing us on, like impotent gods, as we retreat. It inflates our importance and exaggerates our betrayal. We are omnipotent, in comparison, yet witnessing their poverty we do nothing to change it. I think of Tenzin's constant harping on the god-state. Suddenly I get it. To these children we are gods. Yet we are incomplete and dissatisfied, charging around in gasoline-driven chariots.

I wonder how I might possibly convey this sense of opulence to Cynthia, panicked and alone with a first baby in a stranger-filled Portland. "How can I help them, when she doesn't want my help?" I wonder. "And how can I help them, when she does?"

The next afternoon I hit bottom. Sure, I've hit bottom before, but on the eleventh of October, stuffed six in a jeep, grinding up a washed-out gravel bed of a road, I began to despair of ever not despairing. I didn't invite complaint or compliment. I didn't laugh or cry, didn't take pictures or make notes or read anything. I know for a fact that we stopped just beyond Paryang, but I have absolutely no recollection of the last camp before Kailash. My last clear remembrance is the morning, watching a pair of black-necked cranes doing a herky-jerky mating dance amidst the streamside bog-humps. Jock got his camera up and they flew off for a more private seduction. I remember feebly helping Lobsang pick up other trekkers' trash and burying it in a blackened fire pit. Then the big truck wouldn't start, and even Tenzin could not sufficiently wind the huge crank to make the engine catch. Thinking through the failure that this failure would induce was the start of the shutting-down process. So that even after one of the jeeps was tied to the truck, careened around in a circle, and jolted the truck awake—I had already gone into the morbid mode of thinking: "We are one fuck-up away from disaster."

I awaken from this twilight zone on the twelfth of October, our eighth day on the road. I'm in a jeep with those I feel safest with: James, Richard, Jay, Jock, and the sweet, tall driver whose nervous tick of his head—sideways toward his shoulder—I find out later is the Nepali manner of shaking your head to say yes.

We've been told Kailash will be seen and, if all goes well, reached today. So there's hope suddenly; a second wind starts to blow over us. Jay is back on track, recounting another scene from another obscure foreign film to Richard, who has actually seen the thing, when I interrupt.

"Guys!" I yell out, hardly knowing why. "Sorry, but I really need you now," and I kick into the Vairochaniye color-of-shining-diamonds mantra. Without argument of any kind we're all wheeling through it. Jay puts his arm around the driver, squeezing him tight. Smiles are everywhere. A very cool vibe is coming up from our feet when suddenly the jeep pulls off the road, the driver whips off his hat and starts tapping his forehead, saying, "Kailassi! Kailassi!" and we all turn to where he's looking. And there it is. Where it's been the whole time. Peacefully awaiting every broken-down explorer or pilgrim who's ever heard of it, and so whipped the burro of his being until the beast finally up and delivered it into sight. At last, heaven help us, the sacred mountain!

The other jeep pulls in front of us. Car doors are crunching open, everybody is jumping out, laughing, shouting, embracing. I hear Tenzin say, "Where's Tad?"

Opening his arms he shouts: "We've made it! We've really made it to Kailash!"

There's iron in his hug. Shining eye to eye I shout out, "Finally!" before turning to embrace the others, one at a time, like Burton and Speke embracing their party at the source of the Nile. Why do I think this must be much better? Because this is sacred Mt. Kailash!

After much rejoicing, we set to building small cairns of stones, tiny stupas—monuments to enlightened mind—and taking pictures. Tenzin leads us aside in the direction of Lake Manasarovar to the west. He sits us down on suitable rocks and begins our last session on the Systematic Path: my nemesis, the teaching of the wisdom of selflessness.

TENZIN

At last, here we are at the sacred mountain. As we first beheld it, storm clouds had just lifted to reveal its glory. What a good omen!

See it glitter in the streaks of afternoon sun, like the sperm-drenched crown of a great phallus, or a beautiful white breast oozing with milk. The gleaming dome is adorned with a streaming plume of blowing snow. Lifting bands of clouds stand off to the south and north. Think of how many pilgrims must have reached here with foreboding unrelieved, as dense clouds blocked their longing gaze.

Just now in this dusty field among the many small stupa-cairns, I had a really strange thought. Dim memories broke through from what seem to be some recent former lives as a Mongol or Tibetan. I was completely taken by surprise. But the thought burst forth that I must have been a person who was devoted to Chakrasamvara, the Superbliss Buddha, and I must have developed a longing to visit the sacred mountain, but was never able to get here. So the frustrated desire just now surged out from part of an unconscious I didn't dream was there, mixing intensely with the joy I feel at being here in this life. I lived those lives nearby or here in Tibet. I studied hard, meditated, prayed, and dreamed, but never did I behold the real mountain for myself. It was too hard to travel here. Too many bandits. No government permission. In this life I was born far away in America, on the other side of the globe, yet now I get to the sacred mountain, coming with jeeps and trucks during a time when Tibet has been devastated and groans in torment under foreign domination. What irony!

The minute Kailash came into my sight, the world did change for me. Such strange memories came from beyond my normal barriers; I am not given to psychic experiences. The seemingly impenetrable Western sense of conventional reality that usually forestalls any possibility of the miraculous is showing a tiny crack.

Transcendent Wisdom Meditation

This is our last teaching on the foundational path. So focus yourself, calm down, count your breaths a few rounds. When you're ready, set up the refuge field. See your mentors above you in the mind's sky. Their smiles and radiant faces send liquid rays down through the aperture at the top of your head, filling you up with nectar light. You begin to feel like a new person, not so set in old mental ways. The many beings in the field around you—all your mothers—look at you and see you glowing as if you are their mentor. Your gratitude flows up to the mentors and their pleasure radiates more light to you, completing the infinite circuit among you. Even if you can't see them clearly, know that they're there.

As this is experiential learning, we review all the themes to make them more and more familiar. First reflect on your human embodiment with liberty and opportunity, free of the eight inconveniences. Pleased that you have this human life, with access to the teachings of enlightenment and the intelligence to understand them, inspired by your relationship with the mentor, you then reflect upon the fact that you will die soon. The inner mask that you uphold as your identity is a temporary structure, and it will soon go. You can't know when, so you should be prepared for it at any time. Your soul-essence, your open heart of bliss, your buddha-nature, will continue in a coherent stream. You become inspired to focus your precious human life on positive evolution.

Sure of evolutionary causality, you resolve not to kill but to save lives, not to steal but to give gifts, not to harm sexually but only to benefit, not to lie but to speak truth, not to backbite but to reconcile, not to chatter but to speak meaningfully, not to covet but to be generous, not to hate but to love, to speak not harshly but sweetly, and to hold not unrealistic views but realistic ones. You are made of your past deeds and you make your future with your present deeds. Next bring to mind the suffering of the egocentric life-cycle, samsara. Release your fantasies that a particular egocentric experience will satisfy you. Excuse yourselves from driven ambitions. Love yourself realistically and enjoy transcendent renunciation.

Then turn to the sevenfold causal practice of love and compassion that we have been exploring. Recognize the motherhood in all beings because of your infinite connectedness in previous lives, and aim at gratitude toward all beings. Resolve to repay their kindness by taking away their suffering. As you assume universal responsibility for all beings, the spirit of enlightenment becomes part of you, even when you don't think about it. It becomes the seed of that deep inner openness. No longer are you unconscious of the core of your being. You awake from sleepwalking in self-obsession to the waking wonder of a will for the happiness of all beings. Your core becomes this infinite embrace of all beings, amplified by the sense of infinite unity with all previously awakened beings.

The final part of the Systematic Path is transcendent wisdom. It is the most important of all, because compassion will not succeed in really making beings happy unless we become enlightened, and renunciation itself is not full liberation. We cannot achieve nirvana—the perfect freedom from suffering, total bliss—unless we develop transcendent wisdom. This wisdom is an exact experiential knowledge of everything in the universe, complete and exact knowledge of the self, exact knowledge of the body-mind complex, and the total memory of all past lives and foreknowledge of all possible futures.

Contemplating wisdom is the essential key that frees us. We have covered the first noble truth of suffering and the second noble truth of its causation. Now we come to the third noble truth of freedom. The Buddha said this was his greatest noble truth, his supreme discovery: that a human being can actually become totally aware of reality and totally free from suffering forever, and thereby become the evolutionary engine for all others to find their own release. People talk of freedom all the time, demand it, love it, long for it, but deep down it is only a relative thing to them. A moment of freedom from this or that torment. Very few can imagine a total, achievable freedom. So freedom is the main noble truth, and the essential first step toward it is to imagine it.

Wisdom is called the wisdom of selflessness, but it isn't attained by accepting a dogma that one has no self. That would lead to nihilism. The nihilistic sense of being a nothing-self is the great ideological poison of modern humanity and the real cause of our imminent planetary destruction. Greed is secondary; anger, even in warfare, is secondary. The real catalyst for our suicidal behavior with the planet is the delusion that we don't really exist, and so we will not be held responsible for the destructive consequences of our negative actions.

Wisdom prevents our sinking into nihilism by turning us to examine the self and to realize selflessness. The proper understanding of selflessness is the root of liberation. Mastery of selflessness is essential for universal compassion to be effective. Nothing less than liberation is the goal of transcendence. So wisdom completes the path.

The teaching of selflessness is the Buddha's greatest gift to the world. It is also unique to him; no one else has ever taught it. Many people taught, "You should be selfless and moral; put others ahead of yourself." That moral teaching is a common thread in all social etiquettes and religions for the simple reason that societies couldn't function otherwise. But the complete technical, philosophical, and psychological teaching of selflessness was not discovered by anybody but the Buddha. This is not to praise him as religiously superior, because it's not a religious achievement. It's a scientific achievement: He analyzed the self and the world to its ultimate depths and discovered the real nature of the self, which he usually called selflessness or voidness. He further integrated that insight with life.

The Buddha supplemented the valid teachings of the great religious teachers who exhorted us to be kind to others. He gave an understandable explanation that the reason we don't so easily love our neighbors is that we are caught in a distorted perception about the centrality of ourselves as fixed, independent, isolated entities apart from all others. He discovered how we can each come to understand that as a distortion, see through the error with critical wisdom, and then actually free ourselves from this lack of love, this false isolation based on a misperception of the self.

Dispelling the naive absolutism of ordinary beings, the Buddha did not settle for nihilism and make nothingness the ultimate. Instead he pioneered a practical middle way between absolutism and nihilism. How do we approach this selflessness? Selflessness means that there's no absolute self, but there is a relative self. It's not that difficult, but it's a little tricky. A simple way of understanding this is: "Since I am not and have no absolute self, I am free to be a relative self." This acknowledgment of two levels of reality is the key.

The heart of the second noble truth of the cause of suffering is precisely this "self" delusion, this active misperception of the self and the universe, consisting of the following: "I feel, personally, that I have an irreducible center or core that is me, that is somehow absolutely different from everything else. And I similarly perceive other things as having what is called an intrinsic reality in them. The table, the teapot, even Mt. Kailash—I perceive each as a thing in itself, an intrinsically identifiable, real, objective, and absolute thing." This absolute view of myself and things is the core of delusion.

Once we know that this has been suggested by an enlightened person to be the cause of all our suffering, then we are surprised by the next point: He does not ask us to meditate that we are selfless. Rather, the Buddha recommended that we begin to meditate upon the self, acknowledging that we do feel an absolute centrality about ourselves. We need to discover how the self is habitually held as if within, how it is that when I say "Bob," my mind seems to land up on this "real" indivisible thing that is the real me. I really feel as if something fixed and solid were there. I must start by becoming clear of my sense of it.

This attempt to acknowledge the way the self is held requires you to develop a split consciousness in your meditation. If you try to examine your self-habit with your main consciousness, putting your main attention on yourself, you will not find a self, because, of course, it will be your self that is doing the looking. Then you'll say: "Oh, that's what selflessness means—that I can't find myself." But the "I" that has just had this experience is still feeling this unitary, isolated self. So you haven't gotten anywhere. Instead you have to look at yourself with a split-off consciousness, what is called a spy-consciousness or a self-observing consciousness.

This is the meditation: With a corner of your mind you watch yourself thinking or meditating. Try remembering a time when you were falsely accused, when you were gripped with the emotion of injured innocence and indignant righteousness. Observing yourself innocently injured, you notice the I landing on some sense of solidity in the center of your chest and you feel a tightness in your throat and solar plexus. Your strong sense of the absolute centrality of yourself emerges very powerfully.

Observing the self held in place by the self-habit is the first key practice of the meditation on selflessness. The second key practice is to realize that the person who is looking for that self, of course, is also you. You resolve to look for yourself with your full energy: "If I absolutely exist then I should find myself. And if I cannot find an irreducible self when I put this full effort into looking at myself, then I must acknowledge that there is an error in the core of my programmed view; that I make a mistake when I consider myself thus absolute." This second key is called the commitment to a comprehensive binarity, very similar to the law of the excluded middle—that something either is or is not, with no third option. This is a complete surprise to those who think of Buddha's teaching as some sort of vague mysticism. It is essential for achieving a clear realization ultimately, since otherwise the quest of the self will remain endlessly indeterminate and the self-habit will not be broken through decisively.

The third key practice is the looking itself. Buddhism abounds with models of the mind and body for introspective meditation. Most schools use the scheme of the five systems that constitute the mind and body of a living being. These systems are (1) the material system, the five sense organs and their objects; (2) the sensational system, feelings of pleasure and pain all around the body; (3) the conceptual system, different ideas and notions that float around in the mind; (4) the emotional system, the cloud of emotions we swirl around in; and finally, (5) the system of consciousness.

You begin to look for the static self by going through your body, thinking, "Well, I usually think of myself as this body, so where in this body is myself? The real, solid one that is absolute and isolatable. My body itself is constantly related to the environment, it's constantly getting cold or hot, it's getting injured or healed. Blood is flowing, food is going in, and other things are going out. My senses are functioning, my eyes seeing sights, my ears hearing sounds. I look within that body and I assume there is a very stable thing in there that is me, I'm 'Bob.' But I felt that was 'Bob' when I was fifteen! I felt that was 'Bob' when I was twenty-two. And everything about my body is different now than it was then. My body is actually a completely changing impermanent process. So I can't find any single, absolute 'Bob' in the material system of the body and its environment."

Then you look into your sensations, through all your feelings of pleasure and pain, and you don't find anything stable in them. Then you look through your conceptual system, all your ideas and images, voices and pictures inside—you don't find anything stable in them, either. Then you look at your emotions and find that they are far from fixed or stable.

The hardest part of this meditation is when you look into your consciousness. Quite quickly you see that most of its contents are reacting to sense stimuli, with no one consciousness fixed on anything. So you focus on the sixth, the mental consciousness, which organizes the inner impressions and picks out inner, conceptual objects of thought. You realize again that there is nothing fixed in it either. Your thoughts are constantly flowing—especially when you first start meditating and you realize how easily distracted the habitual mind is: Thoughts are like a swirling Sargasso Sea, a whirling cyclone. Indeed, there's nothing stable in it.

The witness to all this instability, the watcher, seems to be the only stable thing. When you realize this, you begin the most difficult effort that a human being can make, or so it's said. This is the effort that the Buddha successfully made; it is how he became enlightened. You turn the witness on the witness. You become like a dog chasing its own tail. Because you are the self you feel like a unity, but when you look back for that solid unity of self, you don't find anything. You then notice that you're still feeling some sense of solid self. Then you look back at what you're still feeling, and you start to spin like a whirling dervish inside the center of your mind. It's very tiring and strenuous. Just looking and looking back becomes a twirling, and then that twirling effort becomes what is called the diamond cutter.

The diamond is that sense of a unique, absolute, and substantial inner core, and when it spins around looking for itself it becomes a drill and it drills through itself. Descartes provides a useful example, because from the Buddhist perspective he made a huge mistake right here. He said, "The reason I can't find my 'self' is because I'm the one looking. I'm the subject, not an object, and that's why I can't find myself. But because I'm the subject, I'm sure I exist." Don't accept this mistaken reliance on self-evidence, a guaranteed way to remain stuck in illusion. You are using your presumed absolute self to find itself, and surely an absolute can find an absolute. You cannot be sure of what you cannot verify—especially if it presumes to absolute certifiability. "I think therefore I am" was an assertion of the utter conventionality of the self, its relativity and, hence, lack of absoluteness. So not accepting the Descartes maneuver, you persist in looking for the assumedly solid self, and you enter the diamond drill mode, and eventually you become dizzy from the spinning. You might even feel as if you're about to faint, because suddenly you lose all idea of who is looking and who is being looked for. Yet you mustn't cop out and say: "I'm nothing, and it's all nothing, it's all meaningless." By this time you should have discarded any thought as really being you. Don't listen to any thought, just keep concentrating on looking for the absolute you.

Then suddenly you feel like you're open as the sky. Suddenly you can't even find the looker who wants to look, and you can't find what the looker hasn't found, and you can't find the not finding. You just suddenly melt and become like empty space, as if the wind is blowing through you; it's as if you are floating, what's outside your skin no different from what's inside your skin. You have the experience of being like water flowing into water.

You feel released from the knot inside, the struggle of the absolute self looking for itself. It is not that you have stopped the search, walked away from it saying: "Hey, there's no one here." You never step out of it, you keep intensely bearing down. Your second key practice still works to keep you on target here, your commitment to comprehensive binarity—either it's there or it's not. And then your absoluteness melts itself, like fire sticks rubbing until they kindle themselves into flame, like a diamond cutting through itself, like nuclear fission or solar fusion.

In this vast spacelike equilibrium, you realize that you don't know who you are in any absolute way, nor do you know that you don't know. You transcend all subject-object knowing, entering another way of being where everything knows itself without your interference, sharing itself freely with you. All labels, all words dissolve—words become useless, meaningless. You don't identify with any thought inside yourself. You feel vast and infinite and one with the vast infinity, and everything disappears, including yourself. And you don't just disappear in a way that things are left behind, because things dissolve with you. Everything goes. So it's not like you're losing balance and forgetting who you are, where you might fall down and hurt yourself. Because up and down dissolve. The ground dissolves. Your mind goes into the state of liquid diamond infinite clear light. This is called the space-like equipoised *samadhi*—a state of unbroken concentration.

Enjoy this miniliberation but do not get attached to it. Your omni-dissolving critical awareness also drills right through the spacelike voidness. The minute you stop aiming it at the elusive self and aim it at the experienced voidness, the voidness itself dissolves. The world of beings and things returns as if reflected in the mirror of voidness, illusory and yet crystal clear. And because you have felt no you apart from things, your you is also just another mirror image, consciously both infinite and also totally interconnected with all things. This is called the dreamlike aftermath samadhi. Because now you don't really feel different from other things.

You come into this dreamlike aftermath state as if you were dreaming the world and yourself. Both you and the world are transparent. You're not even sure whether you're you or the next person, or the table or the mountain. And you feel completely blissful in this translucent state. You don't seize upon this happiness, which strangles any happiness, naturally, as you know. It's the happiness that is just you apart from grasping. Amazingly, you reemerge transparently secure in the calm of happiness.

Then you restore your boundaries and you feel different again. But you suddenly realize that the difference between you and other things is habitual. It's arbitrary, it's relative. There's no absolute difference between you and other beings. This is the first inkling of what is called a nonconceptual understanding, that is to say, an experiential understanding of selflessness. But don't expect this to be the final, big, obliterating blow of enlightenment and everything is all completed. Not at all. There's still the dualism between the aftermath world of objects and the emptiness of everything, but having experienced a kind of moment of enlightenment, you also know there isn't a real difference between these two states.

Now you get involved with beings and things again, but since you've had a first experience of the melting of the self, you naturally become more compassionate, more generous, more tolerant. Because you have experienced it yourself, compassion is integral, spontaneous, and not merely intellectual. You're no longer locked up in some isolated, absolute sense of self.

But then you will become egocentric again. You don't automatically become some vast being. Your old habits will reassert themselves, but then you can go back into the meditation of selflessness, and while you're in the dreamlike state you act compassionately to other beings.

This is the process, then, of trying to unite wisdom — ultimately the skylike state — with compassion, which belongs to the relative, seemingly solid state of things. You integrate them again and again, until you arrive at the inconceivable state known as the reconciliation of dichotomies, where you're committed and totally active while still floating in the sky, like Milarepa. You never budge from your blissful vastness, yet you're fully present to every being and thing. This state should not be described as egolessness, because the ego is just the pronoun "I," which you get even better at deploying when you no longer mistake its referent as something absolute. When you're in the relative state — the aftermath state — you know who you are. You're "I," you're the person who just had the equipoised samadhi. You don't think the equipoised samadhi is your essence, any more than your alienated ignorance was your essence. You don't cling to that timeless feeling of infinity as if it were some sort of soul. Your mind and body ultimately maintain a calm unity of wisdom while fully engaging with the creative diversity of compassion.

Now we've had an inkling of this vast state. Our mentor is flipping out by now, smiling broadly like the sun because we've now tasted the realization of the nondifference between ourselves and our mentor, the nondifference between ourselves and all beings. The mentor, who has long ago realized this state of selflessness as nondual with total interrelatedness, melts into light and dissolves into us, sealing our feeling of oneness with him or her. We feel delighted. We then dedicate the merit of this little bit of understanding of selflessness, the third part of the Systematic Path, to our coming to a total realization of buddhahood as soon as possible, for the sake of being able to really help all these other living beings. We then dissolve the refuge field and, arising in our ordinary bodies and minds, we're ready to camp beneath Mt. Kailash.

TAD

I've heard this before, but never the whole way through. Back at Amherst I'd interrupt with a "Yes, but" at selflessness. Today Kailash, home of buddhas and bodhisattvas, shines out in loving proof: "Hush your silly mouth!" it tells me. "Listen! Learn!" The great scar down the front face of the snow-capped pyramid glistens with a light not of this world; Tenzin rattles off a technique not of this world. But both are right here before me — Tad — most certainly of this world. Here is my tiny reconciliation of dichotomies.

But what duality rears up immediately following this great guided meditation just down the hall from the sacred mountain? We drive through an enclosed garrisonlike village, nodded through by an unofficial-looking sentry. I suppose he could have been a yak counter with no political duties, but we've got our guard up. I get the feeling that ominous types are studying us from every doorway, an impression that, unfortunately, is not entirely unrealistic.

Back out on the flats before Kailash, the glow returns. Our jeeps trade off pulling over and photographing the ever-white one, as below the brown altar a golden carpet of rye bows on either side of a meandering tributary, bound—we know—for Mana-sarovar, lake of compassion. I climb up a little bluff behind Jock, who's clicking away. I call his name and get a shot of him, camera in hand, looking away from his portraiture of Kailash, caught as if a moment before kissing the bride, happy as can be and powerless to explain why.

We drive past a solitary figure who salutes us with a proud, upraised arm. He is Asian, yet I could swear that dangling from his neck hangs a cross. We press on up the widest, flattest, most desolate desert yet, up a road that isn't a road, merely a sand track running past hundreds of dangling wooden crosses—not telephone but telegraph lines! In the distance a medieval wall and gate take shape before the mud-wasp pods of Darchen, over whose purgato-rial squalor towers our piece of heaven. The deep scar Kailash wears is now partially sunk in shadow, though the snow-filled channel refracts intense light at its eastern edge. Cross striations, caused by the cakelike layerings of sedimentary stone, catch the snow in straight, even lines. Wind and gravity knock the icing from these tiers at vertical edges, and the resulting montage of horizontal and vertical lines to some eyes takes the shape of a great swastika, the ancient symbol of happiness and goodness. Thus the Bonpos call Kailash Yungdrung Gutse, or the nine-story swastika mountain.

All along this long, neatly arranged brown terrace, equally symmetrical minor peaks kneel with perfect posture east and west, in obvious subservience to this god-king of mountains. These altar boys and girls would seem quite remarkable in themselves were they not dwarfed and otherwise diminished by the preeminent lord of earth blazing before us.

I force myself to use a masculine description, since Kailash is considered the great lingam, or phallus, of rock that impregnates the heavens with sexual-spiritual energies. Even so, to refer to this as the king of mountains is difficult for me. For how could any-thing so jewel-like, so ermine-decked, so effortlessly faultless and radiant not be a woman? Something to meditate into proper per-spective, no doubt.

Do we stop and consult? No. The Dharma-mobile heads straight for the gates. I'm glancing to the east where pilgrim trucks unload gypsy caravans full of Tibetans from every corner of a tyrannized nation, to do as their hearts tell them. To make the *kora*—the sacred pilgrimage—around Kailash and do prostrations. To pray for the return of their leader. To make offerings at altars and cairns. To spin prayer wheels and say mantras. All day long and in their dreams to save the world and every being in it. *Om mani padme hum.*

I want to camp over there with them. And I'm certain Jay, now in the Dharma-mobile ahead, wants the same thing. To sleep out in the open and sit around a Tibetan fire, to understand nothing of what is said and to understand it all. But we can't do that. This is occupied territory, we're behind an iron curtain. There are rules to follow, and for the transgressors of such rules, harsh consequences.

Tenzin, in the lead jeep, charges forward through the open gate. We follow, driving into a rocky, lifeless, empty lot. I start to laugh. Here we've endured a solid week of grueling travel, facing hardships real and imagined. Now, at last, we've actually reached our long-sought-for goal. We pull up at the foot of what indeed looks to be a manifestation of the divine, shimmering in a pale white veil above, and what do we get for it? We're in jail!

PART TWO

Circling the Mountain

Nobody can approach the Throne of the Gods, or penetrate
the Mandala of Shiva or Demchog, or whatever name
he likes to give to the mystery of ultimate reality,
without risking his life—and perhaps
even the sanity of his mind.

—LAMA GOVINDA, *The Way of the White Clouds*

CHAPTER EIGHT

The Southern Gate of the Mandala Palace

TAD

*P*iling out of the jeeps into the prison yard we greet one another's disbelieving faces. Western trekkers must camp here, in this five-hundred-by-seven-hundred-foot rectangle within which a few concrete slabs have been poured. I choose to have my tent pitched on such a slab, opting for uniform, rather than erratic discomfort. It's a bad call. I've unpacked my gear, hung my still-damp laundry from an interior elastic, and am just plumping my sweater-for-a-pillow when I hear the tea bell. Suddenly a loud, squawking "Hell-oh!" makes me jump.

I'm expecting Poe's raven perhaps, but what I find upon unzipping the front flap is a brightly smiling Tibetan woman, big and wide and getting on in years, decked out with all manner of neck-laces, pins, headdresses, rings—the lot of which festoon a form and face extraordinarily beautiful not more than fifteen years be-fore. She smiles with the boldness of her departed youth, and holds up a rope of silver-clad stones. "You buy!" she says, without asking, as a generation before she would have put a hand on her hip, winked, and said: "You like!"

By the time I clamber out of my nylon cave, she's roped in Wolfgang and Jay. Wolfgang peers at her wares and states matter-of-factly: "The coral is fake, and so—I'm pretty sure—is the tur-quoise." With that he's off to the mess tent. Jay listens to her patter, which has taken on the tone of the wronged lover who might forgive some transgression for a price. He stares at me with large, black, melancholic eyes and states calmly: "This is the first Tibetan I've ever met whom I thoroughly dislike." Then he too, is gone.

I won't buy. Still, something holds me here. The chill of eve-ning sets in, regal Kailash glows softly from above, dogs trot by growling at each other, and the tea bell is heard a second time. I indulge the age-old ritual of offering an affordable price for a huge gob of blue stone. She laughs at the ridiculousness of such an offer; I hold firm. She screws up her face, pouts her bottom lip, places a curled index to her eye, and pretends to weep. I take her cold hands in mine, press them once, and leave her wiping away false tears.

While pouring antiseptic-laced blue water over my hands, as we must before entering the mess tent, I find myself wondering whether this disturbing creature is local or came with the pilgrims camped against the hillside outside the gates. She said something about being "off to Lhasa" tomorrow. I fear she's a rotten apple in the rolling barrel of a caravan. Still I can't shake the creepy sensa-tion of her eyes being a mirror and of seeing in them my baser self. Just as I was so confident at having left that bastard in a latrine a hundred miles back.

Inside the tent a Sherpa pumps the Coleman lantern, then lights and hangs it from a hook. Its arc of flame casts a lovely glow over the folding table, creating a hiss that is instantly soothing. It's been a long, important day. We're happy, tired, relieved. Dinner falls even faster than usual upon tea. Tenzin stirs himself to speak more thoroughly about the mandala we are about to enter. The dishes are removed, we fill our water bottles and mix our tea expectantly.

TENZIN

Welcome, pilgrims! Here we are at the foot of Mt. Kailash! Don't despair at this prison-hole of a town. This tourist campground of Darchen feels more like a slaughterhouse pen. But we can imagine it to be part of a ring around the mandala palace of the Superbliss Buddha, which, as we will get to know better, is believed to be eternally present within the mountain. There are eight sacred charnel grounds outside the mandala palace—they represent the way the world of ordinariness looks from within the perfected realm of the mandala. Hence, this grim camp turns out to be highly appropriate to this site.

The Blade Wheel of Mind Reform

Now that we have reached the mountain and have finished an experiential run-through of the Systematic Path, we can begin *The Blade Wheel of Mind Reform*. This makes the second session in one day, but we are now beginning the full meditative retreat of the serious pilgrim, and intensity is appropriate. The *Blade Wheel* is a powerful spiritual alchemy taught by Dharmarakshita, one of Atisha's teachers, almost exactly one thousand years ago. We will work with it following an eighteenth-century commentary by the fourth Panchen Lama.

The *Blade Wheel* contains the teaching we will practice as our inner pilgrimage around the mountain, parallel to our outer one. We're going to study and contemplate this at the eight main devotional places on the compass points of the circumambulation path. I don't want the path taught here in this holy place just to be my personal interpretation. I want to follow an ancient pattern, from the written legacy of an enlightened sage. Dharmarakshita taught Atisha, who you will recall elaborated the Systematic Path we have been studying. Dharmarakshita came to Tibet at the turn of the last millennium, fleeing the Islamic invasions of North India. He had to watch as his monastery in India, his monks, and his library burned before his eyes. Now in turn, all the Tibetan monasteries have been destroyed by the Chinese communist invasion, occupation, and cultural revolution of the last forty-five years.

The great lama Tsong Khapa was especially helped by this *Blade Wheel* teaching, as was the Great Fifth Dalai Lama in the seventeenth century. And the mind-reform tradition of Ganden Monastery maintained it as the essence of Dharma practice. So we're going to work on this mind reform together, in the presence of this wonderful fraternity of high beings.

Let's start at the beginning. What is meant by mind reform? In general, all the steps toward enlightenment are mind reforms. This mind of ours must be cultivated and transformed. These are methods of doing so.

Why is this practice called a blade wheel? A blade wheel is a weapon for doing battle with an enemy, like those little metal stars called *shiken* that ninjas use, with eight or twelve blades sticking out. This blade wheel hits our real enemy, which is our own inner habit of self-preoccupation. It causes damage—serious, blessed damage to narcissism, vanity, the self-habit. A blade wheel is a very fierce image for mind reform, a fierce form of the surgical blade of critical wisdom. My root teacher, Geshe Wangyal, presented it to me as the bottom line. And that was after he'd been teaching me for a couple of years, often giving me hell, scolding me, and exposing the self-preoccupation and self-addiction habits underlying all my other bad habits.

The Panchen Lama says: "In the world there are two kinds of enemies, the physical enemy and the invisible enemy—the only real demon. The invisible demon enters our own mindstream and harms us from within." It doesn't openly attack from the front. The physical enemy outside is easy to identify as an enemy. But for all of us—from our infinite stream of lives—the chief enemy who has been forcing us into one suffering after another is this

126

self-preoccupation habit, which we have had since we were animals, lizards, or whatever other kinds. The usual enemy shoots
arrows at us, but unless they hit our vital points they do not cause
great harm. But this inner spiritual enemy, our self-cherishing
habit cultivated and preserved from former lives, destroys us invisibly from within, like a worm that eats wood from within. We have
to deal with it accordingly, since it works from this very dangerous
point at the center of our heart, from the very center of our self-
perception.

Dharmarakshita begins his text:

I salute you, great ferocious Death Exterminator,
Fiercest archetype deity of bliss-void-indivisible intuition,
You kill Death, the Devil self-addiction and his minion egoism!

Yamantaka literally means Death Exterminator. He looks extremely fierce, dark blue-black in hue with flaming hair, his main
face that of a mahey buffalo, with eight other faces of various
colors, thirty-four arms holding weapons and gruesome symbols,
and sixteen legs standing upon various animals and mundane deities. He is an archetype deity, a manifestation of the gentle bodhisattva Manjushri, ever-youthful prince of transcendent wisdom.
The archetype deities are embodiments of buddhas that symboli-
cally manifest the qualities of wisdom and compassion and power
to provide practitioners with physical templates for realizing their
spiritual ideals. Manjushri adopts his fiercest buddha-form in order to exterminate death, represented by the Indian death-god
Yama, who is both the devil self-preoccupation and its minion self-
habit. Yamantaka is so fierce because his wisdom scourges the
self-preoccupation habit that poisons the inner mind-process of all
beings. The blade wheel is a symbol of this critical wisdom, with
which he terminates the self-addiction, the real devil of death.

Yama, Death, is self-addiction, because egotism brings death.
The way it brings death is not simply when I physically die. The
way it brings death is that self-cherishing narcissism and habitual
egotism cut us off from the rest of the world. They kill the source
of our life and energy—our relationships with the rest of the

world. They isolate our living self, pretending to draw energy from a nonentity, our absolute self, which doesn't really exist. That presumed absolute self, isolated from the rest of the world, is only a mental construction, a fantasy created in a vacuum that actually is not there. Therefore, we are always exhausted, drained, frustrated, dissatisfied, having to struggle to keep up the pretense of enjoying living in this artificial, self-defeating vacuum. Self-addiction is death because it is the essence of self-enclosure, the self-isolation that cuts off our living being from the interrelational weave of life. We are already dead when we are controlled by the devil of self-preoccupation. The *Blade Wheel* releases us by killing that demon. That is why Geshe Wangyal said to me: "This is the real thing." So we are working with it on our way around Mt. Kailash.

Here we are at the start of our pilgrimage in the barren wastes of Western Tibet reading these ancient paeans to Yamantaka, whom you often see in temples. He's so fierce, Tibetans say, that when the gods see him they lose control of their bowels! Tibetans believe in the existence of gods, but they're not too reverent about them, except the highest god, the god of liberation, Devatideva—the god beyond the gods—as they call the Buddha.

There are two levels of Yamantaka: the interpretable level and the definitive level. The definitive level Yamantaka is the wisdom of the nonduality of bliss and voidness. That wisdom is totally aware at all times of all life-forms' inseparability from the great bliss of ultimate reality itself. It is the ultimate discernment of reality as supreme bliss, and it is armed and dangerous to our delusions about the life-cycle of self-inflicted sufferings. It attacks all our self-posturings, all our self-identity habits, all that we use to torment ourselves and persist in misery.

The interpretable level is the fierce form of Manjushri, who arises as the great Yamantaka we recognize in the iconography. So what we're saluting here is bliss-void-intuitive wisdom—the exact and experiential knowledge of the unity of real subjectivity as self-transcending bliss and real objectivity as infinite freedom—in this extremely fierce personification. This wisdom of ultimate reality will not tolerate any of our self-habits. It will overwhelm them. It will liberate us from them. We don't have to worry, "Will this work?" It will completely overwhelm our self-cherishing habit, which means that our understanding has the capability of overcoming our self-cherishing addiction.

Yamantaka is an apocalyptic revelation of liberating wisdom, central in the Diamond Thunderbolt Vehicle (Vajrayana) of esoteric Buddhism. "Vajra" is a powerful word, it means "diamond" as unbreakable, "thunderbolt" as all-powerful; it is a weapon, a royal scepter, and the ultimate Buddhist symbol for universal compassion as well as orgasmic bliss. I like to call the Vajrayana the apocalyptic vehicle, because it instantly rips away the veils of the life-cycle of suffering in samsara.

The Vajrayana practitioners don't wait for some future life in which they'll attain buddhahood. They don't wait until they meet Maitreya, the buddha of the future, or get to Shambhala, the magic land of the new age of the Wheel of Time Tantra. The apocalyptic heroes and heroines won't wait for that. Not because bodhisattvas are impatient and not able to wait for their own release, but because bodhisattvas can't stand to wait while other beings continue to suffer. Bodhisattvas want the power to be able to serve as buddhas for beings, to save them from their suffering as soon as possible.

You can't just sit back and say, "Oh well, if I'd been lucky enough to have been born in the time of Shakyamuni thousands of years ago, or lived down the valley from Milarepa, then I could become a buddha." Instead, the apocalyptic practitioner insists: "No! Buddhahood is here in this life. Bliss-void-intuitive wisdom is here right now, if I can only tune my understanding to its wavelength and destroy the demon of my self-preoccupation."

The relationship of student to teacher is absolutely critical to this transformation because of your ordinary, habitual vision of the world as a garbage heap and addiction to the habitual vision of yourself as an uncut diamond in the heap. You focus only on yourself and constantly think: "What can I get? Where do I fit in? Are they doing what I want? Are they meeting my needs?" These attitudes are the sputterings of the demon self-concern, the bars on your prison walls!

The true, honest guru—the real lama, the spiritual parent—

challenges you to find the demon in the center of your heart and sparks your own intuitive wisdom. He doesn't liberate you, your own understanding liberates you. What the mentor does is attack the devil whom you falsely think is you, which prevents you from releasing your liberating understanding.

On the ordinary human level the teacher or mentor may not be such a perfect buddha. They have a great proverb in Tibet: "The best lama to have is one who lives at least three valleys away." That means that you get the initiation, you get the teaching, the deeper reflection of the buddha-mind, and you make the teacher into the icon of the buddha, without having to see that buddha walk around and fart and do stupid things, and create for you a cognitive dissonance you're not ready for.

Milarepa is an instructive example. Milarepa's guru Marpa was definitely a fallible figure—he caused his own son's death through mistaken initiations, he beat his wife, he lost his temper. He had buddha-experiences, and he had a point in himself where he was in touch with buddha-energy. No doubt he channeled that buddha-energy to Milarepa, but he had serious human faults.

Milarepa, however, practiced seeing Marpa as a perfect mentor from the moment he received initiation, which occurred after a long, arduous, and stormy courtship between them that involved Marpa's overt hostility and Milarepa's grave doubts about this lay teacher. Milarepa ran away from Marpa to join a different guru but couldn't stay away. Finally, working himself to blister and bone, threatening suicide, the exterior drama finally fell away and the true teaching was laid bare. Then Milarepa was initiated into the mandalas of Hevajra and Chakrasamvara, and he saw Marpa as indivisible from those archetype buddhas. Then he was sent away by Marpa to meditate for thirty years in caves— never seeing his teacher again! Never having to deal with the human side of Marpa, he deepened his vision, and the more he became freed of his self-preoccupation demon, the more he saw the buddha-essence of Marpa. He got the full benefit of Marpa's spiritual essence, seeing beyond the human flaws.

When we were doing the Systematic Path you visualized as your mentor the most enlightened being you could think of, Buddha or Jesus or Moses or the Goddess or some personal teacher of yours. I myself think of the presence of a fusion of His Holiness the Dalai Lama, Geshe Wangyal, Tsong Khapa, and Shakyamuni Buddha. Now, with the *Blade Wheel* you can use the wisdom bodhisattva Manjushri, or his fierce form Yamantaka, or else stick with whoever was your mentor before.

Let's all be yogis—real practitioners of this deep meditation— out here on our pilgrimage, as we study the *Blade Wheel*. We're away from civilization, we're away from our habitual life of self-aggrandizement, and we're looking for something more profound. If you take Yamantaka as your guru-mentor, you fuse the human guru's incisive criticism with Yamantaka's terrible tranformative power, and you see the guru's mirror reflection even if it shows your ugly sides and bad habits, the destructiveness of your egotism.

Let's carry the bodhisattva attitude of fierce compassion and insight with us around Mt. Kailash, because it is the Tibetan attitude. This attitude gives you the pure vision needed to see right through the rock and snow of Mt. Kailash to the mountain as the living mandala of Superbliss Buddha.

One last thing. Please do not project me as being your mentor. Just think of me as the secretary, the reporter of the teaching. I do not feel qualified to assume the role of mentor for any of you, including you, Tad. I rather aspire to being your Dharma-friend.

This all develops from the opening salutations of the *Blade Wheel* and we'll move further into it tomorrow. Finally, though it is late, I want to open up for you the vision of the mountain as the mandala palace of the Superbliss Buddha, Chakrasamvara Father-Mother-united and their divine community of bodhisattva-heroes and yoginis. This Superbliss palace is always here at this mountain, and the door is always open. We are now at the southern gate of the mountain. In its visionary dimension, it is a palace of ascending wheels of Superbliss, an alternative universe. It has a divine architecture wherein one enjoys the aesthetic experience of being a buddha. It's the most exalted space conceivable, a pulsing, self-luminous building made of jewel energy. The whole eastern wall is made of a solid slab of diamond. The floor is made of ruby and emerald and diamond in big slabs without any seams. To enter is to experience the most sublime bliss possible.

Within it, you experience all other beings as if they were there with you. It doesn't isolate you from the world. The palace has big staircases leading into it, like Mayan pyramid staircases, that go through the multicolored arched prongs of crossed vajras. You walk up through them. Outside the southern gate where we are now, everything is golden-yellow sapphire. As we go round the mountain we circumambulate the mansion, and depending upon our vision, we can go in and out of the doors. Inside the mansion is the Chakrasamvara Superbliss Buddha Father-Mother, two beings in one, with sixty other deities: the four inner goddesses, eight ferocious animal-headed female protectors, and twenty-four divine couples dancing on jewel wheels. Eight of these couples are sapphire blue; eight of them are ruby red; eight of them are diamond white. And the twenty-four heroes and heroines also have their own palaces where the mandala reverberates in twenty-four other holy sites throughout the Himalayas or throughout the West. The mandala can be multiplied infinitely — it can be found even within an atom if you become an adept. This Superbliss Mandala Palace is a transformed environment, a realm where bliss and beauty and perfection are the norm, rather than some far-off ideal.

Tibetans believe this mountain is the mandala, that's why they revere it. Normally, to see a mandala you have to be initiated. Ceremonial mandalas are diagrams created by adepts with little grains of colored sand. They may even make a three-dimensional building, which is like a dollhouse model of the real jewel-energy palace of bliss. Usually you're initiated and introduced to the mandala, and then you memorize the architectural description and you can visualize it. But here we don't need any lama to create it. The mountain-mandala is always open, totally here all the time.

This Superbliss Spiritual Technology is the highest of the Mother Tantras. It is an Unexcelled Yoga Tantra, because it takes the energy of sexual union and turns that orgasmic bliss into enlightenment, rather than dissipating it in self-concern. It's not the sexual union sought by the ordinary frustrated mind of self-preoccupation—it's extraordinary, a union that embraces all reality within it, the ultimate fulfillment of generosity, love, and freedom.

Circling the mountain is an initiation into this incredible world. The reason I gave a teaching on selflessness as the culmination of the Systematic Path is that you must have at the very least a clear intellectual understanding about selflessness in order to experiment with this kind of Tantric visualization. You must be aware that any sense of self or reality is constructed, relative, interactive, and not absolute. If you have never dislodged the habitual absolutism of the ordinary self-habit and then begun to imagine: "Now I'm going to be the Superbliss Wheel Buddha," you will experience what Jung called inflation. You can become a megalomaniac, which soon leads to paranoia when you find the world does not agree with you. Selflessness is essential to ground the creation of the buddha-self.

I'm not pretending to give you this initiation. The mountain itself is the mandala palace with open doors, and the actual Superbliss Buddha-deities are here in their subtle light-body forms. You might as well have a peek at what they're like, because the ultimate goal is not to just sit back and worship the Buddha as Superbliss dancing within the mountain. The reason for the mandala is that the Buddha invites beings to join and become Superbliss Buddhas themselves—male and female in union, in the female form, or in the lone hero forms.

Enough introduction to the Tantric vision of the mountain. Tomorrow we begin our actual circumambulation.

TAD

We greet this vision with stunned silence, like a bunch of gypsy guitar players passing a battered instrument around a campfire and unknowingly handing the six strings to Segovia. Listening, we marvel, even as we're told, "I am not your teacher, do not meditate on me as the mentor!" Back in Woodstock, your guitar teacher is the best player you know. Your teacher, therefore, needn't agree to be your teacher. Did Marpa agree to be Milarepa's teacher? He did not. Was there ever a time since their meeting when he was not Milarepa's teacher? There was not.

I therefore take Tenzin's rebuttal with a grain of salt. I have a feeling Jay is coming to a similar decision. It isn't so much that I insist upon being Tenzin's student, it's that I am Tenzin's student, whether he cops to it or not. At the same time, I am not his acknowledged student. So Tenzin is and is not my teacher. This is no contradiction. His face flickers in and out of focus as my mentor. Thomas Merton and His Holiness the Dalai Lama also appear. I haven't figured out how to proceed exactly—but that's nothing new for me. A similar state of philosophical paralysis typifies most of my days.

I start to wonder how I will handle the crushing pressure of the *Blade Wheel* channeled through this go-between of a Westerner. It's too huge. I'll either have to learn the Tibetan alphabet and start at the beginning or run back to America and lose myself in tawdry affairs, hangovers, and the partial redemption of fatherhood. Is there any middle ground? Can't I just walk around the mountain and let it work its magic, without having to understand the entire Tibetan universe? Or is this my chance to use the *Blade Wheel* to cut my usual denial and face all my crap?

Looking up somewhat furtively, I solicit Jay's glance and motion out of the tent with my head. After a cursory "goodnight to all" at the edge of the lantern's glow, we explore a bit of the enclosure. My tiny, powerful flashlight in one hand, walking stick gripped like a club in the other, we tiptoe to the northeast corner. Dogs growl from the shadows, a drunken figure urinates unsteadily on the wall, cursing the dogs. We proceed west, scanning the barrier for a way through to the electric lights and human movement we can see over the wall. More growls greet our maneuverings. There's a nervous silence between us, a vacuum that demands filling.

"It's overwhelming," I blurt out, finally. "It's too much! Like learning to read when I was a kid. I never thought I'd ever read. I didn't advertise my fears, but secretly I knew, all those squiggly marks on the page would never make any sense to me."

Jay puts his hands to the back of my neck and squeezes. "I think it's meant to be overwhelming, Tad."

Having surveyed a nocturnal prison wall, we return to our sleeping bags. Keeping a hand on my walking stick I fall into thin sleep, invaded by nasty dreams. The dogs of Darchen will bark all night.

CHAPTER NINE

The Great Freedom Pole

TAD

The next morning, as every morning, we're awakened with Lobsang's two-tone call of "Teeeea Wa-tah!" Ten minutes later comes "Wash-iiiing Wa-tah!" and ten minutes after that, "Breeeeeak-fast!" I rush through hot cereal with muesli and Ovaltine mixed in it, pack my day pack, my duffel, say, "See you when I'm a virgin again!" to my uncomprehending favorite driver, and check my uniform for vitals. So far every waking hour, I've been in a suede leather vest Cynthia gave me for Christmas. Whatever the conditions, I've worn it over a wick-dry thermal shirt, a regular shirt, a sweater, and bare skin. Four vest pockets, for vitamins, pain killers, calculator, pens, and pencils; a fanny pack dangles at my right hip holding a dozen other necessities like my knife, toothbrush, toilet paper, sun cream, harmonica case. A camera bag is attached at the belt on my left hip.

There's a bandanna and my glacier glasses around my neck and one or two hats on my head, and finally I've got my Day-Glo sleeping bag and parka in my day pack in case of a blizzard.

We've met our yak handlers and their yaks, seen our purple duffel bags tied alongside the tents and stoves. The front guard has already taken off. I'm trying not to be a pain but I cannot wait to follow. It's a little after eight. There is not a single cloud in the pale, milky blue sky. I can see Richard is raring to go, too, so I raise my chin fast and grab his eye, as he chants, teasingly, "Beat ya' to nir-va-nah."

Out we go on foot, straight through the main gate onto the flat Barka Plain, a whole new creature in the morning light. Pools of violet shadows hang mistlike for miles, then the as-of-yet-unrevealed sun spills a tanned rose strip splashing brighter patches and darker shadows on the ridges and ravines of foothills. These presage the classically wide and snow-topped Gurla Mandhata rising eighty miles away, more than twenty-five thousand feet high. Seeming to nestle at its western feet, a long, narrow band of cerulean blue is Lake Rakshas Tal, behind which the snow-saturated Great Himalayas stretch to the west to the edge of the horizon, like some primordial definition of dignity.

Somewhere to the southwest along this gauzily lit ridge lies the invisible crossbar of a capital T. North of the crossbar is Tibet, west of the stem is India, east is Nepal. Therefore, somewhere snaking through those mountains are the Lipu, Chyangio, and Tinkar passes, through which hundreds of thousands of Hindu pilgrims have traveled for over a millennium or two by foot, donkey, yak, jeep, and probably elephant to get to this very spot. This is the start of the great circumambulation, their Hindu *parikrama*, or the Tibetan kora—this last, the Tibetan word, is perhaps the easiest for "once round Kailash."

And so we start it, at fifteen thousand feet above sea level, on October 12, 1995, at roughly 8:30 A.M.—the thirty-two-mile circumambulation of Mt. Kailash. For each and every one of us, this is the first time around the holiest of mountains.

Buddhists circle a holy relic clockwise. The left hand is considered unclean; thus, one eats with the right, and approaches reverential objects on the clean side. Somewhere over the last eight days Jay told me my prayer beads were on the wrong wrist. I had them on the right, clean, wrist. As I switched them, I recalled Jesus advising his critics that saints had no need of churches, which is why His were filled with sinners. Similarly, I reasoned, the clean hand has no need of prayer beads, and the unclean hand has every need.

The sound of my feet on the trail and my lungs sucking air are all I can hear. Richard in his salt-and-pepper pullover and sailor's cap is kneeling, examining a rock. I push on, a little too fast maybe, over the top of a knoll. Even the leaves of bushes are coated with dust stirred up by pilgrims' feet. And there they are, heard before seen, four women chanting, long hair tucked in colorful buns, dressed in full-length black dresses, with long tan aprons. The first loses her balance, trips and falls, as the second, raising her hands in dismay blunders into the same trap. Then the first gets up and the third falls, as the second rises, and the fourth falls. My God—I suddenly understand—they're walking around Kailash on their knees, over thirty-two miles of rock and sand! I look more closely. Yes—they have gloves or pads on their hands, which they slap together over their heads with a sharp note of praise. They take two steps forward, and, with a lower song, down they go onto the third step, and back up onto the fourth.

I wander off the trail and steady myself on a boulder, feeling a slight pang of shame as I snap a picture—the shutter falls all the same. Richard has already cleared the hill. I let the parade go by, then Tenzin, then Jay. They haven't noticed me. Clearly, there is much to digest alone as, walking by the prostrating women, I am passing those who by their faith have already by far passed me.

Over one more hump, I see the first customary prostration site. The spot is marked by a cairn-stone pile holding up a half-raised flag, like the famous one the Marines were raising under fire on

Iwo Jima. Below this bent flag is strewn the usual assortment of cast-off clothes, shoes, shattered glass, yak horns, and fluttering prayer flags. Tenzin is on his knees in front of it, prostrating not once but three times.

Jay has arrived and is doing the prostrations too. I wonder if I should join them. Wolfgang and Jock, too, are putting down their packs and lying down on their stomachs three times. Jock then busies himself photographing sacred herbs that grow in abundance here. There's the local bush, *khenpa,* which is used as incense to invoke the nearby protective deities, and *shengpa,* which sports small red flowers. Richard picked a lot of juniper (*shukpa*) above Nyalam, which he burns in his tent to kill the stink of his socks, producing an even warmer aroma. Wolfgang has brought his own sacred herbs. He places some on a single piece of charcoal and blows.

All this spiritual busyness is making me slightly nervous. I pick up a stone, and cast it halfway up the pile. All right, damn it, no more stalling. I walk out toward the glowing dome and find a spot between cast-off sandals and a baby bottle and down I go. I've seen it done. I know how to do it correctly.

I stand back up and clasp my hands together over my head, and as I look at the mountain, my neck starts to get hot. I bring the clasped hands down to my chest, my elbows lock, I look at the mountain. My eyes are getting tight and my lips are trembling. I bend my right knee and hit the sand with my palms, as my left knee follows, and I look out, straight ahead of me. Here I am, on my knees, looking straight out at Kailash. And I wonder: Have I ever been on my knees before? Yes. In a taxicab when I proposed. What's wrong with this picture? Am I proposing to a mountain? Breaking with my agnostic past? Taking a chance on magic? Prostrating before this perfect cum-covered cock of stone fucking the most perfect blue of bluest skies in the most distant, most difficult, most wonderful and perfect damned place in the entire world? Yes. All that. Please.

Closing my eyes, I kiss the ground, and as I open them, two tears hit, and I kiss where they hit. Then I get up and do the whole thing again twice, without the kissing. Then I prostrate three times toward Manasarovar, to the southwest to a sacred spot on the Sutlej River, and, finally, toward Darchen. Indeed, the whole deal, twelve times in all—but without the kissing. I've only kissed the ground once. The first time I bowed down before Kailash.

As with losing virginity, there is a clumsiness to this, my first time round. But I am not ashamed of my inexperience. Instead I feel a dignity in it, a little like the calm following long, hard labor on a wall of words or a wall of stones. But this is different. This is a calm at a beginning.

Suddenly I trust whatever conspiracy it is that's brought me to my knees to push me around this sacred rock. Because having started on my knees, I am proceeding correctly. At present, there is not a hint of a doubt concerning this, not in a single cobwebbed corner of my mind.

Today, I am a pilgrim and this is my progress.

Over the next ridge the architecture comes clear. Two sets of high, austere cliffs, with a valley between. Those to my right, charging off the western ridge guarding Kailash, are reddish-brown and horizontally tiered, with pyramids of eroded sand and rubble gathering at the bottom of seventy-five-degree faces. These cliffs are knob-topped, some of them quite torsolike in shape. They are called the sixteen arhats, a group of transcended saints of the Mahayana tradition.

Across a valley a mile or so wide, west of these jagged-topped guardian cliffs, rise up even steeper, higher, more irregular, and more foreboding cliffs. This is Nyenri Mountain. By some circumstance of nature the Nyenri cliffs are not as smooth as their eastern neighbors. Though mineral deposits lend occasional aquamarine and rose glazes, the entirety of the massive wall is streaked with horizontal lines and countermarked with deep downward striations, resulting in a cruelly cubed and diced look. Also the debris that gathers at their slopes is rockier, cruder, less refined. Thus the rule of holiness holds true: the farther from the jewel of Kailash, the less perfect the manifestation.

I can't yet discern the exact character of the valley between these two sets of walls, since it is blocked from view by the comparatively squat walls of an amphitheater spreading three-quarters of the way across my field of vision. Neatly terraced stone seats tier the steep hillside, inviting the impression that deities might gather here to view the reverential offerings of men. It's completely sensible, then, that directly below the amphitheater stands the *Tarpochey*, or great freedom flagpole, a thirty-foot pole that is lowered and raised again each spring at the Sagadawa Buddha Enlightenment Day festival, held on the full moon of the fourth lunar month.

Weeks in advance, Tibetans from near and far pour into the area hawking and trading wares in a carnival-like atmosphere. To start the festival, the flagpole is lowered and festooned with new prayer flags, then pointed toward Gyandruk Monastery (in the inner kora) from which blast Tibetan trumpets, longhorns, drums, and cymbals blessing the raising of the Tarpochey. Learned monks study the angle of the newly raised flagpole, a yearly oracle of good and ill events. There is an abiding belief among Tibetans (defended by certain radical physicists) that the resonant dissonances of these longhorns were once used to levitate extremely heavy objects. The accompaniment of the trumpets during the raising of the Tarpochey, therefore, may harken back to ceremonies when such blessed noise actually did the lifting.

Somewhere up those cliffs overlooking the Tarpochey lie several significant sites, the most important of which is a burial ground for monks and lamas sometimes confused with the graveyard of the eighty-four *mahasiddhas*, a set of great adepts of Indian and Tibetan lore, although that is actually just under the brow of Drolma La, the highest point of our journey and another couple of days ahead.

Normally, Tibetans do not bury their dead at all. Instead a specially trained mortician uses a saw or ax to hack the corpse apart, and leave the human meat for birds to eat. Often this grim reaper must work among flesh-maddened ravens and buzzards, who are not so patient for their meal as they loiter about the sky burial sites as seagulls will around garbage dumps. A conversation yesterday about the burial grounds and the sacred stench said to accompany them inspired a nightmare involving my newborn, a dream so brief and potent I refuse to accompany the group up the hillside come morning.

Visible to the left is Kangnyi. Recently rebuilt, this walk-through monument is the starting gate of the circuit, blessing all beings who pass through it and ushering them into the Valley of the Gods. Closer to Kailash, the flagpole pokes up in the distance like a huge, brightly festooned circus tent's mainstay. Thousands of prayer flags pinwheel off this maypole, spokes of cloth roped together like a Rastafarian's hair. So bright! So happy, positively gaudy juxtaposed to the muted earth tones surrounding it. Only the jewel of Kailash, itself, hints at such gaiety.

We've seen these Mardi Gras colors before, in Milarepa's cave and spangled across Dharma books from here to Los Angeles. What does it mean? Clearly, Tibetans do not celebrate the somber palette of their surroundings. The austerity of their day-to-day existence would seem a protective disguise, behind which a carnival-of-mind riots.

Odd how in America just the opposite seems true. We specialize in collecting the most extraordinary array of possessions, behind which an absolutely colorless, characterless citadel of boredom and despair rears up. Here—in Tibet—broken-down old men and women eating the worst food in the world, drinking a poisonous tea, smelling like goats and butting their heads in greeting like goats, hidden off in smoky old holes, half-closing their eyes on their poverty, peer down Dharma's dusty hall to bliss fields, pure lands, Eden.

Today, I've earned my place here, as three times round the flagpole I go, singing my mantra, *Om mani padme hum.* Jay and Tenzin roll in behind me. A white dog that has followed Tenzin all the way from Darchen lies, happily panting, in the shade of a great rope of flags. Tenzin has named the dog Maitreya for the buddha-to-come.

Tibetans love their dogs and they hate the Chinese even more for the fact that dog meat is a popular meal among these colonial overlords. A nice dish of grilled dog and rice is Mom's apple pie to a homesick Chinese. I'm a little confused, frankly, since Tibetans treat dogs with both great contempt and great respect. There are tales of enlightened beings disguising themselves as dogs, but also a view of dogs as lecherous, drunken uncles and cousins who have blown it to the extent of losing human embodiment. Since they have never been truly evil, they are spared a terrible hell state, reborn instead within the comic-tragic life-cycle of a dog, from which, if they interact positively with humans, they will certainly rise.

Amidst grumblings from macho trekkers Wolfgang and Richard, we make camp just down from the Tarpochey, near the river. Jock wants everyone to conserve energy and ease into the strenuous northern part of the kora, and Tenzin wants to explore the cemetery and also to spend time near each of the eight sacred compass points around the circuit. Tenzin leads us out onto a reddish rock in the moraine by the river in the late afternoon sun, with the light reflecting ruby red off the amazing cliffs of this western valley. Back to the spinning of the Dharma wheel.

TENZIN

Last night I must admit I felt depressed, trapped there in the tourist pit in Darchen. But when I sat up in my tent to meditate before sleeping, I could not believe the rush of energy I felt, as if it came from the very ground. From beneath the concrete tent-slabs, beneath the broken glass and dog shit, there was such a flashing of multicolored translucent lights, at first I thought Tad was playing tricks on me. But he wasn't there. Light seemed to be welling out of the ground. The place itself just glows. I could hardly sleep, I was so elated. We have arrived at a veritable volcano of spiritual energy.

Today we have begun our circling, the formal circumambulation the Tibetans call the kora. After crossing the outer ring of charnel grounds and joyfully bowing toward the mandala mountain, we moved west across the great grassy plain, autumn yellow with well-grazed stubble, the golden southern plain of Buddha

Ratnasambhava. If we were able to see the mandala palace in the mountain, we would have seen the southern yellow staircase leading up to the southern entrance. Looking further within through the open door under the jeweled portico, we would have glimpsed the exquisite, erotic buddha-couple from the side on the highest dais in the center of the palace, the standing storm-cloud body of Superbliss Buddha folding in his arms the ruby-red Vajravarahi, her legs wrapped around his hips, supported on his thighs, blissful in sexual union, her ecstatic face gazing up into his dark blue-black front face. Looking directly down at us, his southern golden-yellow face glowing with glory would have smiled at us as it faced out over his dark blue-black right shoulder that branches into six powerful arms.

When we turned the corner of the circuit at the prostration site, we entered the reddish western valley of Amitabha, where we might have looked into the western door of the mandala and seen the red, passionate face of Superbliss Buddha, looking down at us above his broad blue-black back. These buddha-deities are only remotely visible with the inner eye, which sees each deity from a bird's-eye view, with a kind of star-spangled presence.

Let's now turn to the *Blade Wheel*.

Taking Charge of Evolution

Here we focus on the specifics of mind reform in the areas of suffering, impermanence, the inevitability of death, and the preciousness of human life. We begin with facing all the negative things that happen to us, finding the way not to let them bind us into negative-reaction cycles but turning them to our advantage instead. In our emulation of the bodhisattva peacock here, we have already planted the seed of the infinite spirit of enlightenment. Now we have to figure out how to take all our negative experiences and emotions and make something positive out of them. The first step is to take responsibility for everything bad that happens to us and not to project responsibility out, in order to use all our energies to evolve ourselves internally rather than to vainly struggle with the environment.

When I'm helpless, dominated and tortured,
My bad-action blade wheel has come full circle,
From long having despised and enslaved inferiors —
Henceforth let my body and life be the slave of others!

When nasty words strike my ear,
My bad-action blade wheel has come full circle,
From my past evil speech such as slander —
Henceforth may I criticize only my own faults!

When I'm always living in negative lands,
My bad-action blade wheel has come full circle,
From my entrenched habit of negative perception —
Henceforth may I always use positive perception!

These are the opposite of normal egocentric reactions to suffering. Imagine yourself helpless, trapped, a victim under torture; all you can think of is hatred for your tormentor, fury at the injustice of it, how to resist, escape, and get revenge. Mind reform finds freedom internally, not reacting in this way, taking responsibility for the suffering, using it to overcome egotism. It is important to understand that this is an internal, emotional yoga, which does not foreclose options for action. You consider your punishment an expiation, and develop a mental readiness to serve others. So motivated, you might escape, you might take steps to vigorously oppose your tormentor, serving him by preventing him from the evil action of torturing you. Your motivation would be completely different of course, with no hatred or wish for vengeance, though you might be quite forceful and probably more effective, like a martial arts master.

When you suffer from hurtful speech, you learn to react in the same extraordinary way, breaking the reaction-cycle and using the hurt to prevent yourself from habitually inflicting further hurt on others.

When you suffer the mental anguish of perceiving yourself in an unpleasant environment, you use the energy of that disappointment to transform your situation, beginning with what you can assume control over—your own mind. Since you have always seen everything as negative and imperfect, you seem always to live in negative places, such as devastated environments, violent cities, and ugly houses. Instead of becoming paralyzed by bewailing your fate, you can address this through the practice of positive perception. You develop visualization to make the environment into the perfect world of the mandala; you imagine that you are in a magic universe where everything is made of holographic jewel energy, where the mountains and clouds are all jewel substance, where everything is seamless, blissful void and there's no dirt, no garbage, no badland, no pollution—nothing negative. This mind reform moves you onto a subtle plane where you abandon your habitual investment in the world of ordinariness, you concentrate creatively on the silver lining, and totally reverse all critical attention upon yourself. When the world looks bad outside, you reverse that perception and take it as your own failure of imagination. All the imperfection that I perceive has to do with my negative vision. Every time I have a negative perception of something I'm going to critique it and overcome the habitual perception of ordinariness. This is the purification of perception, the yoga of positive seeing.

You take responsibility for your own creation of an imperfect world. Corrupt politicians, food shortages, wars, and terrorism— all these are critiqued as projections of our imperfections. This is a very radical practice, reenvisioning the world into the best of all possible worlds. But this type of positive perception is how you see through the rocks and ice of Mt. Kailash to behold the always open, always radiant mandala of the Superbliss-Machine Buddha.

"Henceforth I'll only use positive perception." This refers to an internal revolution. It doesn't mean you annihilate your critical faculty. Everything is void, so everything is relative. Relative reality is fluid and not fixed, being simultaneously ordinary and extraordinary. It is multifaceted and ambiguous, easily provoking cognitive dissonance. The purpose of practicing positive perception as mind reform is to stop blaming everybody else in the world, to stop seeing faults as others' problems, and to take all faults upon ourselves. This empowers us to do something about ourselves and to take responsibility for our future and for the world. Bad things happen to us as the fruition of our own negative evolutionary action. Our mind reform is to turn everything totally around. By that radical flip, we realize our vow as bodhisattvas, to make this world into the best of all possible worlds for all beings—sooner or later, since we have infinite time and energy to devote to it. The power and the glory of Kailash is that it is the abode of beings who see it as the best of all possible worlds, as a perfected buddha-universe, a buddhaverse.

How do you meditate everything as a buddhaverse? The Panchen Lama says, When someone harms you, don't get mad or bewail your fate. Think: This is happening in order to purify me of my previous negative evolutionary actions, the buddhas and bodhisattvas are teaching me in this way—so kind of them. Tibetan culture is based to a large extent on this practice of the purification of perception. We must change our habitual way of justifying our own faults by blaming the world into a new discipline of seeing our faults as causing our problems. Then we can use the energy from this challenge to eliminate our faults within.

When you're consecrated in a Tantric mandala, you're seated on a throne. Solemn verses are repeated as you are coronated as a crown prince of enlightenment. You don't actually become the king just by being crowned, but you become empowered to imitate the virtues and feelings of the king, to inspire you to become a king. You're crowned as a buddha even though you're still a bodhisattva; you practice as if you're naturally a buddha and you correct anything unbuddhalike about yourself. Rather than doing something that is causally related to becoming a buddha, you imagine that you are a buddha, and you work to get rid of ignorant habits.

The danger is that some people misunderstand the approach, and think: "Well, I'm a buddha just by being initiated, so I'm perfect and any bad impulse I have is an enlightened impulse, so now I can do whatever I want." This is destructive, because it gives people a rationalization for all their negative habits. The proper way of understanding this is rather to think: If I really had buddha-perception, I would realize that I am now a buddha—and I would act accordingly. Clearly, I don't have such lucidity. I am stuck with my habitual perception, but I will now turn my critical attention against it. We assume that the fruit is something that is already there within, that the goal is already accomplished. We work to uncover it, to see and use perfect clarity, rather than assuming that we must create what is not there. So it's not a matter of being convinced, deluded that we are buddhas and can do as we please. When buddhahood is uncovered and clarified, only real, nonharming good comes forth: Buddhas cannot do harm and have no delusions.

Tibet was so full of people doing this practice that the whole culture became magical; past kings are seen as emanations of the Bodhisattva Avalokiteshvara, and Tara, the savior mother, is seen and felt everywhere. Here at Kailash, Drolma La is Tibetan for the Tara Pass. Tara's Tear is the lake just over the pass. She's there in the pilgrims passing by: She smiles at you from human, animal, water, rock. This view prevents you from demonizing people around you, or from seeing the land as negative, or even from hating destructive things. This amazing culture turns negative into positive, which is why most Tibetans have not turned to lethal hatred of the Chinese, though the Chinese have killed over a million Tibetans in their genocidal programs and intend to assimilate the rest. Accepting all evolutionary responsibility enables them to remain nonviolent.

Some people say, "This is masochistic, disempowering. Why can't they be human, get righteously angry and defend themselves?" Some secular Tibetans are saying, "We only got in trouble because we didn't have a decent defense force, because the darn lamas wouldn't let us defend ourselves, and they had us sitting on our hands when we should have been defending our borders." From the one-life perspective, they are right. But from the multi-life evolutionary perspective, they are mistaken. They could develop hate and perform acts of terrorism, and kill lots of Chinese people—but then in a future life they'd suffer the same thing all over again.

The big carvings of *Om mani padme hum* on mountains and the huge buddhas on the cliffs help people feel the landscape breathe the Dharma. Practicing the purification of perception on a national scale does develop a kind of mass illusion perhaps. All cultures are mass illusions; it's a question of consciously shaping your illusions to create a positive bubbling up of optimism, idealism, enthusiasm, and creativity. There's no nonillusory culture, because reality is pure bliss-void-indivisible, and nothing is really solid. And so how you create your world is something that you must take full responsibility for. You're the one who creates your world.

When you embrace the bad things that happen to you, you begin to take that creative power and responsibility. If you demonize the other person, or even god, you can't really change anything. Even if you destroy them they'll just be reborn in your face again and be nastier than ever. The only way you can really change the situation is to completely master your own reaction to it. When you do that, then you have power based on self-control. While this seems masochistic to the materialist, it is actually a loving thing to do for yourself. Like chemotherapy to kill a cancer, or extraction of a rotten tooth, it is painful in the short run. But in the long run this intellectual surgery will remove the potential for far more misery.

There's a wonderful comment by the great Indian master Shantideva, "If you don't like to step on thorns and sharp rocks as you walk around the planet, you have two choices. You can either pave the whole earth with shoe leather, or you can make yourself a pair of sandals." Those are the two choices. So what we're doing with this mind reform is not practicing masochism, not being self-destructive; what we're doing is making sandals for our souls.

The next dozen or so verses detail the specific negative interpersonal actions that revolve back to make us unhappy in specific ways, the negative evolutionary actions serving like a vicious blade wheel that comes back full circle at us like a boomerang. It would take us too long to investigate the commentary of each verse, but the details reveal the mysterious ways of karmic evolution in ways that are all too real to us emotionally.

> When beloved friends turn against me,
> It's my bad-action blade wheel come full circle,
> From breaking up friendships of others —
> Henceforth let me never break in between friends!

I have long evolved negatively by making friends with people by taking them away from others to make them mine. I can feel that negativity whenever I feel sad at losing friends: The blade wheel of negative evolutionary action has come back full circle.

> When holy persons disapprove of me,
> It's my bad-action blade wheel come full circle,
> From long shunning them to be with bad friends —
> Henceforth I will give up negative friends!

Associates are very important for cultivating yourself and making life meaningful. Part of the reality of selflessness is that you are highly influenced by associates. If you associate with enlightened people, who have more insight and more kindness and more wisdom, it rubs off on you. If you rely on people who mess around, have wrong ideas, are self-destructive or nihilistic, you will become like them. You are who you hang out with.

On deeper reading, the original negative friend is the voice in your mind that urges you to do negative things. When you purify perception, you give up conspiring with your self-addicting voice of negative impulses.

> When I am falsely accused of negative deeds,
> It's my bad-action blade wheel come full circle,
> From wrongly scorning my mentors —
> Henceforth may I never underestimate others!

> When I never can manage my daily needs,
> It's my bad-action blade wheel come full circle,
> From constant neglecting the needs of others —
> Henceforth may I always fulfill all their needs!

When I just cannot function, anxious at heart,
It's my bad-action blade wheel come full circle,
From always obstructing good works of the saints—
Henceforth may I give up obstructionism!

When whatever I do never pleases my mentor,
It's my bad-action blade wheel come full circle,
From cynical flouting the reasonable Truth—
Henceforth I'll lessen my disregard for the Dharma!

Facing this blade wheel of negative evolution doesn't disempower us, it empowers us. You get accustomed to taking on faults, and eventually there is less and less fault to take on. Then, instead of this blade wheel always circling back, you can get it to wheel forward, slicing through your ignorance. And how does it slice forward as well as back? By your realizing the great advantage of not committing the thousand and one selfish acts that usually fill up your day!

So *The Blade Wheel of Mind Reform* becomes our weapon for liberation. We realize that we can't fight the negative actions of other people all the time, because then we're fighting everyone, and it gets worse and worse. Instead we accept the fault. Then we turn the blade wheel of karmic evolution into a weapon against our inner enemy of self-delusion. This is why it is empowering, not disempowering. Instead of fighting with the world we begin to work with the world to overcome our delusion of separation. We use obstacles as spurs to our practice, turning harm into help.

When everyone turns and denounces me,
It's my bad-action blade wheel come full circle,
From ancient neglect of conscience and shame—
Henceforth may I always avoid insensitivity!

When friends leave me as soon as they gather,
It's my bad-action blade wheel come full circle,
From my previous inflicting hurtful behavior—
Henceforth may I always embody gracious good humor!

These verses give us a case-by-case handbook for the interpersonal transactions that make up daily life. They address exactly the issues that Buddhism is commonly thought to skirt. It's one thing to go and meditate alone in a cave, and it's another to develop a mind reform that works on interpersonal problems. Compassion can only come through interacting with others. The special thing about human beings is that we're always interacting with each other. This teaching goes through all these specific cases, so we can use them to develop mindfulness about how we actually behave, an enlightening practice integrated with our daily living.

> When I suffer demonic harm and goutlike diseases,
> It's my bad-action blade wheel come full circle,
> From past careless or criminal theft of donations—
> Henceforth may I avoid any theft of a gift!

When we get demonic or inexplicable sicknesses, we think they come "out of the blue"; we're just innocent germ-breathers. But if we accept that they come from our previously acting recklessly, carelessly, unethically, and lawlessly, we can use each sickness as a constructive practice.

This relates to the bodhisattva practice of give and take: You give away your happiness to others and take all their sufferings upon yourself. When we are injured, we can turn it around into the meditation of give and take by not compounding the suffering. Instead of suffering over the initial suffering, you say, "How happy I am that I have this; every ounce of pain it gives me is great, because it enables me to expiate the negative things I've done to others. And particularly the harm I dealt in the past. Now in the future I should meditate that in no way should I ever deprive anyone or heedlessly misuse or abuse them."

> When I am suddenly hit with strokes and diseases,
> It's my bad-action blade wheel come full circle,
> From formerly breaking my solemn vows—
> Henceforth may I give up negative actions!

The ethical and the pragmatic are really the same. Ethical behavior is not thought to be some virtuous thing you do even though it hurts you or is against your interest; it is pragmatic, because it molds you evolutionarily as a being. You damage your evolution when you act unethically and you advance your evolution when you act ethically. Even a seemingly random disaster, such as a stroke or sudden illness, can hit us because we're evolutionarily vulnerable due to our own past failures.

> When my intellect fails when seeking knowledge,
> It's my bad-action blade wheel come full circle,
> From my treating the Dharma as merely optional—
> Henceforth I start learning and increase wisdom!

There are three wisdoms, which come from learning, from critical reflection, and from meditation. It is important for people to realize that they can't just jump into meditation when they don't yet know anything. If you meditate when you don't know anything you're simply going to heighten your originally erroneous state of mind. First you have to learn something. Then you can think it over critically. Then you can meditate fruitfully.

To develop wisdom from learning, you have to compare your ideas with those of enlightened people and also try them out in reality experiments. You will debate with yourself and go back and forth between your ideas and Buddha's ideas. Eventually, your understanding will deepen and you will want to meditate, and you will penetrate to transformative realization, to real wisdom.

> When I delight in addiction, intensely distracted,
> It's my bad-action blade wheel come full circle,
> From ignoring death and dangerous fates—
> Henceforth I'll transcend unconscious living!

Students of the Dharma must recognize the dangers of the samsaric life-cycle. We don't realize how deep suffering can get, how impermanent pleasures are. That's when that blade wheel boomerangs back on us. For example, if I enjoy orgasms, I'm going to give up the addictive search for temporary orgasms that just lead to more dissatisfaction and more relentlesss passion. Instead I'm going to look for the supreme orgasm of bliss-void-indivisible wisdom that feels at one with the universe, that feels orgasm in every cell, in every fingertip. I'm not going to dissipate it by genitally organizing it, and therefore becoming the slave of my organs. Instead I'm going to master it, to learn to feel my whole body as an organ of bliss. Localizing release in the genitalia, we strip it out of the universe. Nirvana itself is orgasmic. Buddhahood as bliss-void-indivisible experience means perceiving all of reality as one huge blissful orgasm that doesn't decline.

Tantric celibacy is a very special type. The Tantric yogi and yogini and the buddha-deities in male-female union are united in a manner that symbolizes the undissipating orgasmic intuition of bliss-void-indivisible. One of the vows they must take is not to ejaculate, or if they're female, not to dissipate their orgasmic melting process. The melting process must turn back, without leaving the central channel, and go up through the central nervous system; then the entire body melts into oneness with the universe. There's never any coming down, smoking a cigarette afterward, feeling vaguely dissatisfied, and waiting to build up to try to get back again to that place. Instead of that, the orgasm is this bliss-void-intuitive wisdom that enfolds all beings within the pleasure and satisfaction.

Buddhism is not a killjoy. Nirvana is not an anaesthetic, desensitized nothingness. Nirvana is bliss-void-indivisible, it is permanent orgasm. That's why it's a great prize and a high goal, and that's why to the selfless being, the noble being who has experience of selflessness, the worldly pleasure of ejaculative orgasm seems like a suffering compared to nirvana. Just as the doorway to the central channel of the subtle nervous system opens in orgasm, melting the boundary between self and other, beings are dragged by their self-centered instinctual programming to dissipate their sensations in genital spasms and thus they reaffirm their boundary, returning to the split between self and other. They miss the full melting. The passion of buddhahood, the passion of voidness, and the passion of compassion are liberating passions. They are infinitely satisfying, and hence not addictive—they do not promote craving. "Henceforth I'll transcend unconscious living!" doesn't mean you give up real pleasure, it means you give up unsatisfying pleasures for true satisfaction.

> When my prayers to the Three Jewels do not succeed,
> It's my bad-action blade wheel whirling upon me,
> From not really trusting the Buddha and his company—
> Henceforth I'll rely only on the Three Precious Jewels!

One who takes refuge in the Three Jewels—Buddha, Dharma, and Sangha—is a Buddhist. The Buddha is the teacher who points the way. The Sangha are the companions who help us along the path. The real refuge among them, of course, is the Dharma, because the Dharma is the reality of freedom in ourselves and in the world. When it seems the Buddha and the Sangha and the Dharma do not hear us, it is because we have not really trusted the buddhas in the past. The refuge in the Buddha, Dharma, and Sangha really is refuge in freedom itself. It is a great thing, a spiritual refuge, where our universe gets purged of terror. When you take refuge in the Dharma, you come to understand that the deepest level of reality is something open, free, full of love and kindness and goodness. Realizing that relaxes our deep sense of fear and tension and paranoia, and releases joy in the center of the soul. What really saves us is the reality of openness in the heart and soul.

TAD

The *Blade Wheel* states that "obsessed with pleasure we drown in suffering." And that about says it all. For a while pleasure seems worth it, until the cycle becomes too obvious. Like a hangover following a binge, or a broken heart following the seduction. For me the hangover's shadow lurks over even a first drink—so drinking is ruined for me. The misery tied up with womanizing is easier to forget. Yet it is, actually, just as predictable. Children come of womanizing—and yet they are its antidote. The child makes a child of us again. We get back our innocence, in tiny, homeopathic doses.

I'm really too stunned to share much at dinner. Jay is full of world events. He brought several Indian and Hong Kong magazines printed in English providing the Asian slant. He reads from them here and there; it's always interesting to view America from outside America by non-Americans. The combination of hero worship and derision reminds me of a gossip columnist. Yet Jay, while obsessively keeping up with the world, also recites vows three times a day. He is studying both the world and the antidote to the world, already purifying his perception in a sort of global use of the blade wheel.

Tonight, I take my heart apart and put it back together again like a blindfolded Marine cleaning his forty-five. Yes, I will strip it down, though I do not like what is revealed, that I've been placing the blame everywhere else but at my feet for thirty-nine years. "As a baby I was abandoned! As a child I was tossed back and forth!" Tonight it lands squarely on my shoulders. These days it is I who abandon, I who vacillate. I who run back and forth. I swear it will be different but I know that after a few months I will get addicted to a certain woman. And it will go on a long time until I get addicted to another. Three children by three women and I'm only a good father to one. To the other two I have passed the baton of deprivation, the frantic life of single parent and child.

How do I reverse this? Retrieve it? Turn the wheel around? After dinner the boomerang of the harm I've done comes slicing through my tent and strikes at the base of my throat. I feel like I'm going to choke. A phrase from the *Blade Wheel* whirls: "When my heart is unclear may I never be the cause for others' sins." Hah! When my heart is unclear I am always the cause for others' sins! One pair of bedroom eyes fast recognizes another. Misery likes company, especially when it's disguised as ecstasy.

So far on the trip I haven't listened to any of my tapings. Now I lie in my sleeping bag, plump up my parka in a pillowcase, and play today's talk back at low volume: When I delight in addiction, when whatever I do goes bad, may I abandon all sinful friends, may I rely only on the Three Jewels.

What did I mumble to Jock midmisery in the altitude haze? That this world was making ceaseless jokes at my expense. Actually it's more the stupid jokes I've told come back to haunt me like the ghost of Christmas past jangling the chains before a terrified Scrooge. But I can change the past, by purifying the present and polluting no more. A short time goes by and behold! I have a small sin-free history. I have changed the past.

For what is sin? Judeo-Christians, Buddhists, Hindus, Moslems, Jains—all can agree. Sin is what interferes with the infinite. Sin is what intervenes and blocks the figure-eight circuit, breaking us up. If I could only make give-and-take a habit, as reflexive as a martial arts move that strikes and defeats selfishness before it manifests. For the blow is not against other or self, it is against differentiating between other and self. All outward enemies would be seen as manifestations of old business. Suddenly nothing outside me can harm me, because I refuse to acknowledge the old border of me. There is no secret weapon anyone or anything can pull on me. For the smoking gun always comes from my own holster. And all ammunition fired upon me is bullets I shot in a previous life, winging around the world and catching me in the back in this one. It all comes back to me. Momentarily reassured I snuggle deeper into my bag and sleep until awakened by a nightmare involving my newborn. Panic remasters me, the blade wheel shifting from chop to mince.

CHAPTER TEN

The Mansion of Hayagriva

TAD

We've camped just beyond the amphitheater. After breakfast and a short rest and cleanup, we will head northward up this western valley, stopping at Choku Monastery, on the far side of the valley wall. I pack up, make notes, and then find a small promontory overlooking the Tarpochey pole where I throw down my denim jacket and sit, as I hate sitting, cross-legged.

Strangely enough, in spite of my resistance to meditation, I suddenly feel I see Milarepa in the sky, a naked yogi with green-ish-hued skin, wearing a white cotton robe and a red meditation belt wound from right shoulder to left knee, just as his paintings portray him, floating effortlessly on a fluffy cloud-cushion. His magic must be great indeed for me to get this far! For I feel the circuit, the figure eight Tenzin speaks of, between me, the mentor, and the beings around me. I've zoned in, finally, just a little. I'm not thinking any of these thoughts. No soap opera bubbling forth, only crows seeming to glide on monofilament lines over crazed clay cliffs onto the white-domed pyramid of Kailash against the blazing blue sky and a naked green Milarepa above the flagpole utterly delighted with my delight. It's like I'm eight again, skiing down a novice slope and not falling, until, so proud of my progress, I fall. So proud of actually getting a glint of meditation, I fall out of meditation. I notice the expedition has packed itself up and everyone is heading north up the trail.

I turn to the trail, beaming. Pulling past Jay and Tenzin, I mutter *"Om mani padme hum"* instead of "pardon me." Rounding the amphitheater's stadium edge, I take a last look, feeling something go thump in the psychic playground below. Jay's dark eyes are brimming with joy.

I'm in the middle of the valley, with little or nothing by way of standing vegetation, except in the wrinkles of a dry streambed. Up at the far end, miles off, the cliffs all but meet. Between here and there Lha Chu, River of the Gods, twists south. This river favors the west side of this flatland, the whole of which lightens to mustard in places, darkens to cinnamon, and most of all reddens to the color between: to paprika shaken out over the tan, unleavened crust of earth. The mustard is actually the roots of grass that have been grazed flat. The red is a very sturdy lichen. The rest is sand and gravel, along with the occasional boulder. Up a dry streambed even lichen has forgotten how to grow. I'm smiling at the dust kicked up by Richard's distant feet. I can feel his happiness soaking in, separate yet simultaneous to my own.

This is at once the most barren and the most splendid place I've ever seen. Turquoise above, diamond beside, cliffs walling off the reddish-gold earth for a base. Between devotional trammeling and the occasional flood, nothing blooms in this gulch but the Dharma itself.

Plodding up the ancient valley, under an inverted ocean of air, walks the only man among us who first saw Kailash in his dreams. These were not normal dreams, sleep-movies, but his paintings. For what Richard was trying to paint would best be described as a pure land, a buddha's pure universe. So there he is, making first tracks. Getting the first whiff.

Not far off, a quarter of the way up the foreboding left wall, sits Choku Gompa, the first of the original five Kailash monasteries, all of which were destroyed in Tibet's "liberation." Curiously, it was also the first of the monasteries to be rebuilt, thus becoming a repository for an eclectic collection of treasures. At the turn of the century one huge cube broke loose from the cliff face and crushed a meditation room at the back of the monastery. The cliffs are just plain ominous.

All up and down the valley small pockets of people take shape and disappear again. Nomads, who design their yearly migration route to cross this valley. They worship, do some trading, pick medicinal and sacred herbs and—slapping the rears of their beasts—go on about their wanderings.

An hour or so more and we've drawn abreast of Choku Gompa. Richard crosses the bridge over the river of the gods. This river, not much more than a fast-moving stream this time of year, meanders in closest to the ridge just under the gompa as if to do it praise. An all-woman nomad camp, just below the gompa, is camped a few hundred yards upstream. Half a dozen women are close by, bowing to the white-splashed brick structure above, while casting wondering glances our way.

I look up from scribbling notes to find most of our party gathered around, lunch spread out on the hillside, with James and his Sherpa just crossing the bridge. Our temporary dog Maitreya has found a black twin, the two of them smiling where the arch stone meets plank, sniffing the holy breeze, preening before Kailash.

"Hate to say it, Tad," James laughs, shaking his head, "but they look like one of those old New 'Yawker' ads for Black and White Scotch."

"*Om mani padme hum, Om mani padme hum, Om mani padme hum,*" I answer cryptically.

"Shame on me! Couldn't have said it any better myself," James murmurs. "Yes, now where is Potang with my water bottle?"

After lunch we break up into groups and climb to the gompa. James opts for a nap, which alarms me, since I know he's as Dharma-thirsty as any of us.

The trail up is the steepest I've attempted, yet at this altitude—sixteen thousand eight hundred feet—and I'm winded almost immediately; but the nearness of the monastery robs the difficulty of any dire associations. Instead I'm a bit slaphappy and, without stopping to explain, force two Hershey's Kisses from lunch into the hands of a nomad husband and wife coming down. I can hear them questioning one another about the strange white man, and whatever Kailash-shaped ornaments he's thrust into their hands. Twenty yards up the hill the mouth-music ceases and I turn to see them nodding happily, their jaws grinding as they wave.

Ahead the trail zigzags through mani stones and boulders big enough to obscure pilgrims coming down. All at once a young girl comes around a corner and cries out in alarm at the sight of me. I back out of the way, leaving room for her to pass, but at fourteen or so she is terrified of me and will not budge. In part, it's a hilarious moment, especially as her family bunch up at her shoulders, pushing and jeering at her shamelessly. In the mother's and grandmother's eyes I can see and hear the comedy: "He's not bad looking, girl, and probably very rich—go on—GO ON!" But she shakes her head no, glancing at me with fascination and fear, teetering on the edge of tears. Behind my smile I'm wondering, "What does she know that they don't? Are my wolfy-ways so transparent?" In penance, I actually climb onto a rock, leaving the trail entirely open, and now wave my arm and bow as would Cyrano to Roxanne. With a swift push from behind, the girl rushes past, wild-eyed and coltish. Now the rest of the party follows, laughing and nodding at me fondly.

Just short of the monastery I find the conch-shell-marked stone said to have fallen out of the sky and melted into the boulder. I touch my head to it, feeling like I've fallen out of the sky

Appendix - 11
(Related to rule 33)
His Majesty's Government
Ministry of Home
Department of Immigration

TREKKING PERMIT

In accordance with the rule 33 of the Immigration rules 1994, the permission is hereby granted for trekking in the area of .... of the ....district (except the restricted area) from 20. OCT. to 26 OCT. '95 (7 days) for

8. Point of starting of Trekking: KERMI
9. Point of ending of Trekking: SIMIKOT
10. Name of the agency, if trekking is organised by trekking agency: MOUNTAIN TRAVEL
11. Trekking permit No.: Aw | 494 | 052

Date:

Route of Trekking:-
SIMIKOT - DHARAPERI - KERMI

1. Name: MR EDWARD E. WISE III
2. Nationality: USA
3. Permanent Address: USA
4. Temporary address in Nepal: MOUNTAIN TRAVEL
5. Passport No.: 100 211243
6. Date of Nepalese visa validity: 28-10-95
7. Place of Trekking: SIMIKOT- KERMI

Immigration Officer
Code No.

3rd

CALM IMMIGRATION (TREKKING)
255673
Valid until 26.10.95
Passport No. 100211243
Trekking Area Aw
Date 02.11.95
Immigration Officer

Tad Wise's trekking permit.

Landslide above Zhangmu, just inside Tibet.

Our first view of Mt. Kailash, prayer flags in foreground.

Crossing the Brahmaputra River.

Milarepa's meditation cave outside Nyalam.

Mani stone near Mt. Kailash.

Robert Thurman
circling the
Tarpochey,
the Great
Freedom Pole.

The western valley of Mt. Kailash.

Kangri Lhatsen, fierce protector
of Mt. Kailash (Choku Gompa).

Tad Wise in front of the western
face of Mt. Kailash.

The young abbot of the Karmapa monastery (Drirapuk) at the
Female Yak Horn Cave.

The edge of the diamond, Mt. Kailash.

Robert Thurman performing the fire offering before ascending to the Tara Pass. *Copyright © Jock Montgomery.*

The Vajrayogini Cool Grove Charnel Ground.

Robert Thurman
near the top of
Drolma La
(Tara Pass) at
18,500 feet.

A purified Tad Wise
backsliding into sin
in Darchen.
Copyright © Jock Montgomery.

Robert Thurman prostrating at Lake Manasarovar.

Lake Manasarovar.

The mind of the Buddha, Boudhanath stupa in the Kathmandu Valley.
Copyright © Jock Montgomery.

A pilgrim collecting holy water from Lake Manasarovar.

myself. Inside and on the terraces above, nomads dressed in wildly eclectic clothes and headgear mix with old monks in plum-colored wool robes.

Jay and I make prostrations at the altar where magazine photos and ten-rupee postcards of the Dalai Lama blend with irreplaceable treasures. We drop a few bills in an alms dish. This seems to satisfy the monks, who buzz a little more quietly. Wolfgang tries, unsuccessfully, to take a picture of the altar. The monks are particularly protective of a large, pale statue made of solid jade, depicting Choku Rinpoche, who is considered an incarnation of a buddha; it is considered one of the greatest treasures of Kailash. Several magical stories account for its presence, one of which involves the statue being hidden in the hills for years, and its commanding a woman *terton,* or treasure finder, to bring it here. It also seems to have been more recently hidden from the Chinese. Or perhaps mysteriously returned by them. The stories are somewhat confusing, but one thing is certain: The monks are very nervous about it. I'm reminded of Milarepa's contempt for all treasure; of course the irony is that everything Milarepa ever touched is now an invaluable Dharma treasure.

Before the statue sits a silver inlaid conch shell that is said to have flown here from Bodh Gaya, in India, where Shakyamuni attained enlightenment under the bodhi tree. Like the conch-shell stone on the walk up, it symbolizes the speech of Buddha.

Behind the central altar stands a glass bookcase holding a brocade-wrapped edition of the *Kanjur,* the complete Tibetan canon of the teachings of Shakyamuni Buddha, 108 in all. Along the left wall are three forms of Shakyamuni on metal *chortens,* as Tibetans call their stupas. Beside Choku Rinpoche, heavily wreathed with offering scarves, are peacock feathers and the tusks of the sacred elephant Sala Rabten, associated with the great figure Padma Sambhava, who brought Buddhism to Tibet.

Lastly, a large copper pot said to have been brought here by the Sanskrit arhat Tilopa sits reflected in a mirror. Tilopa's offering is said to represent the mind of Buddha. It has been returned most recently, appearing—where it had many times been sought before—in a meditation cave below the gompa. Good omens for the future.

Any and all of these relics would command a fortune on a back street in Lhasa. Explaining this, on the magnificent terraced rooftop overlooking the snow-topped pyramid and the sand-weeping cliffs below, Tenzin mentions that criminal bands disguise themselves as parties exactly like our own. Professionals thump old men on the head and make off with the relics eventually found gracing museums or wealthy homes around the world.

We've done a tour of the public sections of the monastery. Restored in the mid-1980s, the outer walls are hastily mudded-up stone and plank. I'd like to have seen the kitchen and the bunks. Taking one last circuit of the terrace, I snap a picture of what looks like original scrollwork off a pre-liberation beam. It's now a doorstop. Distracted, I almost stumble into a rooftop chimney.

Out on the terrace nomads file by Tenzin, who is in his Santa Claus Dharma-suit, a bright red down parka. He is quite a hit with the wanderers, whose mafioso sunglasses, cowboy hats, cabbie's caps, and nylon jackets make for a regular fashion nightmare, blended in, as they are, with indigenous blouselike *chubas* and pantaloons. I get a picture of Santa-Tenzin and the somewhat off-put, long-jawed, dark-faced abbot of the monastery standing a foot and a half below the fiercely smiling Westerner. Yellow-and-red prayer wheels and the ubiquitous faded prayer flags send blessings on erratic, Kailash-buffeted wind. Off to the north a shrine room sits, like the wheelhouse of a ship. Valerie is hastily escorted out when from under her manly hat falls a feminine show of hair. No women should see the fierce deity. Meet Kangri Lhatsen: painted wood; red-and-blue faced, lion toothed, devil eyed; big, bad, and not the least bit shy.

He is one of several unruly Bon gods tamed and converted to Buddhism by Padma Sambhava back in the late 700s. It is to this tamed monster that the women at the banks of the river below are praying. Tenzin's talk has loosened things up some. Kangri Lhatsen is the protector deity of Kailash—and this statue is not usually shown to laymen except on special holidays.

Back down the hillside the Sherpas are up and gone; James is well rested. The nomad women may have gotten good reports of us, for they tolerate, even smile into, my camera. I hustle up the valley at a brisk pace that proves to be a mistake. We've gotten into moraine, rocks the size of bread loaves, and my thin ankles are taking a beating. Interaction with my fellows has taken its toll on the meditative morning. It's early afternoon, machismo has reasserted itself, and I'm walking too fast.

Presently I overtake our yak handlers, recognizable by our purple duffel bags. I observe the yaks for a while. They don't chew the tiny blades of grass that grow in their path, but because their tongues are so rough, they actually glean nourishment from licking the ground. They're mowing the lawn with their tongues. Therefore they do no harm to the delicate root structures, unlike sheep, which the Chinese are promoting for their finer wool, but which are pulling up the grass by its roots, further denuding an already bare land.

In the distance, another few miles along the western foreboding cliffs, three huge, impressively hewn crags tower over their peers. These are called the longevity triad, and are associated with the long-life Buddha, and his accompanying goddesses Tara, Amitayus, and Vijaya.

To my right, below the slowly emerging western corner of Kailash, just beyond the sixteen arhats, looms Mahakala, a forward-leaning triangle of reddish stone, hooded at the top. Indeed, stone actually curls over the edge of the face, as if a robed monk sat, the cowl of his hood covering his downward-tilting head. His features are thus mysteriously shaded, and it is said that, looking into that shadow, one will see the face of one's root guru.

This has been a persistent problem: Who is my mentor? Clearly, there is too much interpersonal stuff going down to meditate Tenzin as my buddha-mirror. Lama Govinda is a hero, but he's gone now, and even when he was here he stood too far away. There is His Holiness, but for some reason I am blocked there, too. Indecision breeds confusion, which breeds more indecision.

The valley is funneling to a close, with one path skirting the river to the west, one tamely proceeding up the gap, and a third dancing in and out of big boulders, closest to Kailash.

Nestled on this last path is the largest tribe of nomads I've yet seen, maybe fifty of them spread over a hundred yards. I skitter up to a bunch and break out some apricots. A straggly-bearded, scar-faced old pirate is curious to try one. Happily, he likes them and encourages some others to be bold. Some old women heed his request and chew away, laughing with gusto. A beautiful young girl tries an apricot, and glows unabashedly. When I motion politely to my camera, the old women cover their faces with greasy scarves, but the girl looks down the barrel with equanimity. Not even a smile, really, just pleasantly present. The pirate offers me a cigarette. I laugh in refusal, and pantomime having trouble enough breathing. He lights up and happily spins a hand-held prayer wheel. I squat beside him, counting off my rosary wheel through one hundred and eight *Om mani padme hums.*

When I'm done I stand, shake the pirate's hand, and motion to my camera. He puts up a flat palm, which I think is a refusal, but he is telling me to wait. He reaches up the bank for his hat. It was probably his father's hat, too. A beauty. Fur brim on a battered silver-embroidered cylinder. He taps it onto his head, picks up his prayer wheel, and, swinging it proudly, looks into the crosshairs of mechanized sorcery. This nomad knows all he needs to know of me. He likes my apricots, my smile, and the frail, brave legs of my faith. He nods approvingly at me and, grunting at the girl, the old women, and all who have gathered to stare, he seems to insist upon a formal goodbye.

"Tujeychey!" I say to the old women, to the girl, and lastly to him. He is delighted, and nods, repeating the greeting that functions as thank you—literally "great compassion."

"Tujeychey," I say to a gaggle of kids staring wide-eyed in front of me, blocking my path. I stare them down and they finally run off, but for one who stands aside and gives me my wish: "Tu je che!" he yells, victoriously, as I wink gratefully at him and stride off out of his life, having received from him the phrase's implicit blessing, "May you find enlightenment in this incarnation."

I hang on to this hill, knowing from the maps that we must

soon head east, and so—still awash in nomadry—I attempt to go directly over the steepening slope looming straight ahead. Maybe I'll catch a glimpse of the inner kora twisting back behind the sixteen arhats, guarding Kailash. "Maybe I'll just be alone with you a while longer," I say to the glistening mountain.

Above is another phallic promontory known as Padma Sambhava's *torma,* or offering cake. This, yet another pyramid, at the knee of Kailash. If one were to view the mountain from Darchen as a seated Medicine Buddha, the torma is the charm held upright in the Enlightened One's right hand. This is my own secret view.

My personally chosen path leads me to a cliff, and as I reach the edge I can see the invisible West Door to the mandala, from which magic colored lights are said to shine. I don't feel anything magical. I feel lost. Somewhere around here is the second prostration site. Where is everybody? How did I lose them again? Look at the mountain, I tell myself. It's not lost. The great scar on the southern face lies at such an oblique angle as to no longer be visible.

It will be another three grueling hours on the trail, turned streambed, turned yak-manure pit, before I hobble into camp. James has arrived first. Tenzin, having stopped for tea with no-mads, will be last. Myself, having found complete faith and complete disillusionment in the very same day, I drag my ass into my warm mummy bag, convinced that I have been beaten by extremes. It seems now that an old man will climb the pass, while I may, at best, crawl; that I will fail in a materialist world because I'm an artist, and that I will fail in a spiritual world because I'm a sensualist—which is really a glorified materialist. In short, I am a sorry excuse for a human being, best prepared to sleep and in his sleep to dream.

But there is no dream in the sleep the dinner bell wakes me from. I can hardly stand. Thank God I brought sneakers that feel like bedroom slippers and that there's a routine to fall back on. Sanitize the hands at the mess tent; mix a cup of tea, grab a graham cracker, listen to others' complaints. They are feeling it, too. Tenzin pulls out his Tibetan text from the belly pouch of his trekking shirt and glares at us with mock menace. "Here," he whispers, "camped in the house of Hayagriva—a fierce deity—it is very fitting we continue to recognize the blade wheel of negative evolution coming back to cut us."

TENZIN

Today was a very hard day. James was wise to pass on Choku Gompa and rest. This long walk up from the flagpole is much more exhausting than it looks. I was almost losing hope of making it myself without climbing on a yak's back, but then I came round and saw the great rock of Guru Rinpoche, with the camp nestled at its foot. This camp is at the prostration rock called the Mansion of Hayagriva. Tibetans believe a mystic doorway opens from this rock here into the pure land of that fierce Buddha.

One of my very favorite archetype deities, Hayagriva is the bloodred, three-faced, green-and-orange horse-head-crowned, dreadfully fierce form of Avalokiteshvara, the bodhisattva of universal compassion. Hayagriva is the divine embodiment who liberates this concrete world, no matter what. Padma Sambhava, the St. Patrick of Tibet who tamed all the blood-drinking mountain war deities of the land, is associated with Hayagriva. Hayagriva is also a close colleague of Yamantaka, and he also loves the art of the *Blade Wheel*. It is auspicious that we rest here before entering the northern valley of the circuit.

Facing the Blade Wheel of Negativities

In the *Blade Wheel*, we're still in the purification mode of internalizing all faults, accepting them as brought with us from our past, as our remaining negative evolutionary patterns. When Westerners first encounter this kind of practice, they tend to feel that descriptions of karmic evolution are too fatalistic, and lead people into passive acquiescence of the status quo. Of course, anything can be used to bolster fatalism and passivity, if that is your preconception. The karmic descriptions are intended to empower you to not blame others in the world out there, which you can't do much about after all, but to put the focus on yourself, which you can get to work on no matter what the circumstances.

Buddha acknowledged at the outset that no description of relative reality is absolutely true: All such descriptions are only relatively true, though we must carefully recognize that they are true enough to make all the difference in daily life. It is important to understand this and to remain empirical and open-minded; otherwise we tend to become dogmatic. The descriptions of karmic evolutionary causality emphasize our own contribution to our situation, in order to help us from now on to use positive deeds, words, and thoughts to develop positive situations. We use the outlook of compassion to steer us away from rationalizing the suffering of others and doing nothing about it, dismissing it as their fault. If I am poor, I acknowledge my past stinginess and I make efforts to be generous now. If others are poor, I do not blame them, I try to be generous with them myself, but I also help them find opportunities to be generous themselves, with whatever they have. The main point is to enhance our individual freedom and to take responsibility for determining our own life situations. We learn to see our own misfortunes as the blade wheel thrown at us by our own evolutionary past in order to turn our present into a blade wheel we can use to destroy the causes of any negative evolutionary future.

> When I'm powerless, forced to wander in exile,
> It's my bad-action blade wheel come full circle,
> From my driving holy beings away from their homes—
> Henceforth I'll never push anyone off their land!

My wandering in exile comes from previous lives when I persecuted holy beings, spiritual persons trying to develop themselves; my displacing them obstructed their positive development. So when I am homeless, I can use that homelessness to reflect upon how never to dislodge people from their homes, not to drive them into exile.

When disasters happen such as frost or hail,
It's my bad-action blade wheel come full circle,
From not keeping properly my vows and ethics—
Henceforth I'll purify all vows and disciplines!

When we suffer natural disasters, instead of bewailing our fate, we reflect that our own unethical conduct and vow-breaking exposes us to this type of thing. At first they seem to come from nowhere, we don't deserve them, and we feel out of control; but we can regain leverage if we recognize our own failings in the past as underlying causes. Buddhists think there are angelic beings powerful enough to avert storms or divert floods. What happens to us is never a random accident. We can embrace even a natural disaster as a circumstance and an opportunity to renew our energy and intensify our spiritual development, rather than simply complaining in vain. We learn to consider even thoughts as significant deeds, causing effects far beyond the subtle medium of electromagnetic energies in the brain, in order to develop the subtle mindfulness about negativities within us even at the most subtle level. Mind reform involves radical attitudinal change, requiring that we not waste our primary energy struggling with external reality, but focus it internally in ourselves where we can become the masters rather than remain constant victims. This does not mean we should do nothing about external circumstances, just that we should keep our priorities straight.

When I have desires yet am mired in poverty,
It's my bad-action blade wheel come full circle,
Not having given and made offerings to the Three Jewels—
Henceforth I'll strive in giving and offering!

It's not bad to be poor if you're a monk or a nun and have a vow of poverty, because then you're using poverty as a liberation; but it is a problem when you want things and yet are stuck in poverty. When it constantly seems to happen to me, I should realize I did not give enough in previous lives, I made few offerings to the Three Jewels. I may have given to relatives, to persons I identified with, but I didn't bother to give to beings I thought irrelevant to me; most importantly, I neglected offerings to the Buddha, Dharma, and Sangha. From that negative karma, every time I try to get somewhere, I lose my money, I have bad luck, I remain poor.

This is why Buddhist monks prefer to beg their free lunch from poor people, because poor people have been stingy in previous lives to become poor, so monks and nuns want to give them the opportunity to be generous to a holy person so that they can be wealthy in the future. The rich should not be resented; their wealth comes ultimately from their past lives' generosity. However, if they hoard their fortunes stingily in this life, they will become poor again in the future. So they should be encouraged to give gifts.

The paradoxes of life are always like this. When we're stingy we always feel poor, because we never have enough. Even when we have billions, if we're only focused on how much more we can get, how to beat our rivals, we still feel dissatisfied. We lose a few million and we feel deep agony, in spite of our remaining billion. Whereas someone with nothing can be happy with that nothing, if they are preoccupied with how someone else is. Wealth is contentment, the happiness of forgetting about how much you have.

> When I am ugly and despised even by friends,
> It's my bad-action blade wheel come full circle,
> From making poor icons or angrily burning them —
> Henceforth I'll make deities both lovely and durable!

I know it's shocking, but I love this idea. When I am ugly, it's because of my cultivating hatred in this and previous lives. Hate makes beings ugly in the moment of its expression. They look ugly because they're destructive. Karmic evolution can usually be read on the face. When someone is beautiful, previous lives' tolerance is the ultimate source. Tolerance lies in not reacting violently even to injury, and it is the cause of beauty. Kind and loving people are beautiful at the moment, because they are helpful. So if we want beauty, we should cultivate tolerance.

Making icons of buddhas and bodhisattvas poorly also has a negative evolutionary effect. You develop a subliminal attraction toward that ugly form and may become ugly in future lives as a result. So always be cautious—never commission or own badly wrought buddhas. They should always be beautiful. When I am ugly, I must have been an intolerant religious fanatic in past lives, I must have destroyed images of buddhas. To correct this for the future, I must not burn anything and must make icons beautiful and durable, also respecting the icons of others.

> When everything I do creates lust and hate,
> It's my bad-action blade wheel come full circle,
> From my past errors and stubborn self-seeking—
> Henceforth I'll cease the self-concern habit!

This verse returns to the only devil that has ever mattered, stubborn self-seeking, habitual self-concern or self-addiction. When everything I do makes me more dissatisfied and others more frustrated, it's because of my ancient habit and present stubborn persistence in self-preoccupation. When despite everything I do I can't put a stop to bad attitudes, such as lust for things and anger at others, also pushing them to the same reactions, I should recognize the hand of my inner enemy and secret master, my self-preoccupation.

This completes the mind reforms that develop transcendent renunciation. From here forward, the verses aim to cultivate the spirit of enlightenment, the altruistic attitude of the bodhisattva.

> When every practice misses its goal,
> It's my bad-action blade wheel come full circle,
> From thoughtless immersion in small selfish vision—
> Now may all I do just be altruistic!

Motivation is key here. We always need to examine and constantly reform our motivation. I do great things and they never seem to succeed. Perhaps my motivation was narrowly selfish. Seeking only fame and profit for myself, the greatest deed goes sour. I feel unsatisfied with it, I want more, and others sense the lack of heart in it and lose interest. But when I give up focus on myself, even without great deeds I feel good!

Remember a time when you were content with what you had and forgot your self-preoccupation, constant thoughts on what more you could get. Since happiness basically amounts to freedom from self-concern, this vow is immediately beneficial: "Now may all I do just be altruistic."

May I always attend to the world. May I be concerned about whether others are happy. This is the crucial messianic turn-around. When we wrongly understand it, we think that if we are altruistic we're going to be destroying ourselves, suffering more and more, because there's so much misery out there. But the truth is that when we take on others' problems we forget about our own and become happier and stronger.

> When despite all practice my mind stays wild,
> It's my bad-action blade wheel come full circle,
> From my basic focus on the goals of this life—
> Henceforth I'll control myself with real love of freedom!

No matter what I do that's good, my mind stays totally wild because something is wrong with my motivation—I'm trying to get ahead in this life. We are totally preoccupied with the goals of this life because we don't believe there is another life, at least not viscerally. We think this life is all we have, we're conditioned to materialism. Though it's possible for materialists to be altruistic, their worldview assures that their underlying motivation is for benefits in this life.

With a little effort of critical thinking, we can go beyond this and realize that this moment itself is infinite. Within this moment are all the qualities of all of our past and future lives. It is like Nietzsche's eternal recurrence: Everything we do we should be willing to redo for eternity. Everything we do reverberates for eternity, so we should live in ultimate concern for the quality of our living. We should never think the consequences of what we do are finite: "Well, maybe I'll blow my cool today, but I'll be better

tomorrow." The way we behave today will be infinite in its consequences. We should live in the infinity of the moment and find the
power of taking responsibility for infinite consequences.

When our mind remains wild, no matter how much we meditate, no matter what we do, it's because we're preoccupied with
the goals of this life. "Henceforth I'll control myself with real love
of freedom." That freedom, the true sense of the infinity of the
moment, is right here now.

> When I have second thoughts at each start of practice,
> It's my bad-action blade wheel come full circle,
> From being shamelessly fickle, with shallow attention —
> Henceforth I'll deepen friendship and focus in full!

When we start a retreat or do something good, at once we feel
doubt and regret and wonder if something else wouldn't be better.
This happens because in previous lives we were fickle, we were
hopping from friend to friend, project to project. So now we have
no staying power of motivation or effort.

> When others' hypocrisy fools me,
> It's my bad-action blade wheel come full circle,
> Avenging my arrogance and selfish ambition —
> Henceforth I'll lessen my greed and pretension!

Having been ambitious and arrogant, we become a victim of
others' hypocrisy — because they can flatter us easily. So we need
to intensify detachment to overcome our enemy of self-addiction.
The less greedy we are, the more content and happy we are,
the less we're fooled by others. Gullibility comes from selfish
ambition.

> When greed and hate taint all conversations,
> It's my bad-action blade wheel come full circle,
> From not taking to heart the faults of the devil —
> Henceforth I'll know and abandon all evil!

Buddhists believe various gods and devils exist, a main devil being Mara the Tempter, who has tricked us many times in previous lives not to follow virtue and the path to freedom. Far more harmful than he, of course, is the devil of self-addiction each of us carries within us, mistaken for our very self.

> When all my good deeds turn out negative,
> It's my bad-action blade wheel come full circle,
> From ungrateful responses to others' kindness—
> Henceforth I'll cherish each kindness on top of my head!

Sometimes it seems nothing ever turns out right, that everything is unsatisfying, even the best thing. We come walk around Mt. Kailash. It doesn't work out well, we get altitude sickness, headaches, diarrhea, we squabble, the cars break down. Even when we're here we don't appreciate it, we think we should be on the other side, we should go faster, we should go slower. We should have more people, or fewer people, the weather should be better. This comes from our ingratitude toward others in previous lives. So from now on we should be grateful for any kindness.

Mt. Kailash itself is the great kindness of the Superbliss Buddha Couple, and of Shiva and Uma. For these great beings have blessed us by sending out this blissful energy. It looks like a mountain, an ordinary part of nature, but they created out of it some sort of nexus where we can come and rediscover life-in-nature and the blessing of nature. For just being here, without even knowing what is happening to us, our whole mind-stream is blessed immensely, we're freed from many mistakes in our future lives, we're going to have a much better life from now on. Let's be kind, let's be happy, and let's accept others' kindness on the crown of our head.

> Whatever pleasant and unpleasant things I experience,
> It's my bad-action blade wheel come full circle,
> Like a swordsmith killed with his own creation—
> Henceforth I'll be mindful of badly evolving acts!

When we achieve the realization of ultimate reality we become more aware of the fine details of actions. We know that the slightest badly evolving act will have immense consequences. "Mindful" means we must know the subtle details, the little ways that have allowed each tiny bad motivation to creep in, because each has a huge negative effect.

That's where knowledge of the absolute comes in. Knowledge of the absolute is not a matter of floating away into the universe. The notion that the ultimate or nirvana is some place into which you float away is based on your flawed sense that you are a separated thing who could withdraw into the inner room of your falsely absolutized self. This—the delusion that we are or can be separate from the world—is the source of all negative things.

There is no such isolated nirvana. Nirvana is this world as experienced by an altruistic being—a truly other-preoccupied, infinitely expanded being—and so enlightenment means super-mindfulness of minute facts and minute consequences, not an awareness that is just blown away and collapsed into nothingness.

> Whatever misery I felt in the three hellish states,
> It's my bad-action blade wheel come full circle,
> Like the fletcher being killed by his very own arrow—
> Henceforth I'll be super-mindful of badly evolving acts!

We meditate on the suffering of the unenlightened life-cycle and we open our imagination to the hellishness of the existence of the animal, ghost, and hell life-forms. This can give us tremendous power to transform ourselves. Westerners who are escaping from centuries of fire and brimstone preachers want to say, "It's all a state of mind. There's no such thing as hell." Fine, if it gives encouragement. But when we feel ready to gain the energy necessary to achieve the infinitely positive, we have to be open to a healthy fear of the danger of the infinitely negative.

> Whatever suffering I experience in the family,
> It's my bad-action blade wheel come full circle,

Like the cherished children killing their parents—
Henceforth I'll always see reason and flee the world!

This is a very Tibetan Buddhist way of acknowledging the violence innate in the family, seeing unflinchingly that unenlightened family life has murder in its depths, at least in the unconscious part of people's minds. Leaving the unenlightened home life means we give up self-preoccupied identity, self-centered sex, self-aggrandizing possessions, self-seeking killing, and self-promoting lying—especially spiritual lying.

We might say, "Well, that's very culture-specific. In Tibet it was great to be a monk. In ancient India it was so great to be a monk. Now we have to be nondual and transcendent, and we can have a family and pursue enlightenment perfectly well." But no. We can't have a family life that fits with the Dharma unless, in a deep way, we're sort of monks and nuns in the family. We must at least mentally renounce the world. We must transcend righteous possessiveness even about husband or wife, renouncing the right to sex, never forcing an unwilling mate. We must renounce ownership of children, or we will turn our children against us. If we're going to live successfully in a family today, we must renounce backward ideas, avow our unconscious negativities, control them, and exchange self-preoccupation for other-preoccupation. The home life is the home of the bad habits inherited from our lineages, ancestries of family selfishness, violence, cruelty, and righteous misery. We must break these deadly chains to become true friends with our family members, making our family life into the performance of the Dharma.

Tibetan culture is so steeped in transcendent renunciation that their home culture has become quite relaxed. Where do you think that cheerfulness comes from? It took generations of individual attainment to change the cultural atmosphere. The Tibetans are unique in mostly having transcended the usual human focus on ancestors; they don't care much about them. Tibetans feel that their ancestors have been reborn and are the living beings around them now, who could now be from any race or even any species. This is not an insignificant achievement by a nation. Racism is anchored in ancestor worship, it's a self-identity developed by taking exaggerated pride in one's physical genes, and it's deadly in our pluralistic world today. It's a lifesaving achievement to see that your ancestor is me, and my ancestor is you. Then we can worship our ancestors by treating each other well, and getting away from the root of racism, egotism projected into lineage.

In the unenlightened world, the home has been built up by generations of beings who are following the demon of self-concern. Therefore those demons cannot be conquered without renouncing home life. In a liberated world the wife is a nun, the husband is a monk. Their interaction would be on a higher-bliss level, where there is no demand on each other. This is the only way to have a truly loving, noncoercive relationship. If there is to be a new level of relationship of bodhisattva wife and husband, bodhisattva parents and children, bodhisattva brother and sister, it has to be beyond transcendent renunciation, not short of it.

That is enough Dharma for tonight. We have approached the recognition of the self-addiction enemy and begun to counter the karma blade wheel with the Dharma blade wheel of selfless wisdom. Our inner journey is moving along very well. Now, rest for the outer journey we continue tomorrow.

TAD

Tonight, even as a gauzy, supernatural twilight glistens from within the temple of Dharma above, even as realization twinkles in the jewel light playing off the mandala mansion walls, rose-tinted, long past sundown, still a part of me is excluded and remains outside, in shadows. Were we in a certain part of India I'd look at the stone of the temple wall to see what I long for. Carved in rock. Beautiful and broken. Enough remaining, however, to discern, in this posture and that, the primal dance of Man and Woman riding the cock of ages through precious birth after birth, over centuries, through eons, into light-years. Fucking away intelligence, liberty, and opportunity.

Though I am being led through the *Blade Wheel* and the Dharma glows above and faintly still within, I cannot break loose from this shadow.

I've been in bed unable to sleep for at least an hour when I panic. I throw on parka and boots, grab my stick, zip and rezip the tent, and skitter off like a scorpion on shadowed shale. Out of sight of the tents I hunker down, grab my knees and, going up on the balls of my feet, hang my ass three inches from the hard, cobbled ground. Finding balance, poised there, I relax my spine, aligning it with Kailash. I unwind the rosary from my wrist and, studying the silhouette, the immaculate power in the shape of the rock and snow pyramid before me, I start off on a hundred and eight mantras.

Blinking at what I first think is an optical illusion, I see the mountain gaining luminosity like a phosphorescent lamp coming on, brightening before my popping eyes. I'm smiling so hard it hurts, as the night's first undeflected lunar beams of light splash Kailash's western tip rose-silver. I bring the last prayer bead up and, sighting the mountain over it, kiss the two goodnight, turn, and bounce beaming back to my bag.

The inside of my tent has a strange look to it. The elastic stretching overhead is clogged with clothes in different states of dampness. Lighter items dry in a night or two, heavier items reappear with the ritualistic regularity of a shaggy dog story. On one side of the tent is my day pack and duffel with clean clothes in a garbage bag. Dirty, unwashed items are spread at my feet to insulate my sleeping bag from the dew that collects by dawn. My parka and a sweater are pillows. There's a dynamited piece of slate mani stone that holds a stick of incense, also the pills I'll take around three in the morning, and a couple of candles I use for soft light instead of my flashlight, which resides in the tent flap nearest my head, used for nocturnal wanderings and making notes.

During dinner I fill my water bottle with tea water and use it to warm my feet for the first portion of the night. By the three-o'clock-ice-pick hour when Diamox and Alleve are reapplied, the water is tepid and goes down fine. In unlaced boots and parka I rush outside to pee, and rush back in for the warmth of the bag.

Reaching for my bigger water jug, I find it has a half inch of ice at the top. And this is inside the tent, quite near my bag. It's probably ten degrees Fahrenheit tonight. I crunch my parka around my head, and lying flat on my back, fall back to sleep.

I dream that I'm awake, staring straight above me into the chaotic cave-hangings of the clothesline. In this amorphous mess a hooded head appears. It's frighteningly close, within a foot of my face. It's black, silent, and totally grim-reaperish. Yet even as I'm lying here—petrified by this featureless phantom—I realize the shape of the hood is familiar, and that it's not a hood at all. It's a lama's helmet of the type Govinda wore on the cover of my copy of *The Way of the White Clouds*.

Immense relief sweeps over me as this nightmare turns so abruptly benign. I release a long-held breath of terror too soon, as another shock hits: Two rectangular lights flash from within the helmet—a visitation from Darth Vader? But these shapes, too, prove familiar to me. And I realize, with a shiver of delight, that this is no evil. These rectangular lights are the exact shape of the Dalai Lama's spectacles. It is His Holiness in the hood—without a doubt!

I awaken with the dampness of my breath condensed and frozen all around me, but with this clear and most rare sign from my subconscious mind, tinged even with a frosting of humor, glowing all through me. I remember my search yesterday for a face in the shadow of the hooded Mahakala stone, and I think of the inspiration that Govinda's books have been to me. This makes it most fitting that Govinda be the vehicle to dispel the terrifying hints of death heads that echo my fearsome, nihilistic first glimpse at the Dharma. With the telltale signature of those spectacles, a guiding personality takes shape and the message comes clear: In this world of illusion he who wears these symbols of wisdom will shed light upon the darkness. The proper discernment of his view will bring terrifying teachings into happy perspective. All of it warms me on this coldest of mornings and provides a meditation-worthy point of departure for so mercurial a pilgrim, for this dream feels like my deepest experiential insight to date in Asia.

CHAPTER ELEVEN

The Female Yak Horn Cave

TAD

Daylight finds me happy and content, but I keep the dream to myself and try not to bubble. Stepping out into a Jack Frosted campsite, I catch sight of myself in a frozen-solid washing dish. Two weeks of black beard have grown in fast.

We put in a short day, only hiking a few miles up the kora. Before the kitchen crew leaves, Tenzin writes a letter in Tibetan, to be delivered by them to the monks in the next gompa. It requests preparations for a fire offering that Tenzin will perform the following dawn.

For the remainder of the morning we hike slowly, peacefully, past the stream called Belung Chu. Kailash is hidden behind a hill named Vajrapani, which, like its companion, Avalokiteshvara, is a black pile of earth probably dumped by a glacier. The hills resemble the heaps thrown behind a madly digging dog in search of a rabbit already fled out another hole. We camp in the shadow of Drirapuk, Cave of the Female Yak Horn, a monastery of the Karmapa order built in front of the sacred cave where the adept Gotsangba meditated during his retreat, when he opened up the path for circling Kailash in the thirteenth century. He was led here by Tara (Drolma, to Tibetans) in the form of a female yak, who disappeared into this cave leaving the signs of her horns and hoof. On his adventures Gotsangba was led by numerous magical incarnations including jackals, crows, and twenty-one Tara-wolves that melted into the huge Drolma La stone at the highest and most difficult point of his vision quest.

The gompa is reached over a footbridge near the juncture of two inflowing streams. It marks a hard right turn on the kora trail, but tell that to the winds charging up the Valley of the Gods. Walled windbreaks switch up a steep, boulder-strewn slope. Inside the drab, hastily reconstructed building of stone, mud, and beams, a riot breaks out. Tangkas, photos, colorful magazine ads, and postcards conspire in a blaze of Dharma around color-spangled beams amidst veils and dragon-laced pillars. Statues of Milarepa cocking his ear, heavy-set Marpa, and Naropa peering slant-eyed upon meditative wonders are all decked with scarves. All the way in the back is a doll sitting on a venerated shelf. This is the replica of a statue, destroyed by the Chinese a generation ago, depicting the pioneer Gotsangba. The monk in charge is young and brightly clad under plum robes. His eyes seem languid and exude a bit of the twinkle associated with his order.

On the roof, prayer-flagged chimneys are elaborately horned with gold. After much friendly discussion Tenzin broaches the subject of his letter. It seems to have fallen on deaf ears or wasn't properly understood. A slight chill tinges our farewells, as sectarianism rears its head.

"It's usually like that," Tenzin concedes without rancor, as we plod down the hillside, past the prisonlike guest house (riddled with bed bugs, we are warned). "I met the late Karmapa—the head of this order—twice, and it always went well—a very high being, I felt. Quite a power emanating from him. Both times we hit it off and shared a short and friendly exchange. Then, invariably, some worried-looking monk would come over and whisper in his ear, 'Dalai Lama's man.' He looks like he doesn't care, but his attendants coolly urge me along. The old rivalries are unending." He smiles and shakes his head sadly. "It all goes back hundreds and hundreds of years. Wasn't really their fault, you know. Some Tibetan warlord claimed he was going to overthrow the Gelukpas for building too many monasteries. Told the Karmapas they'd be the kings of the hill if they backed him, and also allied himself with a Bonpo king from the east. The Mongols came down to protect their friend the Dalai Lama, and the Tibetan warlord got his head handed to him. The Great Fifth Dalai Lama instituted a lasting peace, disarming all the warlords, and tried to prevent all religious persecution, once things cooled down. But from then on the Karma Kagyu have been slow to get over their missed chance to rule Tibet. They made such a great contribution. It was the Karmapas who developed the technique of finding the reincarnations, or *tulkus*, of high lamas. We owe them the very form of reincarnation by which the Dalai Lama is rediscovered in his next life!

"How appropriate that we're in the northern part of the mandala, where emerald jealousy is transmuted into wonder-working wisdom. So meditate on that. Use obstacles that occur to increase progress in the path, that's the teaching."

The next morning we ease up the pace and only hike a few miles. Straight ahead is forbidden territory, the North Door. Like the inner kora, it is only for those who have circled thirteen times. I fill a bean-cooking tin from my unused mess kit with the mountain's clay flesh. Fearless faith-filled pilgrims eat a ball of this earth, which is renowned for its healing properties. I think it better to make a poultice of the mud with water from Lake Manasarovar.

Some return to camp, a small band of us take a day hike to the northern face. Up the minivalley between the dark mas-

ters of earth Chang Dorje and Chenrezig (Vajrapani and Avalokiteshvara). In this light Chang Dorje looks like coffee grinds
and Chenrezig like volcanic sand. Between them, draining out
from the foundations of Kailash itself, the Kangjam Chu trickles,
sometimes disappearing under a drainfield of boulders, sometimes
ice-covered, sometimes moss-matted and flowing free. Following it
up the gap, we trudge through a notch several hundred yards
across. On the other side of this notch a bowl opens up with
millions of stones softly glowing under a stratified ice-and-snow
wedding cake. From here the tetrahedronal north face of Kailash
rears five thousand feet straight up.

To the right and west a couple of plump, sugared, puddinglike
snow hills are hand-speckled with cinnamon stones. In the east
a small glacier hangs on Kailash. Farther, a steep stone field
marches up a slide between flanks of white. It looks negotiable.
Tricky for a little way but then leveling off, easy as can be. From
up there I could see beyond these cinnamon-pudding hills. I'd see
to the very feet of Kailash!

The slide itself is God's dandruff, flakes of stone, wind- and
weather-chipped from the rock-wall skin. You'd get a surfing action with a few sliding underfoot, but I've picked through enough
slag heap quarries to know how to navigate.

Everybody else is clicking away with their cameras. I want to
get closer and rough out my plan to Jock, who laughs at the idea
but does not countermand it. Off I lunge, but my feet are gyro-
scopes, attempts to climb to the rock slide fold around, and I end
up where I started, punch-drunk, not knowing what hit me.

Jock is still giggling. Suddenly I get the joke, and the whole
afternoon becomes one huge déjà vu, and I succumb to pulling out
my camera. Realizing I'm falling back into line, doing what everyone else is doing, being less unique and more magical.

Jock is still quite amused, looking at me like I'd sprouted fins
and gills and says, "Did you just see a fish go by?"

"This is as close as we get," I mumble to Wolfgang's camera.

"*Ja*, probably," he concedes, dropping the camera and flashing
a smile at me.

Trying to get any closer to Kailash is like trying to force two positive ends of a magnet together. There's a force field in front of me that won't let me any closer, like a Tai Chi master who won't let any blows land. I can feel it! And Jock felt it even before I did. He was laughing at me because I hadn't felt the wall.

You can't manhandle magnetism. If I really tried to force the force field something bad would happen. A turned ankle. A terrible headache, I don't know. For Lancelot it was getting blown out of the chapel and waking up in bandages, the day he tried to ambush the Holy Grail.

Breaking up into small groups we head back. I languish and go last down the dry streambed with huge, seal-like red and black and brown stones flopped onto each other, soaking up sun. Lying atop these to get a picture, I lose track of my mission and space out, peering up at the mountain—the spiritual vibrations taking a terrible, wonderful toll today. I'm stoned, all right, and I wonder if a rock might simply be a thought blessedly free from a thinker, balancing delicately between being and nonbeing for centuries and centuries on end, until, debate over, it's ground to dust.

The sun is spectacular, as if a filter of smoke on even the sunniest day in America was suddenly ripped away, and dodging your eyes across it, you glimpse the actual flames silently roaring. A true furnace in the sky. I make my way wordlessly down the slope, stopping and peering around at the mountain from time to time, like a baby exploring the world but turning now and again to see the smiling parent's face.

I race the rocks across the waters of the gods back to camp, and succumb to Richard's smile. Did he catch it from me or the other way round?

Tenzin asks me to help him build a fire pit with a little seat and rock table above it. He has had a truck and yaks lug a load of firewood all the way from Nepal in order to perform a formal fire offering ceremony in this spot, the place where, he says, Lama Govinda said a wish for the welfare of the world will have maximum effect. I guess it's his dream wish, bringing another wish of mine true too: to build a wall before Kailash.

After tea Tenzin brings out his *Blade Wheel* text, and we all gather round, everyone sun-bronzed, more acclimatized, and filled with anticipation. The others seem to be getting the *Blade Wheel,* really responding to it. I, as usual, am hoping not to resist it.

TENZIN

We have arrived at the place Lama Govinda considered the peak of the spiritual world accessible to humans. He said that here on the north slope of Kailash you should plant your supreme wish for yourself and your world. This is the main reason I decided to make this pilgrimage.

Tomorrow morning I will perform a fire offering to the Tantric Buddha, combining the ceremonial forms for Yamantaka and the Diamond Yogini. You are welcome to attend and use the ceremony to visualize giving up the ordinary world of inadequacy and suffering, entrusting your world to the compassionate hands of all the enlightened beings. I will start before dawn, when it is still bitter cold, so if you choose to stay warm in your tents and participate mentally, that is also all right. It's a free world, and everything is optional, as you know. Now let us turn to the text.

Yamantaka's Wheel of Wisdom

The central refrain of the work begins now, moving from acknowledging the blade wheel of negative evolution to initiating the Dharma wheel of wisdom, Yamantaka's wheel that destroys the devil of self-preoccupation. We've worked up to this through facing the negative consequences of our past and turning toward the spirit of altruism. Now we can go further.

> Understanding this wheel of negative evolution,
> I catch my enemy of self-concern!
> I catch the thief who attacks and robs me!
> I catch the liar who poses as myself!
> Kyema! It *is* the self-habit. I cut all doubt!

Finally, tired of constantly being the target of the blade wheel of negative evolution boomeranging and slicing you into ribbons again and again, you want to use the Dharma blade wheel. You must adroitly grab the blade wheel and, mastering it with wisdom, you catch the enemy—self-addiction. That's the liar who poses as yourself, who has been fooling you all this time. "I catch the thief who attacks and robs me." It's not the external robber, it's this self-addiction enemy. Here we get down to the nitty-gritty.

These root text verses are for memorizing, so you can refer to them in meditation. When you have them in memory, they come to you at deep moments and help you push through certain doorways of experience. Though it may be hard for us to memorize so many verses, we need to internalize the gist of the teaching in order to understand it later in deep meditation.

"Understanding this wheel of negative evolution, I catch my enemy of self-concern!" All the great faults of the self-preoccupation habit that have been explained above are not exaggerations. I am now becoming clear and see that this is the reality of the situation: that my self-preoccupation has caused me all this trouble all this time. Everything bad that happens to me now is caused by all my lives' deeds driven by self-addiction and self-preoccupation. I was under the dictatorship of self-preoccupation. Now, through the blessing of the Dharma and the compassion of my teacher, I have come to recognize my real enemy, the thief who has deceived and robbed me. How satisfying to identify the thief so I can get my treasure back.

It's hard to recognize this enemy who hides within us. So when we do, we feel triumphant and delighted: "Now I see that enemy; now I no longer think there's some evil person out there after me. I recognize the only real devil, pretending to be me or to help me!" When your self-preoccupation mind says: "Oh boy, that is a really good idea, you'll get something great out of that! Go steal that, go get that piece, go take that drink, it'll be great!" it fools you because you think it's your own irresistible impulse. When you're fooled that way you're helpless against its dictates, because it presents itself as your own thought, you see? So, recognizing that demon, you are no longer tricked by it. You feel really happy about seeing that the thief of your happiness is your self-preoccupation, and that it isn't really you, just a mental habit. You say, "Wow! Why, I never imagined that you, liar, pretend to be me and get me into all this trouble. Now I've got you!"

Now that you've identified it, you're never going to doubt again, you're going to call on wisdom to do your devils in. And wisdom has to be fierce to wake people up.

> Now let this evolution blade circle my brain!
> Hey, Death Exterminator, fierce in manner,
> Now whirl three times round my brain
> Your weapon of positive evolution!
> Plant your legs, showing the two realities in balance,
> Your eyes wide open, blazing with wisdom and art!

Let this evolution blade wheel circle my brain and hit me with all my negative results. Because now I know who the enemy is. When the blade wheel of bad karma comes at me, I can let it go right through the real living me to hit my demon of self-preoccupation. So now I let it go around my brain as vengeance against my self-preoccupation, which was the cause, actually, of my negative deeds and their results.

We call on wisdom as Yamantaka, the Death Exterminator, because the self-preoccupation habit is death. Yamantaka is Manjushri—the transcendent wisdom of selflessness—in his fiercest form, tackling the demon of death, who is Yama. Yamantaka is the main archetype deity for the practice of the exchange of self and other. You invoke the Yamantaka archetype to conquer the self-preoccupation habit, to kill your death. "Hey fierce Death Exterminator, now whirl your weapon of positive evolution three times around my brain!"

Yamantaka has all sorts of weapons in his hands, and he tramples around the brain and whirls and smashes them into all the structures of the demon of self-preoccupation. His two horns stand for the relative and ultimate spirits of enlightenment, and he uses both to destroy the demon.

Yamantaka's left legs represent the integration of the absolute spirit of enlightenment, that is, wisdom; and his right legs, the relative spirit of enlightenment, which is love and compassion taking shape as the will to buddhahood for the sake of all beings. You can't save all beings without knowing the nonreality of all existence in absolute reality, and you can't know the ultimate nonreality of all existence without embracing the infinity of relativity that commits you to save all living beings from suffering and make them all happy; because your infinity is their life, they are your infinity. So abandon any notion of enlightenment as just chopping wood and drawing water, just being here now in the relative. And give up any notion of enlightenment as just being some absolute trance state. When you collapse enlightenment to either extreme, criticize that. Enlightenment is the ultimate tolerance of the cognitive dissonance that grips you when you confront absolute and relative at the same time. Enlightenment is being simultaneously totally present to the relative and totally liberated in the absolute.

Buddha is totally out of here, in nirvana where nothing bothers him. At the same time he's totally present here, concerned for all beings. Seeking buddhahood, we don't give up either being totally out of here or being totally in here. You aim for both the nirvana of the arhat-saint and the engagement of the bodhisattva. That's why Yamantaka has two legs, planted in two-reality balance. There's absolute absentness in one leg, and total relative presentness in the other leg.

Yamantaka's eyes blaze with art and wisdom. Art is simply love and compassion in action. Wisdom is the insight that empowers them. The twin energies of wisdom and compassion blaze forth simultaneously.

> Grind your fangs, the four forces,
> Crush my enemy—cruel self-concern!
> Use the king of mantras—other-concern,
> Smash my enemy within!

The four forces are the four remedies: remorse, repentance, resolve never again to be the slave of the self-preoccupation habit, and the wisdom of voidness. These are the four fangs of Yamantaka, which he uses to crush the enemy of self-concern. First you must genuinely acknowledge the evil things you have done. Really face them. Then, second, you repent that you have done them. Third, you must form a genuine resolve that you won't do them again. Finally, you must see the voidness, that really there was no reason to have done them, they're not ultimately there; that's where you break the chain. Repentance alone, as it tends to reinforce your sense of the concrete reality of the sin, is not enough. Ultimately, you have to see through the sin. When you truly see its voidness, you can break free, and then you really will never do such things again.

Concern for others is the king of all mantras and Tantras and magical methods. It is not just giving up self-preoccupation but also becoming other-preoccupied. You face yourself and see through yourself, then you turn around and ignore yourself and become preoccupied with others, more concerned with them than with yourself. This way you really become an agent of the active energy of the good.

Here we are on the north face of Mt. Kailash. We are going to pray for relief and liberation for ourselves and for the world.

> Frantically chasing me through the life-cycle jungle,
> That vicious demon, the self-habit monster,
> Violates me and others—stop him, O Yamantaka!
> Catch him! Drag him! Fierce Death Exterminator!
> Strike! Strike! Pierce my enemy-dominated heart!
> Stomp! Stomp on this lethal thinker's head!
> Annihilate my enemy self-killer heart!

This is the really heavy verse. It's fierce and frightening, calling on Yamantaka to terminate in my heart the murderous butcher, my enemy who dominates me. It has to be very clearly understood here that one is not talking about suicide, or some sort of destruction of the self. Wisdom does not destroy the self, because the self that is the focus of the self-habit or self-preoccupation is not a self that exists. It is our illusion of a fixed, frigid, rigid self. If it existed, being preoccupied with it would be fine, we'd be taking care of something real. But this presumed self—the fixed, absolute, independent, "real me" type of self—doesn't exist. You cannot destroy it, since it didn't exist to start with.

The self that has always existed and constantly changes, yet can never be ultimately destroyed, is the relative living self. It suffers when it is habitually under the cruel domination of the false notion of an absolute self. It never matches up to that notion of a self. It can't be rigid and fixed—as is this notion of an absolute self. It is not actually disconnected from everything else—as is this notion of an independent self. The relative self is flexible and vulnerable. It changes all the time, living right here in the midst of everything.

No one is telling us to destroy that relative self. That relative self is a process that includes a body, a mind, and even a soul, which just means the also changeable, subtle mind. The relative self is the living self. When we get rid of the delusory overlay—our sense of a rigid, absolute self—we are released! Then our relative self at last becomes a buddha-self.

This is what selflessness is. It does not mean you throw away, suppress, or destroy your ego. Understanding it strengthens your ego and liberates you. Buddha is smiling not because he wants people to commit psychic hara-kiri, but because he sees that it's possible for people to get rid of the erroneous sense of absolute self. You're simply getting rid of a delusion, you're not getting rid of yourself.

The Buddha often taught his great discovery as the teaching of selflessness. Yet he often refers to a person dealing with the self in a positive way, controlling the self, mastering the self, liberating the self. When he declares, "There is no self!" he shocks people into questioning their sense of absolute self. Some people need just such a shock to turn and look for their imagined self and see that it isn't there. But then it is reported out of context that the Buddha said generically "there is no self," and that is misunderstood to mean that Buddha's great insight was simply that nobody and nothing exists.

But Buddha was obviously aware that it doesn't make sense to say that he doesn't exist at all. Then who would be talking? What he really says is that we don't exist the way we think we do. Beings and things do not exist as absolutes; they do exist as relational entities.

The *Blade Wheel* is not talking about killing yourself either physically or psychologically. Killing our self-addiction habits brings us back to life and liberates us from suffering. It is like heart surgery. When the surgeon cuts open your chest, goes into your heart, replaces a valve or an artery, or adds a pacemaker, he is not trying to kill you, though you are inviting him to cut open your heart. He is going in there to remove an obstruction, to recalibrate the delicate mechanism of life, to free you from the suffering of heart attacks. Yamantaka is the skilled surgeon you need to perform the delicate heart surgery of cutting the self-addicted habit out of your heart, to liberate the relative living heart to beat freely and with a newfound power.

Clear awareness about the relative self is one of the keys of accomplishing this liberation. The Tibetans especially have developed great skill in dealing with this, elaborating the subtleties of the relative or conventional self. The self is only the self by virtue of being mentally and verbally designated as the self. It's the mind's creative role and the world's creative role that creates the self. "Self" is a reflexive pronoun. "I" am a pronoun. "You" are a pronoun. Those pronouns actually create "I" and "you." That's a very deep teaching. So the awareness from the beginning about the persisting relative self helps overcome feelings of fear about transcending the absolutized self-habit.

So the harsh tone here, "Fierce Death Exterminator! Strike! . . . Stomp!" means "Kill my death," not "Kill me"! Yamantaka, please terminate my terminator, my dead concept of myself that imprisons my living self. This extraordinary way of seeing enables me to call on terrible wisdom, Yamantaka, Death Exterminator, to strike the vital point, that self-enemy killer heart. Then we say: "Maraya!" which is used in fierce rituals and means "Kill!" in Sanskrit. Then comes the incantatory part of the work:

> Humg! Humg! Great God! Unleash your magic!
> Jah! Jah! Tie this enemy tightly!

Pat! Pat! Liberate him, Great Death Lord!
Slice! Slice! Cut the tangled self-habit knot!

Come hither! Great God Death Exterminator!
This sack of actions and addictive five poisons
Gets me stuck in the bog of life-cycle evolution —
Tear! Tear! Rip it open right this minute!

This follows the pattern of a fierce ritual from ancient India — a ritual of destruction, the destruction of death. Once death is dead, there is eternal life. If you kill Death he can't die: Death becomes a Dharma-protector, a protector of life — because he can't die anymore himself — much less inflict death on others.

Now we come back to the refrain: "Stomp! Stomp on this lethal thinker's head! Annihilate my enemy self-killer heart!" When we invoke gods of superferocity that scare Death to death, we're not only talking on some grand level, we are also working on taking that little triumph in the day when you get rid of your self-involvement and just release yourself into your play or work. You get free of self-constriction and enter the zone of power, which here means breaking free from the dominance of the killer heart. You've temporarily suppressed the lethal thinker's head. You just rip open the self-preoccupied killer heart and you then have the life, the energy, to do some good work or to have some fun.

Now the *Blade Wheel* moves on to invoking Yamantaka to help us with each little bad habit, specifically and effectively.

Though I have drowned in the agonies of the three bad states
I still don't fear them and so commit their causes —
Stomp! Stomp on this lethal thinker's head!
Annihilate my enemy self-killer heart!

The three horrid states are: hell, the pretan ghost realm, and the animal state. We Western materialists have lost our terror of these things, just as we lack the powerful hope to reach any culmination of evolution. To open up the possibility of infinite positive evolution, you must be ready for the imagination of the danger of

193

the infinitely negative. The terror that arises from contemplating Dante-esque infernos can be useful to inspire us to reach the positive. Milarepa found the terror he felt from thinking of his evil deeds to be instrumental in his gaining buddhahood in one lifetime. It's like the adrenaline rush you get to jump out of the way of a train bearing down upon you. It is powerful and useful.

Fortunately in Buddhism, the infinitely negative is less infinite than the infinitely positive. My patented formula is that evil is infinite, but goodness is infinite squared—infinite times infinite. Because the infinite evil beings draw energy from their self-addiction, each works for one person only. But the infinite good beings draw energy from love for others, each works for infinite others. Their energy is infinite squared. That must be why Buddha smiled! On that note, let's dedicate the merit of our deep, deep confrontation with the *Blade Wheel,* and take ourselves off to bed!

TAD

The group disperses and drifts off to rest and wait for dinner.

After I build the fireplace and platform from which Tenzin will conduct the fire offering, it's early evening. The wind runs a single cloud across the first star. Over the Lha Chu, just above a shrine-dotted hill, Kailash basks, in unmolested meditation, its crown bathed in the last rays of sunset. I hold my eyes on her silhouette, then sanitize my hands and unzip the tent. Inside await a hissing lamp, smiling company, and hot cups of tea. Tenzin—throttle open wide—is answering a question concerning Tantric teachings involving the opening of central nervous system energy-sites, the chakras, including the last one.

"It is so difficult that it needs the help of past yogis and past buddhas who have traveled that particular path. That's why one needs initiation and a relationship with a particular guru, a yogi who has accomplished it in the past. They have a pattern for this process already, and they help one structure the pattern. It can't be done otherwise. One can study the Dharma by developing the mind of renunciation and transcendence, the mind of compassion,

and the mind of wisdom, to become suitable for other teachings—
but once one gets into the Tantric teachings, without a Don Juan
there's no hope. It is utterly impossible. To open the door to that
path definitely requires a personal mentor who has mastered this
herself. There's no substitute. Without the mentor it's a no-go."

There's a wry, infinitely ironic look on his face that seems to
acknowledge the adolescent angst of ten million teenagers who
have vowed to figure out life, once and for all, but despite reading
Catcher in the Rye or *Siddhartha* or *On the Road* they never do, never
can, without one of them becoming a buddha and leading the rest.

"There are big strictures about even talking about Tantra, traditionally. But about fifteen years ago, around 1980, the Dalai
Lama began getting very open about it. He felt there was so much
misunderstanding, so much foolish and dangerous stuff taught as
Tantra, that it was necessary, while protecting the initiations, to at
least let people know what it really is. As I've been letting you
know about it."

The Dharma-hook is now perfectly baited, with caviar, the
feeling that this is possible for us too!—as Tenzin nails the moment.

"I have to say, it is the most far-out thing I could ever imagine.
As I learn more about it, I can't believe it. I received different
initiations in my twenties, which is the Tibetan tradition, without
much explanation. Just to plant a good seed. Then you work on
renunciation, compassion, and wisdom meditations; particularly
pushing the wisdom part, to deepen it. That should, in itself—
naturally, on the neurological level—open the system, loosening
the knottedness where the sense of self is held. Around forty, you
turn to Tantric studies, not just the yogas but to figure it all out
and use it as a system."

Our silence calls for a full explanation.

"I followed that pattern. I thought it would mean reading a
few more books or getting more initiations and doing more meditation and then I'd be doing Tantra. But it is such a huge science in
itself! It's hugely complicated, sophisticated, staggering that any
human beings could have elaborated such an amazing art—it is
just unbelievable!"

Dinner comes, goes, suddenly Tenzin starts singing "Happy Birthday" as the tent unzips and we're faced with candles on a birthday cake ushered in by a porter holding an umbrella so the flames won't blow out. The cake is carried by our Tibetan cook, Pawan, who places the minor miracle he's tended for hours in front of Jock. Blowing out the candles, Jock insists that Pawan sit and sample his handiwork. Chocolate cake with coffee icing!

"I pray Padma Sambhava Torma today . . ." Pawan laughs, breaking into Tibetan and having Tenzin translate, cackling: "As he was hiking by the Torma, Pawan knew he must attempt to make a cake. It took two men with bellows two hours."

We begin to cheer and soon the men who had used the bellows are invited for the last of the cake. Pawan and Tenzin have quite a Ping-Pong game of Tibetan going now, and Tenzin's face has taken on the glow of a lamp. In the green light of the tent he looks vaguely Asian—Mongolian or Tibetan. Delighted at something Pawan has said, he announces: "Our honored guest and chef wishes to direct birthday greetings to Jock and to all of us who are here at Kailash for the first time. The monk in the monastery above told him a story this afternoon, which he wants to include in the celebration, of when Gotsangba took a break from his three-year retreat in the yak horn cave right up the slope from here. As he stepped from the cave and looked up at the curiously shaped mountain, he beheld Kailash as the buddhas see it, fully transformed into the mandala mansion. It was only at this moment that Gotsangba realized that Tara had led him to Meru, the center of the universe, and that outside his cave—this very ground—was a vantage point from which millions of beings might glimpse enlightenment and so steer their lives more accurately toward it. At that moment he prayed for the enlightenment of all beings, visualizing completely the ultimate destiny of us all. Thank you, Pawan, happy birthday, Jock, and happy Kailash to us!"

Later, lying in my sleeping bag, glowing like an ember, I keep hearing Tenzin's cough. Finally, I get up, put on my boots and parka and go offer him my tiger balm. By the time I'm back in my sleeping bag, the camp is silent.

I'm up before dawn. Twenty paces from my tent Lobsang's

already laying the firewood in the shape of a tipi, with a section of *The Kathmandu Post* wadded-up beneath. Tenzin, in his Santa Claus suit and with a miner's light on his head, is expediting wizardry: various millets, grains, and spices, plus a boiling pot containing a huge glob of butter.

"Ah yes, Tad—I need a lectern, something to put the prayers on, to read from. Something big. Massive, worthy of such holy scripts." As Tenzin thus commands this all-too-willing servant, Valerie and Leopoldo crawl from their tents, yawning, video equipment and toothbrushes in hand.

"Right," I mumble, stumbling around in the predawn dusk. Sure, no problem. Big. Massive. Worthy of such—got it! A golden stone, the size of six loaves of bread laid side-by-side.

"You can't be serious, Tad!" I grin to hear Valerie's dismay.

After a cup of coffee or two, warmed up by an hour's work, my weight belt on, and at normal altitude, I most certainly would be serious. But none of these being the case, she's right. It's ridiculous.

With hands on either side of the slab and knees bent—it's *up we go*—but something is very wrong here. No air! No strength! No brain!

No matter. Where was I? Oh right, onto the knees, up we go—hitting a wall. Come on, Tad! What's with you? No air! No strength!

"Yes! Very good. Perfect, in fact. Now over to the fire. In the back. No, a little to the right—there! Thank you, Tad."

I retreat in silent agony, lungs bursting, black splotches blooming before my eyes, transformed into the old man from commedia del'arte, stooped, broken, choking, ready to die, giggling at myself.

On the little stone throne, before gold and red and orange flames licking the limbs of trees that won't grow up here, peering over long, narrow strips of paper, slumped in a half lotus, his miner's lamp illuminating new printings of ancient Tibetan prayers, Tenzin sits, ladle in one hand, and wisdom bell to the side, splashing the flames with pungent inflammables, droning the strangest song. As the dawn—a few minutes off—trembles on the edge of our world.

"Tad, melt the butter better," in English, before buzzing back into wasp-nest talk. And no, I'm not afraid of the fire, and yes, I hold the pot over it, and yes, I'm smiling without comprehending. Nomads, drawn by rumor of a white monk, gather silently in the darkness, standing in the offering smoke spilling skyward, to save a world in need. I squint through the smoke while Tenzin ladles butter onto the flames, and throws barley, grasses, wheat, millet, white rice, and wheat flecks in offering to the deities of the mandala, requesting them to intercede to help the world. He rings the wisdom bell and twirls the vajra scepter to bless our journey over the great shoulder. Dawn lights the tip of Kailash like a burning coal just before it crumbles to ash, pink and blue and white.

TENZIN

I got up before dawn to perform the fire ceremony, combining the Yamantaka offering with the Superbliss Yogini offering, as suitable for the place. This is a very ancient Tantric ceremony, used after retreats and during long practice sessions to intensify purification and merit and to develop wisdom energy. Performing it here on the mountain during a pilgrimage would have been unusual in traditional Tibet. Traditional Tibet is no more. Pilgrims here today have no means and few have knowledge to perform such a ceremony. For me, while I'm no adept and this is an unorthodox retreat pilgrimage, performing this ceremony fulfills a dream I have carried for a long time.

I want to establish an omen, a positive symbol for burning away the fog of ignorance, confusion, and self-destructiveness from our world. The Chinese are killing Tibet as an outgrowth of their own self-destruction, totally knocked off balance by Western technology and ideology, mixing in with their own homegrown imperfections. The world is letting it happen, feeling helpless, while the few who are profiting by the devastation deludedly think everything will remain just fine for them.

Here on the north face of Mt. Kailash, we are looking into the ecstatic though the fearsome dark green face of Superbliss

Chakrasamvara Buddha. May the energies of the millions of true adepts fuse with my humble efforts and send an energy of illumination everywhere through the minds of all beings on this planet.

In the icy cold, wearing a headlamp, my large red parka, vajra, and bell taped to my hands, with fire offering ladles I have brought from America, I have readied the fire for lighting and can now begin the ceremony. Last night I performed the self-creation visualizations of Yamantaka, Chakrasamvara, and Vajrayogini. Again, as a good omen, I will summarize the offering and prayers.

Yamantaka Fire Offering

I visualize myself as Vajrabhairava. I salute Manjushri in this form:

"Namo Vajra Bhairavaya! Your sixteen feet dance tirelessly upon the head of devils and yamas, smashing to dust all demon armies, O Yamantaka who conquers outer, inner, and secret devils, be inseparably present to adorn the circle of great bliss!"

I make offerings to the local deities, ask them for the place. "Whoever dwells here, gods or dragons, trolls, ghouls, or others, I request all of you, please give me this place!"

I imagine they give it, saying, "Do what you like!" and then go home. I tell them, "Go on home happily!" I purify the site with various mantras, especially Yamantaka's *Om brih shtrih vikritanana hum phat.* I bless the vajra and bell and all the offerings.

I light the fire. I fan the flames. *Hum.* I pour seven ladles of melted butter, chanting, *"Om brih shtrih vikritanana hum phat."* I pick up a handful of kusha grass and bless it, and make a seat for the invited deities. I invite the Fire God, Agni, who serves as messenger bearing the offerings through the fire to the Superbliss mandala deities.

"Om! Come hither! Come hither! O great elemental! Rishi of the gods! Supreme of Brahmins! To receive the fire pourings and foods, please truly draw near to us! *Om takki hum jah.* Be seated in the fire quarter on the kusha mat on the edge of the hearth!"

I make him comfortable and give him offerings. I ring my bell and praise Agni, combining ancient Vedic hymns with special

Buddhist dedications. I announce his vow to receive oblations and transmit them to Yamantaka and the Superbliss Buddha community. I offer seven ladles of butter. *"Om agnaye adivya adivya avishaya avishaya mahashriye havyaka vyavahanaya.* O, please eradicate for all of us—master, disciples, and retinue—all obstacles to our liberation and omniscience, all breaking of our three vows, all natural misdemeanors, all misfortunes, all unclarities of samadhis, all inaccuracies of mantras, all excess and deficiency of procedure, all such faults. *Shantim kuruye svaha."*

I then offer a dozen other substances, slowly and repeatedly over several hours: kindling sticks, sesame, mustard seed, grains, peas, sweets, and so forth, each with a specific request for blessings for all beings. With each new mantra, I repeat it as often as possible, offering a bit of each substance each time.

Having satisfied Agni with these offerings, I then ask him to transmit the next round of offerings to the transcendent buddha-deities. I visualize that he does so, as I proceed with the longer set of offerings to the mandala palace and its deities. By now the fire is blazing very intensely, and I must sit further back behind the stone firewall between my seat and the makeshift hearth. I repeat Yamantaka's mantra and that of Vajrayogini.

"Om hrih shtrih vikrtanana hum phat. Om khandarohi hum hum phat. Om svabhava shuddhasarvadharmah svabhavashuddho ham."

I visualize the mandala palace complete with deities lovingly held within Agni's heart. I make offerings and I sing the praises of Manjushri and Vajrayogini.

Jah! O Manjushri, your nature is the actuality of all things,
Abodeless, you are free of going and coming like space,
Your compassion neither comes nor goes, like the realm of time,
Your emanations are free of progress like mirror images—
Yet though unaffected by the nature of coming and going,
You are seen wherever I look, like the moon reflected in water.
Now invited here, O God, I pray for you to come,
As Manjughosha, the intuitive wisdom of all buddhas,
As Bhairava Yamantaka, to tame all devils,

Together with the Yama-retinue, emanated agents,
Come hither, attend to me, pray take your place!"

I praise Chakrasamvara Superbliss Buddha:
Shri Heruka, master of the blazing body,
Laughing "Ha Ha," shaking the three realms,
Shriveling demon brains with *Hum hum phat phat,*
Now grant here the luck of the Great Bliss Wheel!

And I praise his consort, the Vajra Yogini.

> O glorious Vajrayogini
> Universal Queen of Dakinis,
> Fivefold wisdom, Three Bodies Incarnate,
> Savior of beings, I bow to you!
> Your emanation Vajra Dakinis,
> Ladies who perform the world's work,
> Who free us from bondage to presumptions,
> I bow to all of you!

I begin the transcendent fire offerings. "Let the kindling sticks
have the nature of the enlightenment tree! *Om brih shtih vikrtanana
hum phat. Om bodhi vrkshaye.* O, please eradicate for all of us —
master and disciples and retinue — all obstacles to our liberation
and omniscience, all breaking of our three vows, all natural misdemeanors, all misfortunes, especially all obstacles to perfection
of brilliant energy, all unclarities of samadhis, all inaccuracies of
mantras, all excesses and deficiencies of rites, all such faults —
Shantim kuruye svaha." I repeat this many times with each of the
many substances. I think of all the beings I know or can imagine. I
imagine them all connected to this event, receiving merit and blessings from the intensity of the joy of the deities here on sacred Mt.
Kailash. The deity's heart radiates buddhas holding white vases
full of mead; the beings sit on a white moon disk, and the deities
bathe them, purifying all sins and obscurations, sicknesses and
demons and so forth, and their bodies become like crystal.

After a long time of this hot and heavy work of offering into the fire, I conclude with various final offerings and praises. I also beg forgiveness for any irregularities, of which there were doubtless many.

"O Protector, whatever slight things wrong I committed in my confusion, as you are the Savior of all beings, be fair and please be tolerant! And you should please forgive any deficiency in all performed here, due to lacking, not finding, ignorance, and inability!"

I repeat the hundred-syllable mantra to repair any damage. I then invite the deities to return to their celestial abodes, trusting they will return again in the future. I go through a third round of complete offerings again to Agni, this time somewhat more rapidly, since everyone is tired and cold by now, and we need to break camp and begin our climb. I conclude with an auspicious verse to Yamantaka.

Triumphing in battle with many, many demon armies,
O Diamond Bhairava, deep, deep, excelling all others,
During the retreat, supreme art to attract your heart,
I made this effort in the essential burnt offering.
By its power, may dark masses of beings' evolution and addiction
Be banished far away by the rays of the sun of compassion,
And may the wondrous image of authentic view, meditation, and
    action,
Become a feast for your all-perceiving eyes.
In all my lives may you, mild and fierce Manjushri,
Never leave me, always care for me! Good luck to all!

CHAPTER TWELVE

The Cool Grove
Charnel Ground

TAD

Over the Lha Chu and along it through the gravel and grass valley, up a gentle slope where the Lha Chu meets the trickle of the Drolma La Chu, we hump it. The Lha Chu continues northeast on a small-stoned drain field, to the source of the Indus River. We veer hard east with some nomads, who are chucking stones to the left and the right of yaks, clucking their tongues, and saying see-you-soon prayers to Kailash—all pretty much at the same time.

From the wide, rocky slope, the northeast face of Kailash has a backstage feel to it. Confusingly convoluted coffee-grind piles for hills sprawled around partially rob the Holy One of some of its previous luster. Yet we've feasted on perfection for three days and nights already, so perhaps now there's a concealed complement to this less dramatic face. Maybe this is Kailash without the royal robes, the holy mountain's less perfect back door.

At noontime, if and when we complete a two-thousand-foot climb, we'll be just a few hundred feet below the eighteen-thousand-foot mark. This is the altitude that separates the wheat from the chaff. No one but professional maniacs goes over twenty thousand feet without oxygen tanks in reserve. So I'm not going to rush it, and neither is James or Richard or Wolfgang or Jock or Valerie or Leopoldo or Tenzin or any of us, over barren, and at the moment undramatic, territory. Kailash is soon hidden by the epaulets of a guardian Manjushri standing off the snowy east shoulder. This is the territory of the lion-faced dakini, who guides those who are fourteenth-time returners through a shorter path right past Jambeyang, past the shrine to the Medicine Buddha, and back out the east side with the Kandro-Sanglam Chu, the Dakini Secret Path Stream. A shorter, less grueling route, but not for us! We stalk up this rear valley, through shadows incredibly chilling, and every Christian-raised Westerner must feel it, if they don't actually hear it: "Yea, though I walk through the shadow of the valley of death . . ."

Sudden blizzards are infamous in this section and potentially deadly, yet today the skies remain clear. Thrilling? Maybe, but not in the least comfortable familiar. Like it or not, old age and death are coming. Sickness, fear, and trembling. It's not human up here. There's nothing standing or growing. Not a single human thing in sight except for us and the occasional piece of trash.

My entire body proceeds to yell at me—not just my head, heart, stomach, weak knees, and tingling tongue, but my kidneys, thighs, dead fingers, and these wobbly Styrofoam feet—joining in a silent chorus, warning: "Big mistake . . . return to sender . . . go back!"

But that's all nonsense. Everything is fine. We've got a good jump on the day. Another couple of hours and the climb is steeper, the dread greater, the sun blinding, the air abruptly thinner, thoughts flintier. There's a lump in my throat. No, my throat is a lump of fear.

Since the beginning I've been thinking about the graveyard of the eighty-four great adepts, also known as the Vajrayogini Cool Grove Charnel Ground, a place where the holy adepts from India are evoked, where the dog-gnawed body of a young girl was left in recent memory, and where pilgrims place the clothes of loved ones, living and dead. It has been my thought to leave a picture of my baby Anna at this place. But resting at an eerie spot already littered with clothes, I start to get the willies at the thought of leaving a piece of my baby in a place so saturated with death. With high-altitude sentences that fall out in strange order, I voice my anxiety to Tenzin, who reassures me:

"You will be back here—probably even your daughter will be here—but if it spooks you, don't do it. It's not really a graveyard, after all. It's the emanation of a graveyard back in India. Don't worry about it, Tad."

"But where is the graveyard?" I ask, only slightly reassured.

"It's right here! This is it!" he laughs, pointing to the rain-soaked, sun-baked tag sale surrounding us.

This kills me. And for several minutes I can't move. "Of course," I'm mumbling. "Of course—this is the graveyard."

Nomad women approach, droning mantras and spinning prayer wheels. Taking garments from their packs, they hold these over their heads, bowing toward Kailash, then place the mementos down to rot among the rocks. Their prayer wheels spin with a dizzy-making swishing. Comrades labor into sight. We don't talk. We all want and need to be alone.

All along the horizon cairn stones pop up, like Indian braves in ambush. And I move among these gigantic boulders, grown quite dependent on my stick, grimacing fiercely at all I see, under the brightest sun yet. The sky itself looks like water, clear, cool Caribbean water, mentholated hues, lapis lazuli, coral blue, and cobalt, too. Stones of no particular color leap out—even mousy-colored stones leap out. Is it shadow that does it? I wonder. Or the still-life quality as under a microscope?

Movement is good, though painful. Each step, a reacquaintance with a memory that's painful, like looking through the family album of a suicide. For it's dues time, as beginnings start flashing at me now, and middles, and, as close as I've come to know, ends. Little histories. Little tragedies. Tangential and eternally interconnected to the missing link of me.

Tenzin is waving to Lobsang, who waves in the yak drivers. Our fearless leader is inspired to camp here, to prolong the agony. I want to keep moving, but he is blade-wheel wound. I feel myself resisting, like the day in biology when we cut up dead frogs and cats to see how the pieces fit. But the animals are our human selves this time.

With his orange-wrapped texts and his mustard scarf over his glacier glasses, Tenzin's steadying a pulpit, overlooking the cast-off clothes of the graveyard. In the distance the tents are set up on lethal-looking ground. What bothers me most is we haven't got Kailash in view here. Despite our height, hills stand between us.

Now Tenzin reads and translates and comments. I wonder if he won't, in fact, return to a monk's robes before this life is over. Like Ahab searching the seven seas for his white whale, the man is tireless and obsessed, though for the most part cheerful.

I don't want to look at anybody, fearing a laugh attack or a squabble, distractions more disabling than my crippled mind can bear. As the blade wheel spins and the spokes of my tiny tape recorder spin, as water bottles are drained, sunblock is smeared, Diamox gobbled, a sort of comic-fury overtakes me. The teaching bids me cease protecting myself—rather, be a surgeon and lance every karmic wound. Then seek out the wounds of others, bathe and balm these, and thus slowly heal and disarm the world. It's in Govinda, and I find it later, at dinner. "He has gained the equanimity of one who knows that nothing can happen to him other than what already belongs to him already from eternity. There is no more need even for any 'armour,' because he is both the dragon and the knight, the slayer and the slain, the demon and the God." Maybe Tenzin is right to ring the Dharma bell so loud and long, but I fear it will drive me mad.

"Now lie down," he says. And for a minute I think he's still reading, but no—he's speaking to us. "Lie on your backs and imagine this precious life of yours seeping into the rocks, and into the rags of other beings, and now reborn into other bodies wearing different clothes. Consider that your bodies are rags too. Tired, worn-out rags, that copy but cannot compare with the livery of enlightenment. Now we know it is considered a great blessing in the West to leave this body in your sleep—not so in Tibet. Tibetans like to die wide awake. They also meditate with their eyes open. So let's be like them now and practice death while wide awake and healthy. Let down your guard, the ever-alert police dog on the chain that keeps us separate from each other unless we have a twin, or a mate of many decades, or a newborn baby, or a precious new love. Let us all be our own precious new love. Let us be merciful and merciless both, like a mother bird kicking the chick out of the nest and forcing it to fly. Die now. Get up out of the worn-out body.

"And when the body is cold and you hang over it, looking down, don't mourn and moan. Be glad. Look around. There's a twinkling everywhere, like a light snow falling. But it's not cold, it's warm. It's not insulting or assaulting—it honors our old form. Nor should we be in a great hurry to find another body too quickly. Be choosy. Let's go window shopping in the highest heavens, giving up the idea of another body for now. Let's see what can be glimpsed without one."

TENZIN

Yesterday we planted our deepest wishes for peace, prosperity, power, and transcendence for all. I prayed for happiness for all I love, liberation for Tibet, relief for His Holiness, freedom from suffering for all beings. Today we focus on all those who seem to have disappeared, having died and left the bodies we used to identify as them. All those people who seem to be gone, yet in fact are everywhere around unrecognized, busy being other living beings. That is the wonderful thing I learned when translating the book known in the West as *The Tibetan Book of the Dead:* all beings are endlessly alive. There are no dead people. Each being instanta-neously goes through a portal at the end of a particular life, then at once is in the between-state, then soon enough must cope with the events of another life. The buddhas and bodhisattvas, too, are limitlessly alive, exploding through death transformations into in-numerable lives, all aimed at liberating beings.

Here is where I naturally think of my father and mother of this life, may you be well whatever forms you now live in; I wish you all happiness. My first lama, spiritual father and mother, Geshe-la, I think how happy that you are here with me, having attained infinity in your lifetime. Some think this charnel ground reeks of death, but really it represents the conquest of death. May the energy the mountain sends you mother beings advance you wher-ever you are in your evolution. In their ceremonies, the Lakota people say, *"Oyatsuke Miyasun,"* all beings are my mothers. All beings are my fathers. All beings are my relatives.

Here is where you should leave photos or other mementos of any departed people you love. Tibetans believe this charnel ground is a sacred place, and the images left here create a resonance that sends them good energies wherever they now live.

As for us, we cannot do anything greater for our departed ones than realize within ourselves the liberating teaching of the *Blade Wheel*. So we might as well get on with it.

Reforming Specific Habits

My desire is maximum, my effort, minimum.
Though I do a lot, I never find success.
Stomp! Stomp on this lethal thinker's head!
Annihilate my enemy self-killer heart!

The "I" is everybody's "I"—everybody's persona. Now we're really engaged in mind reform. We have turned to other-concern, the root of goodness, the spirit of enlightenment. We are bent against the demon of self-concern and its minion the self-habit. We're deeply into this. We've encountered the wisdom of selflessness, the void in all its nonduality, and we're back in the minute details of living in the world, back with an absolute concern for goodness. So "when my desire is maximum and my effort, minimum," we don't accept it, we call Yamantaka to come, we invoke intuitive wisdom: "Annihilate my enemy self-killer heart."

> I really want happiness but I don't perform its causes.
> I can't stand pain, I just hanker after pleasures.
> Stomp! Stomp on this lethal thinker's head!
> Annihilate my enemy self-killer heart!

This is like a chant, where we come to grips with how shabby we are, how poorly we behave and how irrational we are, still in the grip of this demon self-preoccupation.

> Quick to make friends, soon I treat them lightly.
> Loving fine things I scheme to steal or conquer.
> Stomp! . . . Annihilate . . . !

We take friends too much for granted, being full of greed for new things. Scheming and stealing are everywhere in people's minds. There's a black-out for a few hours, and people steal two billion dollars' worth of goods. It's not just some poor people—it's anybody who can get away with it. Everyone is frenzied by advertising, by commercial culture that whips up greed: "I can't live without this. I can't leave home without that. I've got to have this shoe, that dress, that car."

That's the stealing, then there's the conquering. People sit around thinking: "Maybe I'll invent a computer gadget and make a billion." That's conquering. Because when they think of how they're going to make a billion—this great American dream— they're scheming how to get a dollar out of every pocket.

> Skilled pretender, I hint for presents, always more.
> I'm tight with my things, paralyzed by miserliness.
> Stomp! . . . Annihilate . . . !

We learn to pretend as children. When a parent had something we wanted, we could be so sweet. As adults we're still hinting for presents, flattering and stroking people to get what we want from them. Inside, we're always dissatisfied, always wanting more from those we're with, never enjoying just being with them. Even lovers have this problem of constant dissatisfaction.

The other side of greed is stinginess with what we have. I hide things, lock them up, and repeatedly check my hoard to see if it's still there. I worry about losing things, basically paralyzed by miserliness. Why? Because of the self-cherishing habit that dominates us and makes us torture ourselves. So, Yamantaka, please, stomp on it!

> Slight deeds for others make for giant claims.
> Done nothing to shout about, yet I'm full of boasts.
> Stomp! . . . Annihilate . . . !

I do very little for others, but I sit around grumbling, "Well, I did so and so for so and so, and they're not grateful. Why don't they do more for me?" We constantly complain internally—and to others. Because so and so didn't really appreciate me, and "I'm the one who really did that. And they didn't appreciate it." Such little habits come out very prominently on trips like this, where we're at such close quarters, so we'll see these things, how deep they are. This is the way our minds are—we can manage to have a miserable time, even in paradise.

On the other hand, when I do the slightest good thing, I get carried away with boasting about it. Externally and internally I torture myself and others, driven by this bad habit, so "Stomp, stomp, annihilate!"

> I have many teachers yet slight respect or diligence.
> I have many students yet I begrudge them instructions.
> Stomp! . . . Annihilate . . . !

All of us have teachers. They taught us a lot of useful things, and for a moment we saw what they meant. Yet we don't really respect them, we don't persevere in practice. We don't put it into our lives. Even if we think we're practicing Buddhism, we rarely confront these personal habits. Even teachers don't confront them. "I have many students yet I begrudge them instructions." I don't really help my students. So, please, Yamantaka, help us not to be this way ourselves, "Stomp! Stomp . . . !"

> My claims are great, helpful undertakings slight.
> My reputation great, my reality embarrassing to gods
> And even demons who know my inner mind.
> My learning minimal, I'm big on empty talk.
> My knowledge is small, but I make up insights as I go.
> Stomp! . . . Annihilate . . . !

I don't really know what I'm talking about, but I see that people like a talk, so I spin off something and then they think I did something great. So I can make empty talk. And there's a pun in the "empty talk," because, of course, emptiness is the highest, ultimate, absolute reality. But empty talk can be foolish talk about emptiness, as well as talk about nothing special. I pretend I know and I spew, "Oh, it's all one, we're one with ultimate reality. This is the great perfection, this the great seal, the great enlightenment, the great middle way"—but it's just pretension.

These flaws are particularly dangerous when we are given the pretend status of a teacher, because we've assumed some spiritual mantle. We attract people with our credentials, but we can't do anything for them. Since we don't really know what we're doing, people eventually recognize that we're not extraordinary, but then they despair of the Dharma itself, because of our bad example. And that is very negative evolutionary action for us both. But we lie in this way because we're trapped in the self-preoccupation habit. So please, Yamantaka, my wisdom essence, "Stomp and annihilate it!"

> My friends and helpers many, none are responsible.
> My masters many, none really support me.
> My status is high, my virtues less than a ghost's.

I'm a great guru, with greed and hate like a demon.
Stomp! . . . Annihilate . . . !

Dharmarakshita—a highly enlightened person—sees the powerful, negative energies still untamed in his person. Though others have made him a guru, if he gets into the act, he's just fooling people, because he still seethes with lust and hate. This only stops with perfect buddhahood. So he cries out, for himself as well as for us, "Stomp! Annihilate!"

My view is lofty, my deeds worse than a dog's.
However bright I am, my virtue blows away in the wind.
I hide my loves and hates deep within.
I pointlessly project my faults on others.
Stomp! . . . Annihilate . . . !

I'm more stingy than a dog with his bone. Though I'm bright, my virtue, at base nothing but other-concern, gets blown away in the wind of my self-preoccupied thoughts. I don't want people to know that I'm so far from my ideals. I'm supposed to be holy and pure; I'm not supposed to love this or detest that, so I hide deep within my loves and hates. When I see others as being greedy or hating, I scold them, but I am just projecting all my faults on others. I haven't defused my own self-addiction, so how can I complain about their addictions? O Yamantaka, "Stomp! Stomp!"

Wearing saffron robes, I put my trust in demons.
Though I take vows, my precepts fit the devil.
Always on retreat, I drown in distractions,
Receiving exalted teachings I spend time on divination.
Stomp! . . . Annihilate . . . !

Buddhist monks wear saffron robes. Whatever Dharma practice we do as professionals—even take vows and wear robes and official hats and belts—when we just hear about some power yoga, we're ready to make a bargain with any favorable demon, to get some wealth or success.

212

But this is on the worldly level. Spiritually, the main demon we're putting our trust in is our self-preoccupation. We're just thinking our thoughts and following their dictates, putting our trust in our habitually self-addicting thoughts. When that's the demon we really serve, the transcendent seeker's robe is fake! The real source of the robe is the realization of selflessness and the overcoming of self-preoccupation, which is just what we don't do. We don't really put our trust in that, because we don't live that. Though I take the vows—the lay and monastic discipline vow, the altruistic bodhisattva vow, and the ultra-subtle Tantric vow— yet the precepts I actually follow are from my own self-preoccupy-ing thought flow: "Why don't I get this for myself? Why don't I do that for myself?" My precepts fit the devil. So "O Yamantaka, wisdom god of selflessness, killer of that devil of death—O great Death Exterminator—Stomp! Stomp on this lethal thinker's head! Annihilate my enemy self-killer heart!"

I'm very spiritual, always in retreat and contemplating this or that mandala, but my mind wanders all over the galaxy, so I get nowhere. You get very high teachings from people, but your real interest is how to perform divinations, to show off to people how good your predictions are.

The next series of verses continue to elaborate the basic insight that the demon of self-addiction causes all the trouble and suffer-ing, and that other-preoccupation is the antidote. They illustrate how we actually do behave. There is no time to comment in detail, so I will read through them quickly, inviting Yamantaka to help us change our negative habits all at once. Each verse ends with the refrain "Stomp! Stomp!" but I have condensed them so you can get the gist of them.

Dropping freedom's discipline, I maintain a home.
Throwing comfort in the water, I swim in suffering.
Leaving the haven of freedom, I rush to market.
Leaving the mentor's class, I wander the world like a tourist.
Hoarding my own things, I also grab from monks.
Saving my own food, I steal from others.
Amazing! I meditate little, yet pretend clairvoyance.

Far from high paths, I feign magic transport-power.
I hate as foe who speaks plain for my good.
I adopt as friend who flatters me to trick.
When intimates confide secrets, I spill them to their foes.
Spending time with me I shamelessly spy their fears.
Deeply competitive, I'm harshly suspicious.
Hard to get along with, I'm always bad tempered.
Never obliging, instead I oppose and cause harm.
Not accepting surrender, I look further for strife.
Ill at ease with good advice, I'm hard to befriend.
I'm way over-sensitive and always vindictive.
High and mighty, I treat the holy as a threat.
Immensely passionate, I lust after youth.
Short on loyalty, I turn away from old friends.
Hot for new contacts, I do anything to show off.
I lack clairvoyance, yet take up the strain of pretense.
I have no compassion, yet I'm quick to blame trusting friends.
I have little learning and I'm always guessing.
With no religious knowledge, I always suspect the worst.
Addicted to partisanship, I can't stand anyone else.
Habitually jealous, I make too much or little of others.
Unwilling to study, I devalue magnificent books.
Not trusting lamas, despising oral tradition—I'm unteachable.
I don't explain scriptures, falsely set on my own views.
I don't purify perception, I teach conflict and confusion.
I never honestly denounce unvirtuous actions.
I deviously critique all enlightening eloquence.
I never feel shame about what is really shameful.
And I'm wrongly ashamed of what is blameless good.
I don't accomplish even a single good deed—
I'm so busy doing everything improper.

Stomp! Stomp on this lethal thinker's head!
Annihilate my enemy self-killer heart!

These verses elaborate the ongoing dangers of self-obsession
and underline our need for transcendent wisdom. Once we have

faced the karmic consequences inflicted by the demon of self-addiction, we embrace all adversity as expiation of our bad deeds formerly committed under the demon's spell. We then become motivated to cultivate the wisdom that is most powerfully represented by Yamantaka, the Death Exterminator. We summon him with total determination, to come to us at once and free us from our demon of self-preoccupation. We implore him to kill our real innermost enemy, who defeats us by masquerading as our self and then constantly kills our natural life of freedom and happiness. These self-critical sections of the *Blade Wheel* alert us to the way we behave under the spell of this fiend; thus they empower our resolve to break free of it. They are utterly appropriate to think over during our night here in the Cool Grove Charnel Ground, sacred place of the great adepts.

Now let's take a break from Yamantaka's purification and rest for tomorrow's death and rebirth climb up and over the Drolma La, the pass of Mother Tara.

TAD

I am getting more accustomed to Tenzin's overload method and to the heavy fare of the *Blade Wheel*. He says he's planting seeds and not to worry if we feel we're not retaining everything right away, and slogging away in the shadow of Kailash makes such intense procedures seem plausible. Then just as it all gets too much for me, she reappears and I set my load upon her massive, snowy shoulders.

Kailash is a secret, hidden in plain sight. For a man it can be a woman; for a woman, a man. Unless we have had too much of the opposite sex and then it can be the sex we are. Unless we have had too much of ourselves, and then it can merely be the perfect mountain. Like the one Cézanne painted as obsessively as his cronies did their lovers.

"But how far must we travel to untrain our eyes that we might behold such a blazingly obvious sight?" I wonder, bushwhacking along a crumbling slope—slipping and catching the edge of my boots on the jagged, ragged terrain. Cézanne had to paint differently to prove that he saw differently, and vice versa. "And how soon will we forget the blazingly obvious secret?" I ask aloud of the geological proof of cubism blazing in rudimentary geometric glory. Suddenly I remember, with such clarity that tears glaze my eyes, all the times I've said, "I love you. I will never stop loving you," only to lose the love. Not stop loving, no. But lose it.

"But I will never cease to love you," I tell Kailash just over my shoulder, certain enough that I'd marry the mountain if I could. But I can't. I'm a man, this is a mountain. How can a man marry a mountain? I wonder, feeling foolish suddenly, catching sight of familiar-looking human beings below. The answer comes quite simply: by holding the mountain first in your heart.

CHAPTER THIRTEEN

Tara Pass

TAD

*S*tars in the morning are like snowflakes in June. They're ludicrous, gorgeous, and cannot last. A small collection hangs off Manjushri like diamonds on a toad. It really is remarkably ugly, this rubble heap—like a sugar-dusted, hemispheric piece of burned whole wheat toast, chunky-peanut-butter smeared, with nails sticking out of it. The spikes are ground-down turrets of rock, so the mountain is interesting, and important. Indeed, Manjushri is a wisdom-keeper deity with a stick, important to Tibetans and Zen Buddhists. The stick comes in when practice becomes too placid. Whack! So the evolutionary

217

alternatives of heaven on earth, Kailash, and the wake-up call of pain, Manjushri, are side by side, illuminating each other, providing cognitive dissonance even at the edge of the world.

I'm having trouble eating much this morning. Packing my bag is vaguely reassuring. It's become routine and, I realize, such discipline is the backbone of troupes the world over, roving Shakespeareans or murdering contras. What are we? A hybrid, perhaps. Today we're going over Droma La, to assassinate our sins and purge the palimpsests of our souls. And the only way to accomplish this is to start walking again.

One good thing that has happened up here, while I'm busting apart, step by step, over little stones and big ones: I promise the universe something. Up here, I swear it on the least perfect face of Kailash. Sure, I've momentarily defeated vanity, competitiveness, and the laziness that robs me of realizing the world without putting my own agenda first and foremost. And what do I promise? Well, back up a bit.

Have you ever awakened in the hospital or rehab or jail? Or in the arms of a person you don't love and are ashamed to have ever touched in the first place? Right now I wake up here on this trail, a mucus and tear-streaked mess, promising all the people I do love, and even those I don't love, that it will be different. That I will be different, not so blind and self-centered and stupid. Rather I will turn and learn from the *Blade Wheel.* Nor will I only avoid the stupidity of commission, but that of omission, too. It's what they call mindfulness, which is the realization that life is a ten-board chess match—and every move does matter. Especially the moves that don't seem to matter, the ones in which you're thinking, "Oh, I don't really know where to move—so I guess I'll just move this pawn somewhere unimportant." And with that lack of respect for your own incredible potential, you start a downward evolutionary spiral, diddling about, fucking instead of making love. Now I start promising the universe that I will think and act differently if I make it up and over and down and back to home, wherever or whatever that is. I promise to try harder, to do what? To take the bodhisattva vow for the sake of all sentient beings?

Believe it or don't, but this seems a very real option up here. Very sensible. And not even a religious choice. No, a rational, logical one—as Tenzin would say—indeed, a scientific choice. For it's become completely apparent that life simply doesn't work the way it's supposed to. Up here I'm no longer so anxious to defend my place in the world. I'm more willing to admit that my life is largely a sham.

Getting and spending, chasing and seldom catching, falling in love and making more babies in order to live happily ever. But it doesn't happen, does it? Because life sucks. Oh, it's hilarious too, but basically it sucks, or blows. Or just breathes heavy and hangs up.

So what do you do about it? Well, why am I crying my eyes out? It's about all the missed opportunities to love and be loved. About things I stole, or borrowed and broke and snuck back to make it look like they broke there all by themselves. About jealousy and duplicity, about lies I told, about deals I made, about bad stuff done so I could feel good. But it doesn't feel good, now, does it? No, so why don't I start doing what feels good? But what *is* that? Mindfulness, of course.

The *Blade Wheel* says: Give up false friends, selfish plans, appetite's four-star menu. The freedom and happiness you were looking for all along will be the result. How? Keep your ears open, eyes open, heart open. Don't take, give. Don't hide, reveal. Don't horde, share! And keep walking. Keep walking and keep weeping.

Because the world takes over in the world. And it will take over again. Right now I'm out of it, mourning for it, dying at the thought of it—but I know when I come down from the mountain it will seduce me again. So what in the devil's name should I do? There's only one way out of the minefield of karma, and that's over it, through it. On with it.

Below, the slab and crag and cairn-dotted graveyard is gone. The trail swerves north, around a switchback over the steepest terrain yet. With dried mud and loaf-sized rocks chinking under my stick, the day explosively bright, through a croquet course of boulders I click, click along, keeping time with a mantra. Companions toil ahead and behind as, over the brow of the skull-like hill, come nomads and yaks, grinding toward me at twice our speed; as always, pushing cheer before them like song before a singer.

I'm weaving now. The mantra is too complicated, so I go to ground zero, *"Om mani padme hum,"* slowly, slow as my feet are slow. For I want so badly to sit down, or lie down, or wake up and already be down. Except that I know I won't have the strength to stand. *Om mani padme hum* holds me on my feet, barely. That and my stick, coming down on the first syllable of *mani.* With Kailash to the right, laid out long as a skeleton, a skull-pyramid for a head, draped in petticoats of white snow and black rock, the proverbial nun rolling down a hill.

I can't go on anymore. Beckett laughs from the coffin. "I can't go on . . . I'll go on," but laughing will topple me, if I actually laugh. So it's silent laughter in concert with pain. I cease to walk, truly, one foot cannot pass the other, can only draw even and wait for my stick to swing up and past, for the mantra to begin again. But as I attempt a basic step, it breaks in half. For once I don't fight it, I let it break to the gait of a wedding march. Never marched in my wedding. If I do it again, ever, I must remember to march.

Just off to the left, in front of a flat-faced boulder, a mountain goat appears, flicking her sweet tail, abruptly pulling her chewing head up from grass. She's as surprised to see me as I am to see her, cross-eyed with surprise in fact, and she blinks with such outraged innocence that I nearly laugh aloud. Unable to take my eyes from her, I fumble for my camera, blinking once, only to look up and find her gone. But I'm stubborn—seeing is believing, right? "Jesus Christ! Where did she go?" Now I'm turning slowly and completely around, like Inspector Clouseau looking for the hat that is on his head—when suddenly the image of these mountain-goat eyes matches up with a set of human eyes that have been infuriating me for too long. They're one and the same. Bingo! But how could she? How dare she? I'm thunderstruck, trying to blame her even as I hear her flat, nasal voice admonishing: "But I didn't do it, darling . . . you did."

The yaks stream past, their handlers whispering endearments

to them. I follow, mumbling to myself in amazement, limping along in my half step. There's such a short way to go, such a short way, but with a single hallucination I've broken my own heart. So it's *Om mani padme hum, Om mani padme hum,* pulling in sight of the thronging nomads singing, *"La la so gyaltso so!"* around the great stone into which some other animals melted. Some blessed jackals before the blinking eyes of Gotsangba a thousand years ago. Maybe that was Tara I just saw as a mountain goat—not some North American ghost! Does it matter? Look at them! Prostrating, praying, singing, throwing up their arms, falling down on their knees, droning out doggerels of praise. La! So-so-so-so!

But with our group it's not a song that greets you at the top of Drolma La, it's more a sweet, collective sigh. A sigh that declares: "There! You've made it! All the way up the mountain of death. Dying all this way—to truly come alive!" I throw my pack down and fall beside a rock and do nothing but smile and breathe and dry my eyes, as Tenzin slowly pulls into view. Somehow I summon the professionalism to take his picture, with a high white sliver of a moon directly over his head.

Soon we're all taking pictures, congratulatory group pictures. It feels stupid. Vain, self-conscious, and stupid. Between nomad groups I circle the great rock matted with prayers and hairs and teeth shoved into crevices. I take out a lock of red hair and shove it in with the rest for a dear friend. The second time round I place my head to the stone, *Om mani padme hum.* The third time round I take out my prayer flag and secure it to an outrigger rock at a right angle to the great rope of flags. From my passport case I take a color photo of my baby, and using the corkscrew on my Swiss Army knife to puncture a hole at the top of the picture, tie it with a torn piece of cloth to the prayer flag hanging off the great mast. Stepping back, I take a picture of the picture of Anna dancing in the wind atop the holiest spot in Tibet.

I'm called away with an invitation to a stone soup ceremony assembled on near flat ground. Behind me is the glacier, to my left is Tenzin, behind him the climb we've just made, beyond it is Manjushri looking like a Bowery bum alongside royal Kailash. Straight ahead is a pile of rocks denoting the true top of Drolma

La, we're actually sitting on top of the ear of Drolma La. To my right is the southwesterly trail down.

We've gathered in a circle, Tenzin humming in Tibetan. He's collected all the food and tools, now he's cutting and blessing. Passing into open hands various nuts and cheeses, pastrami, apricots, apples, Power Bars, crackers, Slim Jims, and a variety of water-laced drinks. Hungry as I am, the most remarkable sight of all is the sky. World War II movies involving aerial battles are the closest comparison, B-52s surrounded with flak bombs bursting in air, those huge hanging sheets, clouds like blown-to-bits pillows with feathers hanging in space.

I come back to earth to find Lobsang has joined us, and my nightmare as well. A brown bottle of port appears in Richard's hand—a good one, and plastic cups into which the syrupy dark liquid hurriedly sloshes. I feel sucker-punched at the sight of it and look to James, who stares back at me with an absolutely blank face. He politely refuses, as every one else grabs a cup but me.

"Just a taste, a ceremonial offering," Tenzin says, holding the cup before me.

"No thanks," I return, feeling my heart do flip-flops in my chest.

"Come on, Tad," Tenzin chides, smiling, "it's a cele*bra*tion."

"No thank you," I answer, as my hands, starting to shake and tingle, flip together in my lap.

"Just a drop!"

I try not to raise my voice, repeating: "No thank you."

"Suit yourself." Tenzin pours a little port in his hand and splashes it on my forehead.

I close my eyes and the liquor misses them. Its hot perfume cannot be avoided, however, as it congeals in a single brown tear and rolls down the edge of my nose. I feel it trembling there, trembling where my nostrils cannot help but drink in its vapor. I know it's just my body of this life that's trembling and I demand that the trembling cease. I fail in this, and as I hold my breath, the drop falls to the stones below. A chill runs over me, and wiping my face to hide whatever tale it might tell, I shiver with a secret triumph. No matter what else may befall me in Holy Tibet, I've had connoisseur alcohol splashed on my face and did not catch it on my tongue.

Still stunned, I chew tasteless food and smile vacantly into talking faces, perhaps even mouthing a few vacuous phrases before wandering to the edge of the vast boulder field. Glacial cliffs, directly across an abrupt crevasse and less than a mile to the east, glisten liquidly lustrous. Inwardly, I escape across this expanse into unbelievably bright blankets of deep, cold snow. An imperfection in the wind-blown surface catches my eye as, shading the glare with my hand, I make out tracks that meander from one edge toward another, disappearing before they arrive. The tracks are large, obviously, and close together. I secretly cherish the possibility — fantastic as it seems — of snow leopard or Yeti. With my camera's close-up lense for binoculars I scan the cliffs, holding my breath for clarity. I call over Jock and Lobsang. "Have you ever seen Yeti?" I ask Lobsang, who regards me like a bartender asked for milk.

"Many years ago, maybe fifteen, two Frenchmen try to go cross Himalaya in balloon. I work for them. They like you and Jay — very friendly with Sherpa. One morning before hike one ask me, 'Lobsang, you ever see Yeti?'

"And I say to him, 'I been on Himalaya mountain all over Tibet and Nepal all my life and I never see Yeti. I don't think there is Yeti!'

"So we break camp and I am walking back to river to splash face, when right in front of me is huge monkey-man with fur on him, jumping up on top of rock, making signs like I better go away. Then I hear people yelling. I turn, and they are motioning to cameras — I look and on my chest I have camera. Aye yi! Then I look up and Yeti is gone! I go to rock — no tracks anywhere near. But others see it, too! So have I seen Yeti? Yes, on the day I say 'There is no Yeti,' I see Yeti! But those tracks are no Yeti," Lobsang says, examining the ridge. "Maybe snow leopard, maybe blue sheep. Nothing else come up this high."

"Have you seen snow leopard?"

"Yes. I worked many times for *National Geographic.* For snow leopard we have three expeditions. We catch snow leopard on two."

"You caught snow leopards?"

"In traps—then drugged, then released. One time snow leopard come awake, we are introduced. Wake up very fast."

Jock and I are in stitches. Lobsang is laughing too, but almost without breathing, only smiling at the memory and at our reaction to it.

Lobsang is looking across the crevasse, then back to the Drolma La stone, now he points past it to the side we came up. "Very clear—very few clouds! Good luck for us—this weather. Climb is not so very easy." He says, smiling at me with humor-laced seriousness, "But no snow! Little wind! All the storms are here." He taps his head. "The mountain, it is very sunny. Very lucky."

I try to let go into the sunshine, into "very lucky," into the best in us. It's hard going. Tenzin calls us to gather round after the feast, to whirl the blade wheel, here, where we are to be reborn, where the illusion of self is to die. As he pulls the long, yellow-robed Tibetan book from the belly pouch of his fleece, I see before me a man whipped by irrational winds. Even so, he is a guardian of perfection; even so, in his hands rests a faultless document of mind. Yet I am tempted to dismiss it, hate it even. So very tempted.

TENZIN

Congratulations one and all! This worst climb of the journey was not so difficult, it seemed somehow easier than the lower, though longer, hikes. There was no way to think about it, no time to pay attention to anyone or anything. I didn't worry about any of you. I knew you would make it. We have taken our genetic lineage and the coarse bodies we adopted from our ancestors, put them to the test, and hopefully lightened all their burdens. I feel that Kailash must reach back through time to lighten our forebears' load even in the past, as well as reach into their evolutionary situations whatever they are now and give them an invisible lift. As I felt heavier step after step, as I rose up the seemingly crestless slope, I imagined the heaviness to be the evolutionary gravity of all these beings, all my genetic and evolutionary relatives. I hope our ordeal has brought the maximum benefit to infinite beings.

Anyway, we all made it up here. Lobsang came over to me with a real sense of wonder, marveling at the beautiful sunny weather at the top of the pass. He confessed he had been thinking me more crazy than the usual Westerner, since I had them haul that bundle of firewood in the truck and on the yaks since way back near Nepal, to make the fire offering on the north face. They couldn't imagine what I thought I was doing. However, he has been on this pass numerous times in all parts of the summer season when it is accessible, and he had never before failed to experience a sudden blizzard, gale force winds, or other wild weather. "That puja of yours must have been a good puja," he said, "somebody sure liked it!"

With that encouragement, on with the *Blade Wheel*.

The Triumph of Bliss-Void Intuition

> Ema! O Mighty Lord Yamantaka,
> Endowed with the Body of Truth
> Of the Blissful Lord who conquers
> This demon ghost of the self-habit instinct!
> Wield your fierce weapon, your smashing club,
> Your bliss-void intuition, wisdom of selflessness —
> Don't wait! Circle it three times around your head!

Once again we call to Manjushri, the apotheosis of the transcendent wisdom of selflessness in his most fierce Yamantaka form, representing the body of truth of all buddhas—for all buddhas are the same in ultimate reality. His awareness of reality is not just some dualistic cognition that he carries around in his head or something. His wisdom is his most real body, and he feels reality as his being, and in that sense also controls it, molding it to benefit all beings. He is therefore completely happy, completely liberated, effortlessly effecting other beings' happiness. Thus he is called Sugata, Blissful Lord. But when he interacts with us, who are afflicted by self-habits, afflicted by self-cherishing narcissism, he manifests this most terrible embodiment of his wisdom. Since we are imprisoned in narcissism, we are ourselves as if dead. Because we constrict our energy of life by opposing ourselves to the universe, he comes to kill death, to destroy our deadly habit of self-obsession.

Yamantaka comes to our rescue with his nine faces, his fierce black buffalo face, his bloodred face above that, his yellow Manjushri face above that, the blue, yellow, and red faces on the right, and the white, black, and gray faces on the left of his great horns with their blazing tips. His thirty-four arms hold many different kinds of weapons, and his sixteen legs on animals and birds and deities show the ultimacy of sixteen voids completely intertwined with all forms of life.

Using all these, he conquers the demon of the self-habit instinct. He conquers that identity of self that is like a ghost and a demon, it is not the real us, it is not our own buddha-being, not our own living happiness. We invite him to come and do this, and so, in a way, we are inviting our own transcendent wisdom. We are not asking to be annihilated, just to be liberated.

Our liberated happiness is itself the intuition of bliss and void indivisible, that things being void and free by nature are intrinsically blissful. The more we realize that, the more our understanding of the voidness of things becomes a melting into orgasmic bliss in the experience of cosmic union. Voidness is not a neutral dead zone but a door to bliss and to release. It is the most marvelous thing. It smashes every atom, every false boundary or isolating individuation. This bliss-void intuition is the highest way of looking at the wisdom of selflessness. Whirling it around his head like a club, this archetype deity crushes the self-preoccupation habit.

> With your great ferocity please liberate this enemy;
> With your great compassion save us from evolution.
> Pray triumph once and for all over this self-habit.

Here liberate means kill the enemy that is my heart-killer, my self-habit. My self-habit is my jailer, keeping me from really being new, fresh, live, and joyous. But the jailer is just as much a prisoner. A jailer has to stay outside the prison to make sure the prisoner stays inside. So the self-habit isn't having much fun either, sitting around making sure you don't realize selflessness. The self-habit would actually have a much better time being defeated, for that same deluded energy would suddenly realize its delusion and rebound in bliss.

So liberate the enemy, get rid of this jailer, break me free from the prison, and liberate the jailer too.

With your great compassion save us from negative evolution, from negative karma, from foolish actions that perpetuate the wheel of desire. Please, definitively triumph over this self! Conquer my negative self, my confused and self-absolutizing, megalomaniac self. Great compassion is the natural reflex of beings that have wisdom, since they feel that they are the same as others who suffer. Yamantaka doesn't see himself as apart from us. Yamantaka adopts that form to show us the way to break through our isolation.

> All of the sufferings of beings in the life-cycle
> Pray heap them up on this self-habit of mine.
> All others' addictions to all five poisons,
> Pray heap them all on my self-addicted demon.

Take all the miseries, not only mine, but those of all beings, and just make a big pile of them on top of my self-habit. Let my self-habit be the sacrifice. Let my self-habit be the crucified, taking the sins and all sufferings of all other beings upon it. Let that liberate me, the real, relative, and selfless me.

Here, my self-preoccupation is destroying me, so hand it all the sufferings of all beings—all the bad thoughts, all the addictions, all the confusions, the five poisons of delusion, lust, hatred, pride, and envy—and heap them on it. This is a homeopathic teaching, using poison to conquer poison.

I rationally recognize this self-concern habit
As undoubtedly the root of all evil,
Since I still am somewhat commanded by its speech,
Pray, destroy this deeply habitual instinct for self!

I ask Yamantaka to go into my unconscious, into the DNA of my spiritual makeup, to go in there with all thirty-four of his weapons and instruments, and transform this voice that I identify as my own, this voice of self-concern. Free me from it, O Yamantaka!

Let all responsibility fall on this false identity!
I meditate on the kindness of all other beings!
I take upon myself all that is unwanted by others!
I dedicate all my virtues to others!

Now I have seen my self-habit causing me to do greedy things, to do hateful things, to do stingy, prideful, and fanatical things all through my different lives. My self-preoccupation habit must take full responsibility, for it always tells me: "Oh, now I must do this. Now I must do that." I obeyed it because I thought it was my own voice telling me what to do. But I now see it as the root of all evil, and I meditate on the kindness of all other beings. I see that all other beings are trying to be kind to me, that they have no harmfulness toward me, all the harmfulness is stimulated by our self-habits. I will take upon myself all that is unwanted by others. I dedicate all my virtues to all beings.

This is the complete reversal of the self-cherishing, by other-cherishing. The relative antidote to self-concern is other-concern. This is the great bodhisattva exchange of self and other, the meditation of turning the self inside out. It is the key to real happiness, this forgetting about our own desires and our self-preoccupation and becoming preoccupied with others and their well-being.

Thus taking on myself all sins of body, speech, and mind,
Done by others in the past, present, and the future,

Like the peacock with its beauty-sheen of poison,
May addictions transmute into enlightenment!

Giving my virtues to all beings as medicine,
May they be cured like crows healed from poison!
Upholding the life of liberation of all beings,
May I attain enlightenment as the Happy Lord!

Because of my vow to turn the self inside out in the activated spirit of enlightenment, I'm going to be able to use all of the sins, all of the sufferings, all of the poisonings of all the other beings, just as a peacock uses poison for nourishment and beauty, as was mentioned in the first verses of the *Blade Wheel.* These poisons will bring me the supreme beauty of enlightenment. Here we see a trace of the Wheel of Superbliss that turns within the mountain, the beauty of the poisons transmuted by wisdom into enlightenment.

I will swiftly become a lord of bliss—a Sugata—and will overflow with that happiness for others as a stream of medicine that will heal them.

So even this *Blade Wheel* of mind reform and penance has become a happy thing. It's beyond having to bear the heavy wheel of karma, and we're moving into the visionary level. So now we must move on down to camp seven, leaving our triumph and our happiness as offerings to all beings here on top of Drolma La.

TAD

Socrates said that the true and the good are the same, that all people will eventually choose virtue over sin because in the end virtue is accompanied by greater pleasure. The blade wheel turns on much the same logic: When we realize that chasing after pleasure brings displeasure, we cease in this pursuit and reverse the spin, giving not taking. Only when selfishness is recognized as the breeding ground of pain do we cease to be drawn to selfish pursuits. It might be an intellectual exercise at first, like priming a siphon, because we believe it will then continue by itself, but the blade wheel does just that, spinning until the punishing razor becomes a haloed crown.

But when do we start doing it, this saintlike behavior? Right now? Yes, says the wheel weapon. Love thy neighbor. Like a spiritual Nike commercial . . . just do it. Just for now, I do. I love all these people, like them or not.

CHAPTER FOURTEEN

The Dakini Secret Path

TAD

*A*fter conquering the Drolma La, we stagger down the long back slope, moving round the northeast skirts of the mountain, scrambling endlessly downward over rock scree, boulders etched with lichen graffiti, and ice fields.

Tenzin is reading and commenting upon the *Blade Wheel* almost to the degree that it eclipses the mountain. Which, to my mind, is too aggressive. We did not enlist to be the bodhisattvas of this age! I certainly doubt that Valerie and Leopoldo planned on saving the universe for their vacation. Myself, I never said that I'd stake my sanity on this experience. But something is blinking in the memory banks as I try to get myself off the hook. Suddenly I remember that I most certainly did agree to face death at every level, and walk through philosophical fire, if need be, circling the holy mountain. Tenzin had warned me in his roughshod office—more than once—that I'd be up against it. So here I am. Up against it. The others are in safer positions, but me, I'm realistically afraid. I'm alone up here trying to loosen my scared-shitless hold on myself, with a one-eyed sorcerer splashing my addiction in my face while pretending he wants to liberate me and all other sentient beings! The trick is not to let my anger at the messenger lessen my recognition of the message.

We'll soon make camp at the northeast corner of the mountain. Not quite on the full eastern side, but an essential stop just the same. Ankles are wobbly and knees trembling from the pounding descent after the grueling climb, but I'm denying all that, flying down at high speed, disguising my hostility in furious joy.

Little do I realize that, somewhere on the rambling hillside, Jay and James are in a jam. We've gotten a bit spread out and turned around and—in a word—lost. Somewhere on the dusty hillside Jay turned his ankle mildly, and paranoia has set in. Jay doesn't have his sleeping bag in his day pack—isn't prepared for getting lost—and therefore doesn't dig the idea of camping beneath stars. He's feeling, well, abandoned. And wise old James has had his toes smashed by incoming boulders, on the descent. He's not entirely happy either or completely certain if it's up the valley we're headed or down. Jay has paid too much money to be turning his ankle without proper medical attention, to be hobbling along with a charming old man scratching his head wondering which way to camp. Jock's off taking pictures. Tenzin is undoubtedly midmantra somewhere, and Lobsang is probably unpacking yaks wherever it is we're supposed to be headed.

Oh, I wish I'd been there with my trusty Sony recorder running when the lonesome limping traveler finally spotted a guide. Jay went apeshit, howling like a baby jilted by his momma. It went on for ten white-hot minutes straight. Tenzin finally began gently slowing him down, saying: "Jay, you're going to regret this. Really, it's okay now. Really, get a grip. It's okay—I'm sorry things got a little loose, my fault if you like. A bit confusing, absolutely. But Jay—wait. Stop. Listen!" But Jay wasn't in a listening mode. Wasn't on a listening road. He was plain ballistic. Pain is pain and pain was him.

For me, the shadows lengthen on red-painted ridge tops. I hear the high howl of a dog and a shiver goes through me. I'm glad to see Richard kneeling on a crag, high and to the right of me. He's got a new delegation of stones for his collection. He's spread them out against a boulder and is photographing them, practically calling them by name. I hike up to meet him, amazed at how calm and happy he is.

"Wow," Richard says, looking out over meandering Zhong Chu at the brown and black hills behind the river bunching up like the folds in the neck of a Brahman bull. "I mean, Tad, does it ever hit you," he says as if we'd been in conversation for hours, "just how strange it's going to be to not be here?"

"Yeah," I answer. "As a matter of fact, I thought about that a lot on the way up."

"You did good up there," he said, cryptically. "Real good, I was proud of you. Sorry about—"

"It's fine, Rich," I say, cutting him off, knowing where he's going. "For you it's fine. For me it's not."

"And it'll never be fine for you?"

"Not anymore."

"Wow," he says.

I start to change the subject. "So, tell me something, Richard."

"OK," he laughs. "OK! I'll show you my paintings," he says as if they were in his sister's underwear drawer.

"Jesus Christ—I don't know how you manage it—but you have got to be as self-centered as I am!"

"Of course, I am." He grabs my shoulders and looks me dead in the eye: "And we're supposed to be this way, Tad. They don't realize it yet, but they need us to be this way. We're the picture makers. Words, colors—not much difference really. One in books, one on canvas. We dream for them, Tad. They have nice apartments and nice cars and nice parties filled—they hope—with one, at most two, people like us."

"Cut the crap, Rich."

"It's not crap and you know it. You cut the crap, Tad. I know who and what you are, so you cut the crap, sonny boy. Because I'm a treasure finder. That's what I've always been—a terton! Look!" he says, throwing open his arms to his rock collection.

"I have a shell collection, myself," I say—stealing Steven Wright, "perhaps you've seen it. I keep them on all the beaches in the world."

"You are a treasure, my brother!" Richard sings out, stubbornly sticking with his subject. "And we are here at the holy mountain together. So don't underestimate this treasure finder, and don't underestimate yourself!"

"Lo lus," I say, which means in Tibetan something like: Of course you are correct, O great sage! "And you know where we are?"

"Of course, I do!" he shrieks, as we fall together into a low-grade chuckle. He's limping so I lend him my stick, since he knows where it is we are going.

But comic relief doesn't prevent my crash and burn. I've come down too fast. We hit the short, golden grass of the plain, and camp eventually grinds into sight, tents in a perfect row beside the Zhong Chu on a mossy sod. Even as perfection lies prepared, I fall into my tent and onto my bag, without even unlacing my boots. The tea bell rings, and rings again, and the dinner bell rings and I know I should be dragging myself up for *Blade Wheel* and yak fricassee.

But I think, "Fuck it," to myself.

"Wolfgang!" I yell, knowing whose methodology to trust.

"Yes, Tad—" he says from far away, then, "You OK?" he asks, politely unzipping my tent.

"I'm burnt. Do me a favor, tape the talk tonight?"

"Gladly," he says, "anything else you need?"

"A long nap. Thanks," I return, as he rezips me in.

Blade wheel turning. I'm trying to sleep through it, but I can't. There's a great haranguing in the mess tent. I'm half sleeping and half listening as darkness browns the gold of my tent. Jay is laughing through an extended apology, while complaining still — here and there — especially about his ankle. Suddenly I'm struck with the terrible need to play doctor.

"Wait a minute!" I yell, "wait a goddamn minute!"

My name is hurrahed from the mess tent. I can't keep a spaced-out smile from wrinkling my face, as finding my arnica and an Ace bandage, I fumble in to dinner.

Soon I'm seated on the bench, smearing arnica evenly and wrapping the Ace bandage loosely. Afterward I can't eat. Jay is laughing and wired, and suddenly I understand how irksome my being wired and laughing can be. My eyes are glued to a corner of the tent. Someone is asking me when I took Diamox last. Then there is a glass of water before me and a white pill. "Please . . . this one's on me."

TENZIN

Now we're camped where the secret yogini path emerges from the north face of the mountain. Not quite on the full eastern side. We're almost around, so we'll do the last verses of the *Blade Wheel* to ground ourselves.

Compassion and Creativity

Until I and father-mother beings
Attain enlightenment in the Akanishta heaven,
May all beings roaming through evolution in six realms
Embrace each other mutually as if one in mind!

What a beautiful prayer! Unusually, he refers to beings as "father-mother." The usual reference is to "mother beings," since we have been reborn infinite times and all beings have been our mother, since they also have been reborn infinite times: We have been in the womb of every one of them. You know this vision of compassion, of connectedness; we contemplated it in the System-

235

atic Path on the way to the mountain. But also every being has been our father; I must say, I enjoy that.

Akanishta heaven is the highest heaven at the top of the Brahma realm of pure form; it holds the ultimate buddha-mandalas and the pure buddhaverses also. It's at the boundary where mass becomes infinite, everything functions at the event horizon of the speed of light, all energy is available from here, whole worlds can be re-created by the enlightened mind. It's a vantage point from which this more coarse realm can be transfigured by compassion for the benefit of the beings within it. But until I achieve that, this prayer asks, may all beings who wander through evolution in the six realms of existence come to embrace each other mutually as if they were one being of one mind. And thus may they be loving and may they not discriminate between each other too much, may they not torment and harm each other too much. A lovely prayer.

> May I enter the three lower realms
> For the sake of even a single being;
> May I end the suffering of those three realms,
> Not shirking the way of the spiritual heroes!

Here is the bodhisattva vow in its deep and grim and powerfully moving form. The bodhisattva prays to give up her blissful lives in the heavens and enter into the hells so vividly described in the ancient sutras: the icy hells, the molten iron hells, the lonely hells, the crushing hells, the cutting hells. Then there are the ghostly pretan realms where beings suffer from unsatisfied craving and frustration, and the animal realms where they suffer from stupidity and violence. I as a bodhisattva am willing and ready to go to them even to help one single being become free. And may I end the suffering of all beings in those three realms, not shrinking from the conduct of the great spiritual heroes.

> As soon as I place the concept of mentor
> On the demon guardians of hell,
> May their weapons become a rain of flowers
> And all hells harmless, cooled by joy!

236

When we do go down to those hells, we're tortured by the demons of the hells, creatures created by our own evolutionary actions, who inflict unspeakable violence upon us. Such are hells. But the demons who do this are not real, independently malevolent creatures, but rather figments of our own paranoia. We must realize that these beings are teaching us by torturing us; we place the concept of mentor on them, thinking of them as our spiritual teachers and benefactors. When we see them that way, our paranoia is short-circuited and instantly their weapons become a rain of flowers.

Then all the other beings around us in the hells become safe and secure and hell is transformed into heaven.

> May hell-beings gain magic powers to save themselves,
> Obtain rebirth among humans and gods,
> Conceive the precious spirit of enlightenment,
> Feel grateful to me, seek the Dharma-teachings,
> And, using me as mentor, put them into practice!

After freeing the hell-beings from their agonies, I pray that they develop the knowledge and magical powers needed to save themselves in the future, obtaining rebirth among humans and gods and conceiving the special will to become a buddha for the sake of all beings. I pray that they then will feel grateful to me, which is not important for me but for them, because that gratitude can inspire them to turn to the Dharma. I pray that they will understand it well enough to use me as mentor and so be able to put into practice in their lives whatever I have taught them.

> Then may all beings of the high estates
> Meditate selflessness just as I do,
> Avoid extremes of unenlightened living or transcending,
> And recognize their own reality as equanimity!

Then may all beings of the highest estates—the gods, the titans, and the humans—all meditate on selflessness, just as I do. May they avoid the extremes of either routine, unenlightened life or dualistic transcendence into a lifeless absolute, recognizing their own reality as equanimity itself. In other words, may they avoid both resigning themselves to reacting to immediate circumstances in life and getting hung up in some frantic search for a transcendent realm of escape from the universe. May they neither attempt to escape life entirely, like ascetics and gods of the formless realms, nor get caught up in merely drifting along complacently, as the desire-and-form-realm gods tend to do. May they instead recognize their own reality as the totally indivisible nonduality of ultimate and relative and thereby become buddhas.

This is very profound. This is what differentiates buddhahood from theistic visions of the highest deity, a transcendent being who is outside the world and beyond it and yet somehow inexplicably reaches into it. That illogical possibility that there is a nonrelative, absolute being is transcended in Buddhist philosophy by the concept of nonduality, that a buddha is a being who is infinitely present everywhere in the universe and yet simultaneously totally liberated by being infinite. A buddha is therefore neither at the extreme of just living totally relative, nor at that of just transcending and being totally absolute, but incorporates both in perfect equanimity. This is inconceivable in one way, but it is experiential, livable, just as, for example, we can see logically that infinity—the indivisible body of truth of all buddhas—must be here in the immediate situation, because if this circumstance were separate from infinity, then infinity would not be infinite. When we understand that, our interconnectedness with all things becomes possible. We can actually feel that we are all things, simultaneous with being normally present to them in the most helpful, effective possible way. So this kind of nonduality, like a tightrope walker balancing the extremes of living and transcending, knowing the grace of such blissful equanimity, this is the central way.

> So realizing, this enemy will be conquered!
> So doing, habitual thought will be overcome!
> Since free bliss intuition intensifies selflessness,
> Why not then enjoy the buddha-forms,
> The causal beatific body and its resultant emanations?

When all beings in the highest estates realize this, the enemy of self-obsession will be conquered. Remember that the enemy not only makes us worldly, greedy, and grabby. The enemy also makes us spiritually selfish, it deceives us into thinking that there's some place outside the universe it can help us escape to, that we can hide from consequences by getting out of the universe and attaining an absolute nirvana. When the self-addiction enemy thus deceives us, leading us into mistaking a sustained state of deadened trance for liberation, it cheats the world of our compassion and cheats us of blissful interactions with all beings. In fact, it prevents us from becoming enlightened, delays for eons our becoming fully present and fully liberated.

It takes nonduality to beat the enemy, to overcome the habitual thinking of self-preoccupation. Once I realize total nonduality, I can enjoy my infinite unity with all beings as my beatific body of release, and I can simultaneously reflect my bliss as emanations perceivable by those beings, in order to alert them to their deepest reality and exalt them in its joy, manifesting whatsoever is needed to whomsoever.

> *Kyay!* All those things are relativities,
> They occur relative to cause and condition,
> Depend on relationality, lack self-sufficiency,
> Change there, change here, false as magic,
> Reflections appearing like a whirling firebrand!

After these prayers Dharmarakshita goes on to some philosophical reflections on the nature of reality, unpacking this deep, inconceivable nonduality. He says *"Kyay!"* which is like saying "Wow!" It's all like a whirling firebrand that gives the appearance of a solid circle of fire. All these things are relativities, meaning that all things exist only in relation to each other without any intrinsic reality of their own. There are beings and things, buddhas and ordinary beings, heavens and hells, and they are all simply relativities, they occur relative to cause and condition, they depend upon relationality, they lack self-sufficiency. And they have changes, here and there, as false as magic. All are like reflections appearing in a mirror. This is the dreamlike vision of the universe, of all things being like hallucinations, like mirror reflections. The surface of the mirror is the absolute voidness of all things. Within that surface teem the reflections of things and persons and events and happenings and the flow of time, but they're no more real than the ring of fire appearing in the air when a torch or flashlight is whirled around. This ring is unreal, merely an optical illusion, and that's the way all things are.

> Life lacks essence, like a hollow reed,
> Its span is ephemeral like a bubble,
> Like mist it dissolves when examined.
> It has beauty only from afar like a mirage!
> Like a mirror image, it seems so real!
> Like clouds and fog it seems so present!

The illusory nature of life becomes apparent. You realize yourself to be like a person who is dreaming yourself consciously, and that is why, as a buddha, as an enlightened being, you have such tremendous power. You can do magic. You can fly. You can change shapes of things for the benefit of other beings. You have all these different abilities. But the one ability you do not have is you cannot change the internal feeling of others. You cannot enlighten others by invading their minds. If they are sitting there suffering and feeling separated from the universe, you can't overcome their state just because you can feel their misery. Only their own understanding can liberate them. You have to appear to them as a separate being and get them to understand that they are one with the universe. That way they can come out of their fear and their terror and their suffering. But they have to do that themselves, you have no power to do that for them. In order for them to understand the dreamlike nature of the world you have to teach them to see for themselves. You have to appeal to their understanding. It's the only way you can do it.

> This enemy killer-self also is like that,
> It seems so existent, yet never so discovered!

It seems so really true, yet no way found as real!
It seems so apparent, beyond reification and denial;
Then how real could the wheel of evolution be?

Finally, Dharmarakshita himself offers us the way out of total enchainment in the wheel of evolutionary action. Remember we learned first how not to dodge the blows of the blade wheel of our own past evolutionary actions. Then we gained the insight that the enemy of self-preoccupation was the cause of our subjection to such suffering. Then we took hold of the spinning wheel and directed its blades against the enemy self-preoccupation, letting it be shredded by its own negative actions; thus we tasted freedom from its dictates and the bliss of other-preoccupation. Here, we think back about how our enemy killer-self seemed so truly existent, yet was never discovered when we carefully searched for it. When you try to experience the real self, you can't experience it, you can't find it. It seems so existent, so solid, so powerful, yet it never can be experienced as really solid and powerful. "It seems so really true, yet in no way is found as real." It seems so apparent, self-evident so beyond reification and denial; but since something that seemed so self-evident turned out not to be real, merely dreamlike, how real could the wheel of karmic evolution itself be? Here the freedom made possible by voidness loosens the chain of evolution and lets us out of the prison of fatalistic determinism. We can aspire to the real freedom of buddhahood, where our investment in the causal processes through which we can relate to other dreamlike beings is made from the point of view of voluntary, compassionate, blissful participation.

TAD

Mantras, Tantras! How can we possibly manage all of these complexities? How about something solid? Like the cliffs we just descended, which hide Kailash from view. I know that on the other side of those cliffs, west of the Dakini Secret Path, at the northernmost section of the inner kora, stand the remains of the original thirteen chortens built at the very base of the southern face of Kailash. These housed the ashes of masters of the Kagyu lineage — the school that produced Milarepa, his master, Marpa, and the Indian originator of the sect, Naropa. The chortens, like the monasteries themselves, were all destroyed by the Chinese. Since around 1980, however, Beijing has allowed rebuilding and worship to resume. The question is: Why?

One answer is money, tourist money and pilgrim money being the same color. Another answer is public relations. Although the atrocities of the 1970s are still well-maintained blind spots in the eyes of Western nations, token penance on the part of the Chinese does help oil the wheels of foreign trade. Lastly, it's pretty well accepted that China's all-out war against Buddhism in Tibet failed. Starvation, beatings, rapes, torture, public humiliations all back-fired, making martyrs of the stoic victims, whose Dharma remains a treasured bulwark. When guards hammered nails into the skulls of monks asking them, "Where is your God now?" they demonstrated complete ignorance of Buddhism, which credits no creator. The Dalai Lama's flight into an exile from which he might still make a mythic return only increases the magic and charisma of his personage.

Paradoxically, what has been more effective in defaming Buddhism is skeptical tolerance. Though this strategy has taken more than a generation to bring to its present state, the Tibetan youth in a Darchen classroom are clearly cut off from their Buddhist roots. In centuries past, monasteries provided the only school system. Now the invaders say the monks lied and tricked the people. Tibetans are told they are less attractive, less lucky, and less intelligent than their Chinese overlords. Told they should be grateful for the Chinese intervention that ended the feudal tyranny of monks over peasants. Told that after decades of attempting to purge the Buddhist superstitions, the Chinese have shown mercy. Old Tibetans are stubborn as mules; it has become clear they cannot be rehabilitated. Even so, the Chinese have pity upon these crude beasts, allowing "a last generation of dreamers" to mumble mantras and fall off to sleep clutching their worthless idols.

Now, by returning confiscated buddhas and *dorjes*, allowing the rebuilding of monasteries and the making of new tangkas, the Chinese seem to be giving the youth of Tibet a choice. You want to travel thousands of kilometers with your parents in an open truck? Mumble round a crumbling mountain stuck out in the middle of nowhere? Give up your place in line—so a smarter, more progressive Tibetan can grab it? You want to throw it all away for some sleepyhead of a Buddha? Go ahead! Be our guest! Run back to the dusty old monastery. You needn't sneak there in the night—no, no, go with your grandmother, in plain daylight, so we know who is serious about tomorrow, and who is running back to yesterday!

Smart Tibetans can have a better life! With hard study a young man or woman might graduate from a trade school, get a humble job, find romance at a disco or karaoke, drink real beer (not that goat-piss *chang* their grandfather makes). Good Tibetans may take a place in the greatest, most powerful nation in the world!

Even so, Tibetans seem to play both sides of the game.

During the dark days, "rehabilitated" Tibetans would protect political prisoners by pretending to beat them, smearing them with "rotten" food actually suitable for consumption, and humiliating the exhausted by "forcing them onto sticks" so they could rest during the day-long hate-fests. It was, and still is, an Orwellian world. Supposed friends could easily be spies, and apparent enemies, secret friends. Loyalties are ambiguous. Daily life is a subtle, subversive sport. So subtle, I wonder if the players themselves are completely aware of whose side they're on.

Take, for example, our drivers. Here are men who have risen to the top of a dangerous, glamorous, and highly paid profession. To succeed they learn when to bribe, and when to look down and defer, showing weakness—but not too much weakness, lest the bribe be doubled, and vulnerability invite attack. Sure, they hate the Chinese. But are they Buddhist? Or, if Nepali, perhaps Hindu? My instinct is that they are sympathetic to the Buddhist cause but remain, primarily, agnostic. Yes, they point out the Tibetan escape route near Saga, cut off by the Chinese. Yes, they know ten billion dollars' worth of timber cutting has denuded the great forests and worsened disastrous erosion. Yes, they know the lakes are being drained and mined. But do they pray for the return of His Holiness?

During Tenzin's passionate talks they remain stone-faced. Even when he speaks in their language, there is a guardedness, a neutrality that defies a reading, by design. Sure, the lovable driver took off his hat and tapped his forehead the instant "Kailassi" first came into sight. In a week's time I'll notice a rosary slyly clasped by one of the staff as he returns from a walk by the holy lake, a so-I-can-honestly-tell-my-mother look on his poker face. But what are the drivers doing now while we circumambulate Kailash? Drinking beer, hustling women, and playing cards? Or stealing out to the great Barka Plain at first light, kneeling down, and praying before Kailash? I have no idea.

CHAPTER FIFTEEN

Mila's Miracle Cave

TAD

When you're hungry at seventeen thousand feet, even powdered eggs have the charm of being yellow and steaming, with hot sauce, Baco-Bits, and a quarter teaspoon of black pepper thrown on. Ovaltine and coffee with whitener, and chapatis with jam and peanut butter; hot cereal and cold cereal, and even fire-braised bread—not so much toasted as smoked.

Tenzin and Wolfgang are talking Nietzsche. Wolfgang rhapsodizes about the brotherhood of the blue flower: when the young philosopher and company fell in with gypsy girls, drank great quantities of May wine, learned gypsy dances, and did their best to forget their large vocabularies for entire weeks at a time as they howled in the hills.

I bring up the anti-Semitic stuff. Tenzin sets the record straight: "Nietzsche was not an anti-Semite! Not in the least! It was his sister's husband who forged his name to those ridiculous manifestos. No, Nietzsche quite approved of Judaism. He said Europeans had two terrible addictions: alcohol and Christianity. The Jews he commended for having little to do with either. But Nietzsche was unique in his time and place for realizing that humanity is the best opportunity for evolving toward enlightenment.

"The launching pad! Kailash is a launching pad."

"Maybe! Tad . . . one moment please! So humanity can be transcended. This spaceship Earth has a very real mission. To achieve happiness for all beings! But Buddhism's evolutionary path is accomplished only through the royal realization of selflessness. If I ride out my bad karma I will free myself and wonderful things will occur for me, but to get there I have to overcome 'me'!"

"It's kind of like ordering a banquet dinner," I put it, "and then realizing that you're not hungry, and would rather give it to others who are."

"Something like that. I must see through the self. Know it to be a fake. A movie! A play! A charade!"

"Plato's cave."

"But Plato thought there was a real place throwing unreal shadows," Tenzin says. "It's all shadows. The whole shooting match is shadows." Lobsang enters the mess tent. "Please, we pack tents now. A few bags are not yet complete."

"Who hasn't packed their bags?" Jock demands. "Jaaay? . . . Taaad?"

The two of us leap to our feet, smiling guiltily, and run to get ready. Milarepa Gompa is on the schedule today. Maybe we'll even get far enough away from Kailash to see it again.

We move on to the last valley, down the last plain, knowing that Kailash will come back to us again only if we strive with feet through the valley cut by the Zhong Chu. It's a flat little groove about a half a mile wide, between the eastern ridge hung in shade and the western ridge's speckled sunlight. Since yesterday a bluff above the river has been powder-puffed with snow, already browning through with the first heat of morning. The valley itself twists and shifts, rolls and pitches like waves out in the middle of the ocean, except the earth does in a thousand years what the water does in a minute. With earth the waves are even larger, even more ponderous, but pitched nonetheless and graded with a lovely heaving rhythm; a land like molasses.

We're walking in the footsteps of saints, where grace can be borrowed for entire seconds on end. Can I take it with me? Can I take Kailash with me?

But you already have. Leave off the "me," say it as a Minnesotan would: *Can I take Kailash with?*

Now lose the "I." And don't ask. Declare: *Take Kailash with.*

Do you need to 'take' it? It's always here: *Kailash with.*

And now most simply: *With Kailash.*

There. It's nowhere in sight and yet it's in your heart this very second and always just around the corner.

This valley is the afterglow following the passion of Drolma La; it proceeds with ascetic plainness, the gait of a monk. The ridges on our side of the river are snowless; across the river they have snow. Each, a different changing character: the river itself, every nomad, every yak, every dog, and yet we all blend in the valley, this bloodless whirling together of selflessness.

The ridge this side of the river slithers down the hills, as the whole valley starts vibrating like a pointillist painting. Millions of rocks are trembling, and out of the trembling a castle takes shape, a low rectangular mirage festooned with prayer flags, real ones. So this is a monastery, not a mirage, Milarepa's miracle rock monastery, to be exact. The hills behind it are honeycombed with retreat caves.

Sometimes in moments of arrogance I will estimate that I've written a thousand songs, since this was my most furious practice between the ages of fifteen and thirty. In the platonic sense, I have written only one. But my hero, Milarepa, is more accurately described as the singer of a hundred thousand songs. The man retreated from civilization completely, and tuned his meditation as

Shakespeare tuned his tongue. So when hunters, maidens, thieves, or monsters barged into his cave, how did this most remarkable man respond? Why, of course, with humanity's most memorable speech—song! Though he was "Cinderfella" as a boy, a murdering warlock as a youth, a miserable wretch through young manhood, still the awful joke of his name—good news—came true. He was Orpheus. He was the hero with a thousand faces, the singer of one hundred thousand songs.

There is no fanfare here at this monastery. No monks either. The hillside is bare, except of stones, but the light here in this valley, it's like *the last light of day* unabatingly shining all day long. That twilight intensity is constant here.

Suddenly I'm reminded that it is Tenzin who brought me to Milarepa and, therefore, to Marpa. Eventually I even built a wall or two on Thurman ground, was accepted in and then expelled from the magic house. It all boiled over one night in my senior year, when I stalked over to the sprawling apartment, ranting, raving, unwilling and finally unable to stop. I grabbed Tenzin and tried to lift him, six-three, well over two hundred twenty pounds, to hoist him by his lapels. His glass eye grew so large in amazement it nearly lost its moorings and rolled out of his head. He shouted me back to earth, cursed me out of the house. An hour later I smashed my hand against a concrete wall. Surgeons wired it together. I came out of the ether, shouting: "I am Lazarus! Come back from the dead! Come back to tell you all, and I shall tell you all!"

Worked out a little karma, maybe.

It's been long time coming, Mila's monastery. I linger at a falling-down wall, waiting for Jay and James, who hustle in behind me, the three of us silently excited, as Jay puts a hand on the small of my back and ushers me forward. Over the broken wall we go in a loose triad, stumbling under a rough blanket hung for a door, blinking, drinking in the light of lantern and candles. Growing accustomed to the shadowy world, Jay finds the altar and we strike hands together, raise them up and down to the heart, then hands to floor, bodies following fast. Back up, and to floor again, back up and to floor again. No monks are here, just an old couple, neither glad nor sad to see us, just looking on, allowing us our devotion. Jay and I each purchase a butter lamp and light them with a lighter from my fanny pack. No words come. Only the light of flickering candles illuminating the nettle-green body of Mila, hand to ear, listening for instruction from the rainbow-bodied Marpa. With all he would ever need to know brimming in his mind, yet listening still! Listening for the distant drum of a Dharma-hungry heartbeat, for our feet on the sill.

Inside his cave I gingerly put my head where his head was when he forced the roof higher in a duel of magic. I'm wearing bedrock for a hat, realizing that where earlier I put my hand in Mila's handprint and felt nothing, this place has broken me open. Pushed and shoved here, by my teacher and by the misery incurred by my addictions and by the thirst for relief from desire, which is, after all, yet another desire. But this is one that longs for clarity, longs for refuge, longs to see through the mask of otherness, and longs to melt the mask of self. We had to break me to get another shot. And here it is. Here is nothing, here is everything, both blessed by Mila.

Outside the cave in the butter-lamp-lit room, the three of us sit before the altar for some time. No looks or words are needed. The altar is the mirror, shining back at us all we put forth and more. Our meditation is as unforced as true love's grateful kiss. Blowing out pain with each breath, as golden-fresh joy rushes in to take its place.

The statue on this altar is made of the precious brass called *li*, said to have been fashioned by the poet-saint himself, shortly before his Socrates-like death. The protuberance between the altar and the cave opening is called Ngodrub Terbur (treasure lump of attainments). Within his own lifetime it was most rare for Milarepa to use the word "treasure" to describe any actual object of this world. For this reason his disciples were doubly intrigued to find among the deceased's few possessions a treasure map for an inheritance. Could this be the place they dug up? Only to find a piece of cloth and an awl, with a note that said, "Whoever says that Milarepa had possessed gold, stuff his mouth with shit." No, this must be a different treasure corner, for this one is said to bless those who behold it, being itself profoundly blessed.

James approaches the altar to make a donation. "My God, look at that!" he says.

I rise, approach, and follow his eyes.

"Will you just look at that!" he repeats, picking up a coin from the altar plate. It's about the size of a silver dollar but bronzed, with an English-printed prayer on one side. On the flip: "To thine own self be true" around the edge and a large XIV stamped in the center.

"But what exactly does it mean—this coin?"

"It means—dear boy—that whoever left it here hadn't had a drink in upwards of fourteen years. And yet they left it here. All that time, and here it sits on the altar plate of Milarepa's miracle rock gompa. Incredible! Pick it up, Tad. Hold it in your hand and read the prayer."

I heed the instructions.

"Grant me the serenity to accept the things I cannot change, the courage to change the things I can, and the wisdom to know the difference."

"More or less says the whole thing, doesn't it?"

Jay, standing, smiles at us with the sweetest "shut up" I've never heard.

Outside again, I consider the falling-down walls of superb rock scattered around the famous monolith for which the place is named. If it were up to me I'd travel no farther, but pitch a tent and spend a month setting things right here. One stone at a time, one day at a time, one wall at a time. For this is the meditation I am equipped to perform best of all, to lose my self in, thousands of flexings of ego-laced muscles, all conspiring to unmask and unleash the captured, angry hawk of my self. To release into sky, leaving what remains totally free.

What I would give to toil here, in reverential silence. There's no need for hammers or chisels, these rocks would lay up, over and along, like notes that play themselves in a rare, perfect, unpremeditated song. So the prayer-wish is made and voiced to no one. The camera clicks, and the caravan moves on.

The valley rolls and we roll with it. A nomad woman we've seen before approaches our party. We're sprawled in the cool of a dry river bed that seems to hold some of the water's chill still. Her hat is off, revealing a shaven head. With a face deeply lined, teeth browned, she is anything but feminine, and butts into conversation with a manly directness. Talking with her, Tenzin finds reason to smile, explaining to us that she is a nun whose self-assigned task is to keep Kailash clean. This bridges the topic of garbage, which is a sticky wicket, at best. What is offering? What is trash? Smashed glass would seem to be of the latter category, always. But the thousands of abandoned garments—What's what here?

In the end she asks for a photo of the Dalai Lama, and Wolfgang, deeming her worthy, breaks into his store. It's a beautiful picture of His Holiness, and his ever-ready smile. The smile of a saint.

On "the last push" we all succumb to the passion Richard has indulged throughout with enthusiasm bordering upon fanaticism: collecting rocks of different shapes and colors. A Hindu on the plane to Thailand told me of black rectangular rocks from Kailash that are of special significance. He also said, looking at my palm, that I dreamed constantly, but that I was lucky insofar as I would be paid to dream. Presently I gather a collection of every type of rock imaginable, olive green, grass green, bottle green, magenta, turquoise, brown, white, mottled, triangular, globular—all but the black rectangular ones.

When Kailash reappears over the cliff-dune edge to our right, we are already singing her praises, as we did before first glimpsing her, when we were on the road from hopelessness. Now Tenzin pulls alongside of me and we buzz together for a stretch. I feel like an oarsman on a scull-boat, with the megaphone man barking in my ear.

So we hum along, we two, bowman and oarsman. And I let it feel good, all the while knowing we will butt heads again, feud again, growl and bark and laugh, and in laughter make peace again. For such is our deal. I don't get a guru three valleys over. No, I live in his valley. I know his children, I know the politics of his enlightenment, and like all politics, it displeases me. Tough luck! So I must see through the hockey player to find the buddha,

251

just as I must see through the rock and snow of Kailash to see the mansion of Demchock, just as Milarepa saw the buddha in Marpa, and as Tenzin must look past my smoldering garbage to see the buddha in me.

I am the Fool to his Emperor, I make the court laugh and get preferential treatment. But the wrong jest and I lose my head, and I do that with regularity. Always have, and until my practice becomes more firm, I probably always will. Yet from now on, even if I lose my head, even if this is my stock and trade, I will lose my head with Kailash.

Dogs greet us at the outskirts of Darchen, interspersed with children running out to "hall-o!" us for candy and pens. Rounding the low cratelike buildings of this desert shantytown, I meet my misspent youth head on. I'm supposed to be free of sin, and I feel light and bright as a new penny. Still here they are, billiard players spread around numerous battered tables, basking in the afternoon sun. Pool tables! Outside! In Tibet! I hear the dirge of Gwendolyn Brooks's ghetto death-chant in my ears:

"We real cool./We shoot pool./We die soon." Nonsense! This is Kailash-blessed, I think, throwing my pack down and hat and coat, laughing at the barrel-stave-warped cue, the rogue's gallery showcasing rotten teeth butted up beside gold ones. Poverty and wealth; sport and stealth; cigarettes and rumpled up rupees, all smack under the nose of the sphinxlike mountain. Motley balls are shepherded in the rack. Crack! The balls fly, a stripe and a solid die. "Ah!" . . . the impressed hum. As round the wrecked green I run. Other gamesmen from their games are lured, as at it we go. Trading tricks and winks and laughter assured. How good to be alive! Tenzin's telling me to put my hat on. He fades, they all do. The game takes over. What else is new?

Finally, on the fourth, I lose. Now where's the drink? The joint? The girl? From across a bridge spanning a garbage-gunked brook, Jock calls, "Tad! Quick! Hurry! We're waiting!" I'm late for what? Another group photograph. And I thought I had outwalked the world.

After posing together we trudge around a new Darchen. "Jay!" I yell, "this is where we were trying to get that night.

Look—over the wall—it's ye olde prison yard, waiting for us again. The same mangy curs growling, and showing their high-altitude teeth!" Suddenly Jay grabs and hugs me with a terrifying, grieving strength. "I love you, I've been jealous of you—and I want you to know that."

It takes me by surprise, but I confess. "I've been jealous of you, too. So now we've both said it. And we'll forgive each other, being such Dharma groupies. And forgive and forget about the girls, too, Jay. We were kids then. Even Steven was a kid once."

"Even Steven?"

"Yeah." I smile, delighted to have so skillfully set my word trap. "Even, Steven," I repeat as his eyes tear over and he laughs his happiest laugh. We have come full circle, tents and mess quarters all crisp and cleanly saluting us in the wind as we march back into the prison yard.

TENZIN

Now we are going back to the world, how do we perform the miraculous events needed to help the messed-up planet? The great peace conference we are holding with His Holiness in San Francisco will be of some help. It will be a great assembly of the powerless joining to melt the hearts of the powerful. We must work for a miracle. Could there still be someone capable of ushering in the millennium in some direction other than toward the catastrophe that logic tells us is coming?

Today, good friends and fellow pilgrims, we conclude our sacred mountain circling and our *Blade Wheel* teachings. Here, at the end, our author Dharmarakshita shares his most profound visions in the wisdom dimension, giving glimpses of his enlightened insight into the nature of reality.

Ultimate Visions

Although they lack any intrinsic reality,
Like the moon disk rising reflected in water,

Evolution's effects parade their superficial variety.
Though mere appearance, they demand ethical choice!

We continue with the illusory nature of reality when perceived by the enlightened being. Evolution is as unreal as the moon rising in water, like fog, like mirror, like mirage—and yet! Within that unreality, ethical choice is crucial: be good and not bad; be positive not negative. Even though it's mere appearance, still, this is the realm of lived experience. And therefore one must be committed to paying careful attention to ethical choices. The next verse gives an example of this.

> When dreaming, we can burn in explosive flames;
> Though finally unreal, the searing heat is frightful.
> So the hell realms may be ultimately unreal,
> Yet we must increase virtue, to avoid their horrors!

In other words, you can really suffer in a dream, you can burn and know agony, although when you wake from it screaming, you realize that luckily it is unreal. But still, in your dream it burns. In the same way, the hell realms may be ultimately unreal, but as long as you are still caught in the self-habit, they are part of your horizon and you should undertake virtue to avoid their horrors.

People say, "Oh well, heaven and hell. Hell is a bad mood on earth, Heaven is a good mood on earth. Those exaggerated archetypes are an ancient, premodern thing. Who needs reincarnation or judgment day?"

Most Buddhists do not agree. They say, "Sure, hell is unreal, but so is this world unreal. If you can viscerally experience this world as unreal, give up your body as if it were unreal, give up your property as if it were unreal, relax and let it all go, then you don't need to fear hell. It will be unreal, too. But if you think you're real here, if you think what you have hold of here is real, then you will feel hell as very real and you will suffer greatly." You should cultivate the virtues of generosity, justice, tolerance, enterprise, meditation, and wisdom, in order to avoid such horrors.

When delirious with fever, though there's no dark void,
Still we feel ourselves plummet into a bottomless pit.
So though the mass of misknowledge is naturally unreal,
You should dispel its errors with the threefold wisdom!

You can have a horrible time when you're sick, falling dizzily into a bottomless pit. But if you have a knowledge that illness passes, karmic evolution changes, the quality of existence will improve again, you can lessen the horror of illness. A child doesn't know it will get better, and so the horror is more profound. But if we know that the whole world is our hallucination, a mass of misknowledge, then we'll have a better time and can help others have a better time. And we do this with our threefold wisdom — informational, analytical, and contemplative.

When musicians sing and play the lute,
Analyzed, their sounds lack intrinsic reality.
Unanalyzed, their sweet music happens
And lifts beings' minds from sadness!

So when you analyze evolution and causality
It lacks reality either as a whole or in parts.
Yet just apparently things are born and destroyed,
Just relatively happiness and sufferings are felt!

When you analyze any relative thing, trying to find its intrinsic reality either as a whole or within the collection of its parts, you can't find anything at all. It all dissolves under the force of your analytic vision. Nevertheless, when you don't analyze it, when you take it as it presents itself, so to speak, it's still right there in your face. This is why the relative is called superficial and conventional. But it's all still real enough that it matters critically how we live it.

So don't get too transcendentalist and think, "I had such an absolute experience, I don't have to worry about how things are." Voidness makes apparent things all the more real and makes us committed to improving the quality of those relative experiences. Even when we're a buddha and we're beyond being bound by anything, in a way we're still bound by the feelings of others—by our concern that they feel good and not bad. So just apparently, but relevantly, things are born and destroyed. And just relatively, but intensely, happiness and sufferings are felt.

> When drops of water fill a vase,
> The first drop hardly begins the filling.
> None, not even the last drop, fills it on its own;
> The relational process accomplishes the task.

This shows how reality has a superficial nature; anything you point to has the reality of something else; is never its own reality. Where does Kailash stop and the Barka Plain begin? Richard's rocks collected all over Kailash—are they Kailash? Or the Kailash mud? Or the Kailash snow? Or the Kailash sun? None of them is Kailash actually. So Kailash is constituted from many things, none of which is Kailash. But somehow when they're all put together they seem to be Kailash. That's the nature of superficial reality. If you really look for the essence of Kailash you can't find anything. If you don't look at it—there it is. So when we can relate to something that is simultaneously there and not there, that's when we've mastered nonduality.

> So when you feel an evolutionary effect of joy or pain,
> The first instant of the cause did not produce it.
> No instant, not even the last, is what makes it happen;
> The relational process makes you feel that joy or pain.

So all experiences are like that. You analyze them and they disappear, but then you effortlessly reconstruct their relative reality.

> Amazing! Though this natural life all unanalyzed
> Seems real to the unreflective while lacking all substance,

This teaching of the relative reality of mere appearances
Is hard for the less perceptive to understand!

Dharmarakshita is surprised, as he reflects here, that unreflective people can so easily mistake the status of unreal things, creating a false substantiality in them automatically. And yet, once they've had some tiny hint of transcendence, they are quick to discard their commitment to the details of relative reality, dismissing it from their concern.

Once they meet some form of transcendence and have a taste of voidness, many people feel that relative reality is nothing, mere appearances are nothing. They get quite casual in the way they relate to relative reality, and are surprised to learn that the truly enlightened become very mindful to all of the tiniest details of relationality. We are so dualistic in mind, and so nihilistic in our preconceptions, that many Buddhists and spiritual people have basically escapist views of ultimate spiritual destiny. We find ourselves seeking the way out from all relationalities, because our egotistical way of struggling with them is so stressful and tiring.

It can be threatening for this side of ourselves to confront the inexorability of relativity, the infinite interconnectedness of all beings and things. There is no escape, experience will be infinite. We must therefore develop absolute commitment for it to be good, not only for ourselves but for all beings. Even Buddha does not escape, since his compassion will not let him. He voluntarily dooms himself to remain sensitive forever to all feelings of all beings, committing himself to assuring their ultimate happiness.

Now when you stabilize yourself in samadhi,
What still exists even apparently?
What presence exists? What absence can exist?
Who is there holding what premise, is or isn't?

There being no objects and no reality of objects,
Free from all choices, free from all elaborations,

Intelligence uncontrived, in the subtlest subjectivity,
Abiding naturally, one becomes a Great Being!

Thus engaging the superficial spirit of enlightenment
And the ultimate spirit of enlightenment,
Completing unblocked the stores of merit and wisdom,
May both selfish and altruistic goals be consummated!

These final verses describe the experience of the absolute in a nondual way. You don't lack all things, but they are not present either. Everything is apparent but not definitive. You're stabilized in the samadhi state—peacefully balanced within infinite virtual reality—and thus you become the Great Being. And the whole world offers no resistance to your vision of blissfulness. You can transform it with your bodhisattva will into a vessel of happiness for all beings.

It is very important to understand that buddhahood fulfills all our selfish desires as well as our altruistic wishes for others. We're not just martyring ourselves here, we're not just destroying ourselves. Through wisdom, coming to know the nature of reality, we achieve total joy and happiness, and consummate all possible selfish goals in achieving the orgasmic bliss that knows the totally stable and secure nature of reality. This bliss is the ultimate beatitude that cannot be improved on and does not dissipate. This joyous wisdom of reality naturally becomes altruism as it contacts others who feel deprived of it, and it lifts them into its happiness and bliss, naturally. Thus all altruistic aims are accomplished by compassion, as all selfish goals are consummated by wisdom.

This is the delightful irony of it all! When our demon of selfishness and self-centeredness and narcissism is terminated by Yamantaka's bliss-void intuition, smashed by his hammer of wisdom, then we actually fulfill our selfish purpose and we know happiness. Finally we get the very happiness that the demon falsely promised us, while it was addicting us to its poisonous behaviors and unsatisfying states. As it turns out, only by getting rid of the selfishness demon and its self-preoccupied states do we find the really satisfying happiness that we have been wanting all along. What more could we possibly ask for?

Well then, congratulations one and all. We have come to the end of *The Blade Wheel of Mind Reform*. We now have all the elements of our enlightenment in hand. To actually realize it fully, we must purify our negative evolutionary tendencies and we must cultivate our contemplative focus and intensify our wisdom intelligence. May the virtue of our teaching and learning together here at this sacred mountain be dedicated to our rapid attainment of perfect buddhahood for the sake of all beings, including ourselves! We dared to confront the blade wheel, learned to turn negative evolution into critical wisdom and blissful compassion, as we made our circle round the sacred mountain. Here's to all of you! I thank you for giving me the opportunity to ride these wheels once more with you! May we keep on doing it in our boundless futures until we all master it completely!

TAD

Farewells to Kailash and congratulations to each other begin with after-dinner toasts, with the mess tent's green light filtering onto the faces we've grown accustomed to seeing together—Leopoldo, Valerie, Wolfgang, Jock, Tad, Jay, Richard, James, Tenzin, Lobsang, as different parts of the gestalt, the organism that circled Kailash. We are its form, and this is our function. But no sooner do form and function finally begin to fit together than the collaboration starts to unravel. Even though we will be on trek another week, and the most dangerous part is yet to come, still the dream team seems to be dissolving. Will we go back to being our old selves again? Will the wheel remember its shape now, without the assistance of the hub that is Kailash? We're gassing up at the first and last station, as we did coming in. Soon we'll have to turn away.

Not so simple! We are sentenced to each other and to this world. And even those who could escape choose not to until all of us can dance over the rainbow bridge in the rainbow body into Noah's rainbow ark together. Then even Kailash will tumble, but not a moment before.

Tenzin, toasting from the head of the folding table, rhapsodizes: "For we have seen Kailash! We have circled the sacred mountain. It's right outside. And we must leave it here. But also it goes with us—this godly thing travels around in human forms. It inspires us to give life, earth, another shot. To get our jobs here right and then expand from that.

"You know, when you stand up in a world that's sitting down, the ones sitting down say a lot of things about you. People say I'm apocalyptic, nihilistic, hallucinogenic, anarchistic. They say I'm out to save the world or to destroy it. And they're right. In a sense, I am out to both save and destroy the world—at the same time! But even before I awoke to Buddhism in this life, I felt that we have the ability to fix these terrible mistakes we've made. The Sierra Club people say about garbage in state parks, 'If you carry it in, you can carry it out.' Well, we've got all of human history's garbage to contend with. Our past lives are gone—but unfortunately, our past garbage isn't!

"Buckminster Fuller is a great hero of mine—the poets all hate him because he wrote like an engineer, but I love him anyway—because he never gave up the idea that people can solve every problem they've created. I mean, the guy had plans after World War Two for taking the factories that had been creating bombs and bombers and, while hardly changing them a jot, creating homes and workplaces, heating systems, cooling systems, entire ecosystems. Interconnected, rational, ethical solutions to global problems. Big business wouldn't let him do it, but he had the plans. Not just talk—but blueprints!

"So I'm allergic to people who say, 'You can't solve this problem.' Even Buddhists totally frustrate me when they say, 'It's all samsara. It's all suffering. Nothing can be done.' I refute that, and Kailash refutes that! Any world that has this mountain in it can get its shit together. I believe this totally, and I always will. So here's to the diamond of total bliss and wisdom and to the ring we made around the diamond, and to the ring in our hearts where we will wear this blazing diamond for all of this life—and beyond, so that somewhere in the mind-body bubble perpetually born and reborn, we will remember and long to return. To Kailash. Forever!"

"To Kailash. Forever!"

As one we say it. Some of us on the edge of tears, some of us over the edge. Some still afraid of the height. We are standing toasting Kailash as one, when its unofficial mayor, Kailash Dorje, dyed green as Milarepa by the tent's green light, strides in under the zippered flap, with salutations and congratulations for our first time around. He has after-dinner tea with us and hears of our last leg, tells us about his school and about cleaning up the holy sites, repairing what is destroyed and venerating what is repaired.

I ask Tenzin to translate my request to rebuild the fallen walls of the miracle rock monastery. This explained, Kailash Dorje says he thinks it might be arranged. Tenzin's bright eye narrows on me.

"Of course, now you'll have to do it, Tad. All fine and good, the idea."

"I can't swear I'll do it, but I promise to try."

"Sounds impressive, yes, another good idea, but what does it mean, Tad? What do I tell the man?"

"Circumambulating Kailash was a good idea too, wasn't it Tenzin?" I say, looking him in the eye. "An idea you made a gift of on a morning you didn't believe I was capable of realizing the gift."

Tenzin grins with a sly respect. "Circling the sacred mountain is always a good idea, Tad. So I'll tell him you'll be back to do the stone work?"

"I will."

"And when shall I say you'll do this?"

"The year of the horse, 2002."

The buzz of Tibetan resumes and Kailash Dorje smiles at me.

"I will send pictures of my walls," I tell him. "One I built for Professor Thurman here—beautiful! six feet tall, with curves, brilliant, and a sense of humor—like his daughter."

"He cannot keep women out of it, this guy. Hopeless." Tenzin is smiling so hard he can hardly talk. "Once round Kailash and still, hopeless!"

Richard suggests: "Maybe, Tad, you should get up early and run around again."

Jay kicks in: "Maybe go Bonpo style—the other way round!"

"Something, anything!" Tenzin agrees. "I think playing pool refried his mind. You know the Chinese drop those tables off for free. Like a pusher giving away dope. To insure sloth. And did you see the way he leapt to it? The poor guy?"

"Like a babe to the tit," I volunteer.

"EX-actly!" Tenzin spouts, shaking his red, smile-smeared face with pity and amusement.

My tent is pitched off the slab tonight. The dogs of Darchen bark and growl, but I get up to pee in the dark and find it snowing huge, perfect flakes. The dogs lope over, growling, and I "gyu!" them away, wondering how I could ever have been so timid. I wake up at first light to two inches of feather-light snow, which auspiciously held off for our kora.

We've collected some money for Kailash Dorje's school, and he'll give us the patron's tour after breakfast. Then he'll point out the climb from which you can get a glimpse of the inner kora.

The school is a sad, noble affair, filled with stern, silent faces plainly terrified when Tenzin makes exploratory remarks about a Buddhist heritage. Now I see the other side of Dorje: the deal maker, the strategist. The Chinese allow him to educate the local children, but once and for all the monastery as the source of learning is, and must remain, obliterated. They learn Chinese and Tibetan here, but no Buddhism. Although a little history seems to be snuck into discussing the winds and channels of Eastern medicine. Much as the basics of Christianity must be touched upon by any student of Italian Renaissance painting, no matter where or by whom it is studied. But the message is clear: Buddhism is your shameful, archaic past. Communism is your proud present and your hopeful future. If, as a Tibetan, you have the audacity to compete with a Chinese for an all-precious job, then you must submit to Chinese ways. Completely.

Dorje is practically worshiped here. His true allegiance must be to the Dharma, mustn't it be? But what goes down in the name of pragmatism, and compromise, and ends justifying the means?

What is at work here? I feel like I've just entered a Graham Greene novel. No white and black issues, all grays. Is he trying to keep his people alive, first? Hoping for a revolution? Biding his time? Awaiting the return of the Dalai Lama?

But what is it with these power places? The Hopis have heavy uranium deposits in their holy mountain, the Black Mesa in Arizona. Our government wants to mine the uranium, breaking its treaties yet again. Some want to cut down the redwoods, others, the rain forests. I remember the rumors we heard locally of the Chinese wanting to drain Lake Manasarovar for the gold. The Tibetans believe the gold to be the excrement of dragons, the implication being that you mustn't mess with dragons.

Dorje sends us a guide to the edge of town. Five of us forge past pool tables with younger men—cigarettes dangling from sparsely mustached lips—who are at it already, as not far off, old men hunker round a lean-to fireplace with a kettle sitting on weakly smoldering coals. A pretty girl saying her rosary smiles into my camera from over a wall.

We hike out of the shantytown onto the snowy hillside, turning abruptly west at the mouth of a pass and grunting up a daunting series of boulders. From the promontory a prayer-flagged rope extends several hundred yards across the pass, to a similar citadel-crag anchor on the other side, like a necklace at the throat of the magic mountain.

I hail a pilgrim on the other side of the pass who's starting up the inner kora. He waves once and labors on into the heartland of Kailash. The great scar on the southern face is aglow.

We look down on Darchen below, at the snowy metal-brick-mud huts abutting the vast Barka Plain, as behind me the perfect ice-lotus rears up, up the forever slope to the never-seen top. I'm filled with such sad gladness, wondering if I spoke true when I promised to return, knowing how vows of loyalty tend to go south. Yet realizing that far away as I must go, I will be closer in some ways to Kailash in Woodstock than these frightened children a half mile below, detoured from their heritage.

From high above I hear a strange sound, like a sharp rock being dropped into a deep well and the plunking sound echoing off the walls. It's the cry of a crow, high up, now sweeping toward me, riding a puff of wind, wings back in a stall, claws reaching out and clasping the prayer-flag rope, midway across the pass where it is bellied down by gravity. The crow perches on the rope facing Kailash, and seems to look neither for nor upon anything else. Crows are traditionally considered to be emissaries of His Holiness, presently in exile in Dharamsala, India. Its presence here is an omen of the return of the world's only monk king to this, the heart of his rightful domain. He, and he alone, will bring a smile to the frightened faces below. He, and he alone, will polish the tarnished Dharma wheel until it glows with irrefutable, lustrous light. He, and he alone, will someday lead a revolution around the high and holy mountain. But in the meantime, this little pilgrimage is our humble offering to him, its merit dedicated to the happiness of all beings.

PART THREE

Returning from the Mountain

To the religious mind the universe is filled with the thoughts
of the gods, with the powers of great intelligences
and consciousnesses, radiating eternally through
space and really constituting the world that is.
—LAMA GOVINDA

The world is charged with
the grandeur of God.
—GERARD MANLEY HOPKINS

CHAPTER SIXTEEN

The Holy Lake

TAD

Descending west of Darchen down steep dunes dotted with juniper, I break into a run. The beginnings of the kora are to my right. I wish this were the start of my second time around. But once around is fine, for now. I leap out, vaulting on a bamboo pole, eased to earth with a delighted grunt. Switching my stick from hand to hand, I lever myself around improvised S turns, laughing. The Barka Plain pitches and rolls before me. Twenty miles straight ahead, Lake Rakshas Tal is that long, narrow, cobalt-blue band glittering dizzily beneath Gurla Mandhata, a vanilla-ice-cream dream of a mountain over twenty-five thousand feet high, with brethren Himalaya branching off along the heart-stopping snow-slicked ridge that shimmers deliciously in the sun.

On the other side of these vaulted snow heaps is India—mother of wisdom, father of sorrow. But something interrupts the natural flow of thoughts, a small thing on the ground, shining against the sandy, piny loam. I skid to a stop and pick up a pin depicting Mt. Kailash surrounded by stars and line-connected constellations. The back explains this to be a souvenir of a star-gazers club that meets here on a certain date every thirty-eight years. The last meeting was in 1974. The pin is in pristine condition and pricks the denim over my heart as it is clasped in place. Behind and above me Jock is steadily plodding along, Jay a few hundred yards behind and above him. A dust devil appears on the plain as one of our Toyotas pulls into sight. I wave my bandanna-tufted walking stick and the dust-covered jeep veers off the road and bumps through the undergrowth toward me.

Rushing toward the jeep, I hit the flats, happily panting. I stop, turn, clap my heads over my head, and shout, *"La So-so-so. La Gyalo!"*—victory to the gods! I clasp hands to my chest, and then clap them to the ground beside my knees, rise up and clap them together again. Three times I kneel before snow-capped Kailash, then turn and climb into the waiting vehicle. The sweet driver and a strong Sherpa cluck in approval. I greet them with a huge, silent smile, show them the trophy over my heart, and receive noisy congratulations. We head east a short distance toward Jock and Jay, who are making the last push onto the flats. They're waving at us, laughing at the door-to-door Dharma service. Jock greets them in Nepali; Jay hugs the driver, yammering, "My friend, my friend, how are you?"

The other vehicles have already left. We are the rear guard. Jay, Jock, and I zone out, smiling with exhilarated fatigue at the shrub-flecked desert. Safe inside our mechanized whirlwind sporting its own private dust storm, we charge along. Even so, the desert is still. Driver and Sherpa banter as we approach a crossroads. There is some contention concerning direction. Then, as we swerve east, I see the lone wanderer, his eyes closed, lips moving, hands clutched in Christian prayer. The eyes open, hands drop to sides, and there it is again, at his chest—the cross. Our gazes meet. Asian Christian peering at American Buddhist in ecstasy-laced conspiracy at the foot of Kailash.

Five minutes later the Sherpa's fingers tap my shoulder and he points at two wolves loping along the edge of a ridge. The driver is nervous; he doesn't like wolves. A third beast bounds into view. Jock demands that we stop. Outside, while taking a picture of disappearing shanks and tails the Sherpa grabs at my leg and pantomimes a wolf's mouth. At the jab of the hand I'm startled—more accurately, terrified—but the terror instantly melts into a sea of comedy. All terrors are such comedies, I think. Like the monsters crashing Mila's cave: how easy to assess, how difficult to accomplish!

Nepali arguments transpire over a Tibetan map. We turn around. Now, passing the Christian pilgrim a third time, I restrain myself no longer but order the vehicle to a stop, charge out the crunching door, and approach the loner. Grabbing hold of my mani beads I point to Kailash, then open my hand and gesture to the cross on his chest, then raise this hand, too, toward Kailash.

"Two roads!" I yell, gesturing to Kailash with two hands suddenly clapped violently together, "One mountain!" He smiles, neither agreeing nor disagreeing. Frustrated curiosity gets the best of me and I cry out, "Where did you get that cross?" He grins uncomprehendingly. We're at an impasse. I gesture to my camera for permission. He clears his cross of the tufts of his vestments, his chest swells, and he stares out just over my head into the blazing blue as he waits for the shutter. Taking camera from eye, I venture the Tibetan greeting: "Tujeychey." He sustains the same silent smile; this man cannot or will not talk; further, it is distinctly possible he does not hear.

I recross the road and take another picture of him waving before Kailash, telegraph poles disappearing into Darchen like crucifixes doing the bunny hop into a police state. Today, saluting the Asian Christian, for an instant I'm awake, held in the eyes of this man who is also awake. Immediately certain that such wakefulness is in us all, I realize you cannot kill wisdom or compassion; you may die momentarily, but these are immortal. And if you die in their cause, speedily shall you be rushed into their commingled light.

I see that the universe is always perfectly sober even if broken men are miserably drunk. That the lotus is rooted in the mud of misery, though its petals glisten in perfect heavens. That the perfection of the lotus begins in the mud, thus mud is part of heaven, and misery is a part of perfection. That everything is perfect always. Already perfect. But tell that to a starving child, or to the child's starving mother. The Dalai Lama could; this Christian could.

Or so, for an instant, it seems to me as I salute him a last time before turning back to the jeep idling against the Barka Plain, the silhouette of Gurla Mandhata, third-highest mountain in Tibet, rising majestically in the heat waves wafting from the jeep's trek-slopped hood.

"What now?" I wonder. "What more is there?" Now we drive to Manasarovar, the Holy Lake—earthly bookend to the Holy Mountain.

Around a hillock overlooking Rakshas Tal we encounter the other vehicles stopped for lunch. Our driver draws fond abuse from the staff. The drivers smoke and laugh, then hunker down around the Coleman stove, where Pawan cooks an entirely different meal for the Sherpa contingent. On our separate tarp we sprawl, viewing Rakshas Tal and Manasarovar, and the famous zygot-shaped rivulet running between them, the Ganga Chu. It is filled with water, a rare and auspicious sight.

"These lakes twinkling at us in the distance," Jay muses, with a scholarly tone, "why is Manasarovar so praised and the Rakshas Tal so criticized?"

Richard improvises an overview: "Rakshas Tal is sprawling and meandering. Even in the golden time, it had but one gompa honoring it. It is said to represent the female aspect in nature, the moon, the subconscious, danger—it is called the devil's lake. Manasarovar, on the other hand, is a huge triangular circle, sixty-two miles around, representing the male, the sun, the conscious, compassionate mind. The two are said to be bride and groom, with the usually dry Ganga Chu running between."

"Very good Richard, fine party line. Yet . . ." Tenzin pounces on the word, relishing a split-second silence. "A person such as yourself with an artistic intuition should realize that the circular, solar, ovumlike Manasarovar is actually the female manifestation, and the stern, cool, lunar Rakshas Tal is the male. Clearly!" Tenzin calms slightly: "Even Govinda repeated this mistake, which he got from patriarchal traditions. Another challenge for nonduality. Do you remember the sun and moon symbol found on the walk-through chorten that marks the very beginning of Kailash? It's all the union of opposites. The patriarchal cultures equate male and female with sun and moon, light and dark, and life and death, while the Tantrics and Tibetans take the opposite tack, woman with sun and man with moon. So Rakshas Tal and Manasarovar are married. They are separate, wanting to be one. Like us all. Thus when the little estuary is full, this is a very good sign, indeed. It is a microcosm of the Manasarovar-Kailash pair; it's opposites in union, bliss-void indivisible. And here—with Kailash the lingam and Manasarovar the yoni—clearly, the Holy Lake is female."

Back in the Dharma-mobile we motor alone, pulling closer to Manasarovar, visible through the low, wind-swept dunes. With a shout our truck is recognized unloading in the dry gully of a riverbed, a hundred yards from the shore of this blue, white-capped monster. The wind is strong and hundreds of prayer flags are waving wildly from Chiu Gompa, one of five original monasteries, rebuilt on a cresting sand-serpent of rock perhaps a half mile away, overlooking this northwestern corner of the giant lake where the Ganga Chu sporadically washes in. The water we noted a few miles north hasn't gotten this far. Looking back north from here, we see Kailash rise up out of the mini-Sahara of the wide, dry streambed, dominating the horizon with no less authority than a pyramid or Sphinx.

The Sherpas and porters are trying to raise the mess tent in the wind. I rush to help them as Pawan is swallowed up in the confusion of canvas and lines. We all fall to the ground laughing, then leap to, reinvigorated. A gasoline run is necessary. Jay volunteers to go along, five kilometers northeast. The rest of us start throwing sand on the edges of the tents to keep the floors from flying up and pulling out the stakes.

We are called to an early tea where we smile at each other in the fiercely jostled mess tent, indulge in hot drinks, biscuits, and conversation, then bail into our tents for deep sleep amidst wild wind. We're starving again soon, groggy, anxious to visit the lake yet totally uninterested in exploring anything but books and sleeping bags in this weather. Jay and the drivers have been gone for several hours; concern is raised, then dismissed. "Of course, the vehicle is late," Leopoldo reasons, "it contains Jay!"

We're having pineapple chunks on angel food cake for dessert as headlights sweep the tent. Jay hails the mess hall, unzips the flap and enters, a little drunk. Outside the drivers are explaining to Lobsang, who is looking into the tent, most amused. Jay says, "Sorry we're late. My duty to accept hospitality. No problem. Much fun. A few beers. A broken vow. No big deal. Everything's fine. Start over again tomorrow. Nonduality, right? Nothing to the extreme—not even . . ."

"Abstinence?" I volunteer.

"Not even abstinence," Jay concurs wholeheartedly.

"Oh-ho-ho-ho! Jay!" Tenzin snorks, rising up from the table like a sea monster in clothes, "Soaking up a little local color, are we? I turn my back on you one second and you're like prowling around some beer pit and getting the drivers drunk!"

"At least was it Chang?" Wolfgang asks, hopefully.

"Sorry." Jay hiccoughs, then burps, "Pabst Blue Ribbon . . ." as the tent implodes with laughter.

The next morning two jeeps drive us along the edge of the lake a couple of miles and release us to skitter back on our own. The wind is still wicked on the shore. An immensity of water, under an immensity of mountains, under the piercingly blue sky, momentarily stuns us into silence. Not Richard, our northwoodsman, not Wolfgang, our Teutonic spiritual warrior, not even the one-eyed white monk himself is much in the mood for swimming.

"The Sadhus bathe in it, and other Hindus; the Buddhists

mostly bottle and drink the holy water of Manasarovar, sometimes baptize with it," Tenzin rhapsodizes. "Just being here is a blessing. I don't think we need to overdo it, guys," he says, smiling at us, parka-wrapped and shivering. "We'll climb up that dune and get a good view with some shelter and do a talk from there."

Kailash strong, we scamper up a sand slide and, sheltered by an even higher ridge, we sit in the dusty sand to observe the lake. Its center is almost black, with blues, greens, and purples radiating out intensely. Just when you think you've assessed the beauty, it shifts, like the eyes of an angora cat. Small wonder this lake is considered "mind," it is ever in process.

It should by now be clear that Buddhists and Hindus travel around any devotional object to pay it respect and gain merit, but while a circuit around Manasarovar certainly exists, it is a longer, less popular circumambulation than the trip around Kailash. It is usually undertaken during winter, after bogs and inlets are frozen solid. Today, whitecaps froth the beach, while brown mountains crowd down to the shore, drinking; lighter ones kneel, revealing the snowcaps behind standing in fast-moving clouds. So different from Kailash, but equally unworldly, the lake seems to check us out. Tenzin smiles fiercely into the wind, bellowing:

"The *Prajna Paramita Sutra* begins with a famous simile: 'The waters of all the rivers flow down on the rose-apple-gold continent Jambudvipa—the ancient name of India—from the lake-mouth of the great dragon, Anavatapta, and run down watering all the trees and flowers on the entire subcontinent. In this same way, all the beautiful teachings and poems and visions that are expressed by all the bodhisattvas in the world come from the power of the Buddha.'

"So this is just one of hundreds of myths involving our lake as the source of all the waters of life. If you look at an exaggerated relief map of Asia, you'll notice that Tibet looks like a dragon lying on its side. The mouth is curled at this Kailash-Manasarovar juncture. The tail of the dragon curls in a mountainous ridge down into Malaysia, through Thailand, Burma, and Cambodia, its tip becoming the Malaysian archipelago. Any guidebook map will confirm our discussion yesterday, that Manasarovar is a round, female-essence, ovum-shaped lake. Whereas the other, the seed-shaped, or crescent-moon-shaped lake, is male. I found an old book in which Rakshas Tal was called Bindusarovar, or "the lake of the drop," which is a male symbol.

"Look!" Valerie yells as the wind changes in direction, blowing the scales of the water against their grain. Flecks of vapor break the tops of waves, refracting in a sector bathed with a laser beam of sunlight. For two seconds a rainbow blanket covers a few acres of water.

We vocalize as one, like Fourth-of-July folk *ahhh*ing over the flowers of flame in the night sky. The short hairs on my neck stand up, as I realize Valerie had to have called out before the rainbow appeared.

"Incredible! You see?" Tenzin demands. "Does the knowledge of light and lens interfere with that beauty? Not in the slightest! Indeed, all magic is technology. And the buddhas are the highest technologists in the universe. They are all Einstein at Princeton in his most profound thought all the time."

"Then where are the buddhas now?" I ask.

"They're here!" Tenzin reports, cryptically. "That was a buddha rainbow blanket; the female-mother energy, the dakini, the round pool at the base of the great phallus, which is the male mountain. The essence of the great mother of the buddhas, Prajna Paramita, of the Vajra Dakini, and all these female forms of buddha are in this lake, and therefore its waters are a tremendous blessing of immortality. There's a place in Lama Govinda's book . . ."

Richard interrupts, "The place where he speaks of the brothers and sisters of Kailash."

Tenzin's eye opens wide, amazed. "Yes—exactly that."

Richard continues his description, "Wherein all of us who have traveled to and around Kailash have an unspoken understanding and can recognize 'having seen Kailash' in each other— and so are joined in a holy mountain family, who see the world differently ever after."

"Yes!" Tenzin exclaims, "Do we agree?"

There are affirmative grunts, then Leopoldo observes, "I haven't seen anybody in days who hasn't seen Mt. Kailash."

Valerie finishes, "And so the real test will be when people who haven't seen Kailash start mixing in."

Wolfgang observes, "But we have been changed. Are we agreed in this? A little or a lot—it's hard to say."

"Well whatever occurred," James insists in happy desperation, "is still occurring. Therefore I wouldn't be so fast to describe it quite yet."

"Yes, leave it like that!" Tenzin interjects, quite excited. "Tolerate the friction between the dualities, find they are both true and therefore actually enhance each other, like double rainbows. Ideally, that is what the different schools, teachers, and even different religions would do. Amplify each other, resonating with different harmonies. That's why the Buddha adjusted his teaching to suit various mind-sets."

"But people do tend to get bogged down in the differences, rather than the sameness," James observes sadly.

"Too often, yes," Tenzin agrees. "Unless we have practiced nonduality. So let's avail ourselves of these tools we've worked so hard for. OK? The mandala of Chakrasamvara Superbliss at Mt. Kailash is open to us, and to any who take the trouble to get here. I have discovered this to be true through my own experience. What was my experience?

"All down the west valley the rocks were singing, the sun was singing, the river was singing, and the wind was singing, each with a different female voice. Goddesses of Earth, Water, Fire, and Wind—Lochana, Mamaki, Pandara, and Tara—the four primary elements. The rocks are alive, they're deities. The water is a female deity, it is alive as both ice and running water. The wind on my skin is a female deity; the fire in the sky is a female deity. Here we come into an area where suddenly all sensory experience becomes divine. A rainbow-decked lake? How lucky we are to be sitting quietly near this lake of victory and compassion. It is the perfect moment for one of our last Dharma talks."

TENZIN

We've made it round the mountain! It feels like a lifetime achievement—though it will take us all years to really integrate it into our subtle nervous systems, into our cells. As we all now go back to where we were—or thought we were—in our lives before coming here, we will gradually realize that once we are different, everything is different. I am proud of us all for successfully circling the mountain while coping with the *Blade Wheel*. I want to offer a reward for that today, in the yoga of Mt. Kailash, the visualization practice of the Superbliss Buddha Mandala. The *Blade Wheel* invokes Yamantaka's adamantine wisdom so it can crush our egotistical adherence to the ordinary world of suffering. As we discover freedom from egotism and its agonies, we need also to explore the extraordinary reality of liberation. I want you to have a practice that you can sit down with at your shrine at home, returning in your imagination to Kailash, that you can use while driving your car, waiting at an airport, or vacationing at a beach.

But first, I have to tell you the amazing dream I had last night. I saw all the women I have ever known, swirling in a riot of beauty above and in and out of Lake Manasarovar. Mother and lovers, teen-fantasy beloveds, grown-up lovers, soul-mate Nena, and then my daughters and granddaughters, and then many friends, flashing around in colors and tones and movements, all seemingly naturally aware of the Superbliss mandala, as if they were its emanations. I saw them all swirling around together, sometimes happy, sometimes sad, diving and leaping like exquisite dolphins in the sea of life energy. I saw women I have only heard of—Isadora Duncan, Sarah Bernhardt, Draupadi, Lady Murasaki.

Then came the wonder that made the dream indelible. Whenever these women occasionally would die, in dangerous circumstances, sometimes with violence and malevolence from others, usually men, they simply dove into the waters of the energy lake, dipped themselves in its primal broil, and instantly arose again, phoenixlike, in ever more radiant forms. My dream voice sounded in my mind, "Ah, they are life itself; because of them there is no death! Death doesn't bother them! They know it as creativity, as rejuvenation, as the space for life to happen!" and I awakened feeling comforted and exalted. It made me certain that Lake Manasarovar—I still like the Tibetan name, Mapam, Invincible— is a female sea, the sun-shaped fountain of the infinite waters of life.

Enough about my dreams. Now let's move again into meditative mode. We will perform a sustained meditation together. Don't worry if much of it goes by you the first time; Tad will record it, so you can go over it again and again until you have it memorized.

The Yoga of Kailash

Get comfortable, sit up straight, breathe quietly, shut your eyes partway, and visualize along with me. Summon up in your mind's eye the refuge tree host of mentors, all your favorite guides, happily crowding around the root mentor as spiritually one with the Superbliss Buddha. By this time you can visualize me in there at the foot of the tree as the secretary! Add Naropa or Milarepa, or any of the great adepts whose story you know, or any holy being or great artist you like to think about. Imagine them all there shining in the sky around the jewel tree growing above this magic mother of lakes. You are familiar with this now. Even if you can't hold their faces steady, know they're there, they're happy to be there, they're happy you're meditating here, and they're pouring down their blessing light rays upon you—diamond rays going to your brain, ruby rays to your throat, and sapphire rays to your heart. Feel secure, peaceful, clear, and blissful in the light orb of the Superbliss mentor refuge host. The entire host melts into light and dissolves into you.

Now, feeling so good, your ordinary body and mind dissolve into voidness. Instantaneously you arise as a sapphire-blue Heruka—the wild man buddha-form—muscular, powerful, graceful, and handsome, holding vajra scepter and bell. You are in full union with a luscious ruby red Vajrayogini, who holds a vajra knife and skull bowl filled with elixir. You feel magnificent and you let your mind forcefully affirm a buddha-confidence, joyful,

277

serene, and loving toward all beings, as if you were a perfect buddha, present only for the love of them all.

As you think of all beings around you looking toward you as you have done before, add to your usual crowd all the local deities and spirits of your home region coming to attend you. Light rays from your heart emanate as Superbliss heroes and goddesses, and make exquisite offerings of all delightful things to all buddhas throughout the universe, as well as giving delicious food and drink to all the local spirits and world deities. Then mentally command the throng to cease any negative activities, to protect all beings, to give you the use of this place, and to sustain and defend the mandala palace you will create here. Command them further to resolve to become buddhas themselves someday. Then send them away happy.

Having made yourself at home here, take refuge in the Three Jewels and renew your bodhisattva vow—to free all beings from suffering—in the context of performing the Superbliss creation visualization. Repeat three times, slowly, with me: "I always take refuge in Buddha, Dharma, and Sangha! I always take refuge in the three vehicles, in the dakinis of the yoga of secret mantra, in heroes, heroines, and initiation goddesses, in the great heroic bodhisattvas, and especially in the mentor! Myself becoming Heruka for the sake of all beings, may I establish all beings in the exaltation of Heruka!"

Now do the Vajraheruka visualization for purification: Visualize a white diamond scepter on the crown of your head, radiating brilliant light rays that bless the universe. Turn it into a miniature, living, diamond buddha-couple seated in union on your crown, dripping with diamond liquid elixir of enlightened bliss. You quietly repeat the hundred-syllable mantra, if you know it, or else just *Om vajraheruka ah hum pat.* Repeat it twenty-one times, imagining the diamond light elixir flowing down into your body through your head, filling you up with bliss and peace. Become translucent like shining diamonds. Pray to the diamond buddha-couple on your crown and they melt into light, merge into you, and you feel pure and perfect.

Affirm the natural purity of all things and your personal buddha purity. Then dissolve into a voidness like that before this universe began. Visualize a thunderbolt cross in space, then a great wind, then fire, then water, then earth, then Mt. Kailash a hundred thousand miles high, and a gigantic billion-light-year force field around you made of fusion energy. Fierce mother goddesses emanate and stand watch all around. You can vary the details as you learn more, but mainly imagine yourself in an alternative dimension of your own buddha-design.

Within this protected sphere, visualize yourself atop Mt. Kailash as Superbliss Buddha Heruka, with the seed letter *hum* at your heart shining light rays of the five wisdoms, sapphire, emerald, ruby, topaz, and diamond, that fill your body, which becomes pure as a crystal egg. Light rays radiate outward from every pore of your Heruka buddha-body, inviting the Mentor Superbliss Buddha along with all beings to be the deity host of the Superbliss Wheel Mandala; all of them fill the sky before you and then dissolve into you. On your crown there is white *he,* at your throat red *ru,* at your heart blue *kah.* These three mean, respectively, intrinsic realitylessness, inexpressibility, and nonlocality. You resolve: "Since beings do not understand how things really are, they roam the life-cycle. So I shall realize the exaltation of Heruka and thus help all beings, naturally free of real subject-object dichotomy, realize their reality."

This is all still preliminary. Now for the main visualization. The *Blade Wheel* has already taught you to destroy the self-habit, replacing self-concern with other-concern. This brings you to the foundational freedom in selfless voidness. But that freedom can arise, embodied, to bring happiness to the universe of beings; you can arise as your own three bodies of Superbliss Buddha. This is the main creation-stage visualization, in which your freedom transforms your death into your truth body, your between-state into your beatific body, and your joyfully voluntary life into your emanation body—these being the three levels of your body as a buddha.

Now imagine your death; dissolve your sense of being into the void of transparent clear-light freedom. Affirm: "I am the natural diamond of the knowledge of freedom!" Then let your self-sense go completely and thus you contemplate the shining void truth-body of ultimate reality.

Without leaving that clear void, arise in space as a very fine, shimmering pink squiggle, aware of the planet built of wind, fire, water, and earth that is centered on the gemlike sacred mountain, Kailash in its mystic form. See the mountain's top with eight towers at the cardinal and quarter compass points, at its center a giant foundation with a lotus pedestal, with a pink moon-disk made of all the vowels and consonants. Float down into the moon-disk and emerge on it as a sapphire *hum*-letter, radiating rainbow light rays, from whose tips emerge the host of Superbliss deities. These rays emanate all the heroes and yoginis, ancient and present artist adepts from beginningless time who delight and exalt all beings and transform them into Superbliss deities. See yourself as the *hum*-letter, radiating artist adepts in an incessant stream flowing forth to all planets and all worlds to perform the liberating artworks that transform the lives of all beings. Affirm: "I am naturally the diamond thunderbolt of the body, speech, and mind of all heroes and unifiers." Thus you contemplate your subtle between-state as the buddha-body of beatitude.

Then you as giant sapphire wisdom *hum* naturally feel like emanating life-forms in order to liberate and bring more happiness to all beings. The whole lotus tableau atop the sacred mountain transforms into the entire Superbliss Mandala Palace, with its deities all made of wisdom.

Imagine this mandala palace of Superbliss Buddha, the mystic reality of the sacred mountain. It is made of jewel substances, square, with four doors with elaborate portico arches, each with eleven-jewel layers, with precipitous staircases leading down through giant thunderbolt scepter-prongs. Inside, at ground level, are guardian deities and giant elixir cauldrons. Four round tiers like a wedding cake, diamond, red, blue, and multicolored, ascend from the base, each layer smaller than the one below. There are eight couples on each of the first three tiers, white, red, and blue, respectively. Four goddesses on the topmost level face inward toward the central Superbliss Buddha Deity Couple. All the couples are dancing and jingling with jewel ornaments as ecstatic music fills the air. I imagine this palace as a kind of super-refined discotheque, glittering, architecturally magnificent, and celestially bejeweled. Around the edges of the mountain outside of the palace are the eight charnel grounds, extremely eerie and macabre, filled with deities and spirits, wild animals and vultures, corpses and zombies. This is the way the ordinary world looks from within the mandala, the zone of endless dying that is the gateway into endless life.

Imagine yourself as the chief Superbliss Buddha-deity in the center of the mandala in union with your consort, surrounded by sixty heroes and heroines. You stand on a solar disk in the center of the palace, dark-blue bodied, four-faced, your (east) front face black, the left (north) one green, back red, and right yellow. Each face is three-eyed, with the third eye of wisdom vision in the center of the forehead. You have jeweled crowns and ornaments. You have twelve arms, holding various symbolic implements with which you transform all beings into buddhas. Your two legs stand on deified embodiments of your own self-habit and self-concern habit. Your first two arms embrace your ruby-red Vajravarahi consort. You look out of all your four faces, your front face lovingly gazing on your consort. She looks lovingly at you, and you are so entwined that you feel her as yourself and yourself as her. Your union is totally mutually intersensitive, infinitely ecstatic, and in perfect balance. Your brain, throat, heart, and navel-centers are woven together by the four main mantras, the garlands of letters glowing ruby red. The mantra-garlands turn counterclockwise, their lights fusing into pulsing orbs. Your subtle senses melt, dissolving from crown to tips of sexual organs, and the whole universe dissolves into orgasmic bliss.

Around you the sixty deities of the mandala are also you and you are they, and they augment your bliss. Enjoy yourself as a community of ecstatic beings, the emanation bodies of your buddhahood. Look out past the charnel grounds around the many worlds, send out laser light rays and infinite emanations, drag all beings into the dance within the palace, anoint them with love and bliss, exalt them in their own natural freedom and joy, and transport them forth once more to bring their joy to all other beings.

Absorb the entire environment and community into your body-mind complex, becoming a field-being, no longer just a point of subjectivity locked away within your own skin. You become a new universe, the buddhaverse environment transformed by enlightenment and by the deities within it. Your legs are the galactic wind bow, your triangular loins the star-furnace of fire, your belly all oceans, your chest the earth, your spine the axial Kailash mountain, your brain the thirty-two-petaled lotus, your whole frame the infinite Superbliss Mandala Palace. The diamond, ruby, and sapphire tiers within the palace become your body, speech, and mind. The central bliss-wheel dais at the center is the center of your heart center. Your soul is a glorious sapphire *hum*, tiny as a mustard seed, shining with rainbow light-rays.

You generate within you all the deities of the mandala, beginning as your *hum*-soul turns into a tiny dark-blue Lord Heruka, four-faced, blue-bodied, and so on, as before. You embrace a ruby Vajravarahi in ecstatic union. The four channels of your heart center transform into the inner goddesses. At your twenty-four body points such as the crown, syllables transform into the twenty-four external holy places of the twenty-four hero-heroine couples, guarded by fierce protectresses.

Subatomic deities swarm toward you from the depths of infinite space, bearing elixirs of jewel energies to anoint you and all the deities in your body mandala. You affirm: "All things are pure yoga, I am pure yoga!" You merge with all, taste orgasmic bliss, and receive the wisdom-intuition consecration.

You hear the voice of your mentor as Superbliss Buddha, saying: "Noble one! That luminance-intuition you achieve through your union with the consort, meditate it as clear light! That clear light is the reality of transcendent wisdom. Not seeing anything with any other intrinsic reality is itself the seeing of clear light. The deities made purely of energy and mind are vivid like mirror images; they appear distinctly; behold them like the moon in water! And that union with your consort Vajrayogini is the inseparability of divine relative reality and clear light ultimate reality; it is the magnificent spirit of enlightenment. This is your highest consecration!"

Understanding this, you embrace the entire universe experienced as the Superbliss buddhaverse and divine community. You are one with the many beings who are mutually interecstatic, and your orgasmic joy is limitlessly open to absorb all ordinariness of things and beings and to transmute them into artist adepts sharing the same infinite happiness. In this time of triumph, you turn the entire universe into offerings and give it over to the buddhaverse. You feast, experiencing yourself as a community of deities, and you include all enlightened beings in the banquet.

Within this imagined creation, you repeat the main mantras. The syllables radiate light rays that turn into the deity hosts, who go out into the universe, make beings happy, and return and melt back into you. Affirming yourself as the essential energy of all artist adepts since time immemorial, you dissolve into voidness. From the void in an instant the entire animate and inanimate mandala is vividly and completely present. You bless your rosary. On a pink moon disk at your navel is a pink *hum,* and as you repeat the mantras, the letters circle and radiate the hosts of the deities of the five wheels. The deities accomplish beings' aims, return into the letters, and repeat this circulation constantly. Your Superbliss Buddha mantra is: *Om shri vajra he he ru ru kam hum hum phat, dakini jala shamvaram svaha.* Your Vajrayogini consort mantra is: *Om om om sarvabuddha dakiniye vajravarnaniye vajravairochaniye hum hum hum phat phat phat svaha.* Say these once with me today. May you repeat them millions of times in the future, in one life or another.

The concluding contemplation expresses appreciation; then it withdraws from the bliss mountain mandala and collects the mandala in your body and mind in a workable way so you can carry it along with you through life. First you make offerings to the mandala host and to the assembled world and local deities. You repeat the mantra of the interpenetration and interfusion of all things. *"Om* — All things are mutually interpenetrating, complementarily interfusing, extremely interembracing — *om ah hum."* You pray, "Valid Goddess, valid vows, valid words expressed; by these truths may the goddesses care for us!" The three circles of the offering assembly become indivisible bliss-void. The guests enjoy the essences of the offerings. You offer praises.

You conquer urges for extreme peace or existence,
Your vision enfolds all things like open space,
Shower me with your heart's rain, O Diamond Yogini,
Blessed with the flood of the protector's love!
O, goddess angels! Be kind and care for me!

The protectors and earth spirits all dissolve into clear light and arise as Superbliss Buddha Couples. They enjoy their offerings. You summon, welcome, and admonish them, and order them to serve. You dismiss them with a finger snap. The Superbliss Wheel Mandala community dissolves into you. You give praise. You don the armor of the subtle energies of the deities, encircling yourself with the fierce energy of the female guardians, the crow-faced dakini and company, repeating their mantras. When you break your contemplation and engage in daily life, you are automatically protected. You dedicate the merit, as always, to your swift evolution to buddhahood for the sake of all beings.

All this might seem overwhelming at first, but it is actually quite simple to visualize in general, once you become familiar with the sequence. Just think of Kailash, think of a fabulous palace on top of it, imagine yourself as a fabulous Superbliss Buddha within it, and imagine joy and confidence radiating from every pore. If you get into it, you can find teachers and texts, get initiations, learn the exquisite architecture of the palace and the anatomies of the deities. We are meditating this now to taste the possibilities, to learn to feel like a glowing ball of bliss and light, and to send out rays of happiness to all beings without exception. Feel yourself within the mystical dimension of Mt. Kailash, in the mystic palace that is its essence, and the energy of Kailash itself will give you peace and inspiration. Now you have transmuted death, the between, and life into the three bodies of buddhahood. The whole divine mandala universe is experienced as bliss-void-indivisible.

Use this visualization to rest in, a perfect buddha-self in a perfect mandala environment, seated in blissful union in the center of the sacred mountain, radiating love and beauty all over the universe in your wish to bring all beings to their own highest happiness. When you end the session, let even this vision dissolve back into voidness and arise as your ordinary self, inspired and renewed. Let's end this session now. This is my gift to each of you, your prize for the incredible determination that enabled you to overcome all obstacles and get here, your heartwarming courage and patience and perseverance that enabled you to get around the mountain and to begin to cope with the Systematic Path and the *Blade Wheel*, and the sweet consideration, enthusiasm, and kindness that makes you all such great companions on this pilgrimage. May we enjoy many others in the future!

TAD

Slowly, faintly, we rouse ourselves from the lushly quiet state we have fallen into on the beam of Tenzin's guided meditation voice. I am thrilled that I can let it go by without grasping for each detail too tightly and yet catch glimpses of shining strings of gems whisking by and deity streams and liquid lights. I can definitely report some progress has managed to settle into my altitude-addled brain in the midst of all the ups and downs of this journey. At the same time, I feel frustrated at the complexity of the visualization sequences, which I can hardly follow, and my mind is also questioning whether it's even necessary. We are reluctant to move from the spot, and Tenzin stretches and leans back but stays seated, lounging happily.

"This awesome visualization is the absolute—the relatively absolute, of course—icing on the cake of our pilgrimage and our path. We have touched on so much, learned so much, gone through so much more than we can immediately digest. Since we did it in such a liminal setting, it has gone deep into our beings, and it will unfold its blessings to us bit by bit over the years to come. In the Systematic Path you already have all the themes you need to completely fortify your spirit to rise to its evolutionary opportunity as well as to develop a profound understanding of your self. The *Blade Wheel* is like a karmic Roto-Rooter that purifies the subtlest layers of negative evolutionary momentum and empowers us to efficiently find what we need. And the Superbliss creation-stage visualization inspires us to achieve the most refined goodness and cultivate the most exalted creativity a human being can imagine. Now we've been through all these. I don't want to do more formal lecturing, so I would like to develop more free-form dialogues for the remaining days. Please bring out your doubts and questions, share your experiences and insights—even you, Tad."

Cautiously encouraged, watching the small, fast waves spill on the beach, I ask, "Couldn't it be said that we've picked ourselves up and come to what C. S. Lewis described as the wardrobe closet that is between worlds and opens both ways? So we're imagining these other dimensions in meditation as if they were very fantastic, but isn't it also just the sun on our faces and the wind in our hair? Like sex. Isn't it better just to feel it than to talk about it?"

"Yes and no," Jay interjects. "A lot of people would have much better sex if they talked about it more and did it less." Wolfgang, who has been critical of Jay's common denominator of humor, explodes in laughter. It is a healing, triumphant moment. "Unfortunately, that doesn't apply to me at the moment, but ah, well," Jay sputters.

I persist in seeking clues to integrating what we've found. "The thing is, tomorrow we will load back into the Landcruisers and drive to the border, then hike out through the Nepali Himalayas, then take a small plane to Kathmandu, then take a bigger one to Bangkok and then a bigger one still, back to the States. We will have left this extraordinary world—and we will be back in the ordinary one. And there will be a lot of things to tempt us back into the conventional view of things and reinforce the syndrome of self versus the world, that painful, ungenerous existence. So what can we do about it?"

"Collect many beautiful stones," says Richard with complete sincerity, "and arrange them all around your house and car and yourself and the people whom you love and want to keep at some extraordinary level."

"Yes," Tenzin agrees, "a fine practice, like hanging tangkas on walls as reminders of the extraordinary level of purified reality. Little windows of crystalline extraordinariness in the gray-

286

concrete-block building of the ordinary. You develop a strong as-sociation between articles of faith and the enlightening practices that accompany faith. This helps us keep the faith. Of course in Buddhism, in a way, faith is not in any object. Yes, you place your faith in the Buddha, and in your root guru. But what have they placed their faith in? Wisdom. For the Buddha there is nothing that has not been revealed. Everything is clear, it's faith in ecstatic clarity.

"That's why sometimes you read that the Tantra is beyond good and evil; here, you don't use the language of good and evil. It isn't that there isn't good and evil anymore, but you use the lan-guage of ordinary and extraordinary instead, and you say, 'I'm going to transmute the vision of the ordinary into a vision of the extraordinary.'

"Some of us will soon feel a let-down. We will think 'Kailash is over.' There it is over the hill, farther away. If so, most likely we are operating on the dualistic assumption that we are unenlight-ened, looking for enlightenment. But that is allowing ourselves to be trapped by our belief in the ordinary, in a dualistic view. That is leaving our new life at Kailash instead of living it ourselves.

"If we stay with the dualistic idea of seeking enlightenment outside of ourselves, then we go around Kailash hoping for a peak experience beyond all ordinary experience, assuming all ordinary experience is unsatisfactory. But now our pilgrimage has helped us taste a transcendent experience that is not apart from ordinary or relative experience, but rather makes relative experience totally extraordinary. So we can incorporate oblivion with ordinary real-ity. We can incorporate deep sleep with waking state. We can incorporate death with life—that's the challenge.

"For example, the whole life-cycle has three phases. Death, between, and life—we're always either in a state of death, be-tween, or life. In our lives we rehearse those phases every day by falling asleep, which is like the moment of death; dreaming, which is like the between; and being awake, which is like being alive. These phases in our daily lives and in our life-cycle bring home to us the intermingled reality of the ordinary and the extraordinary, the relative and the absolute.

"Ordinary death is a door of oblivion that is transmuted into the extraordinary reality of a buddha's truth body, into awareness of the absolute. One minute you're an idiot who's alive, and the next you're a genius who's dead but suddenly quite aware of the void, knowing a complete oneness with the void. Not seeing any sorts of differences in the world, being at one with all things in the world. The between-state, that state of subtle, boundaryless awareness, becomes the body of orgasmic interconnectedness, where you are infinite yourself and also infinitely interconnected with relative things, which are ultimately also infinite. You are then special bliss-awareness infused into things—you are that buddha-mind that's everywhere. That sort of pure light energy that is everywhere is your bliss of being in union with all things."

I blurt out: "The essence of art?"

"It's the visionary source of art. And maybe abstract impressionism and nonfigurative art are trying to tap into that play of pure light. Like Monet's water lilies and beyond that into pure abstraction. So, I don't mean to lecture, but let's get this straight.

"The buddha truth body is like sleep or death, it is awareness of the void, beyond pain or pleasure, good or evil. The buddha beatific body of ecstatic wisdom is like the dream or the between, an awareness of infinite relativity as a bliss-soaked virtual reality. And the buddha emanation body is like the awake state or life, awareness embodied in a coarse, limited body that is rigid against the world.

"The coarse body of the living, wakeful individual is therefore illusory insofar as it seems to be completely separate. At death we become aware of the illusion. We get one last look at the entire file of our life—it flashes before our eyes—then, whoosh! It's gone. After a certain panic and confusion we let go of our life, and suddenly we're aware of the oneness of all things and of our erroneous misconception of self. In the between you become aware of the ecstasy that lurks in everything. We are all very smart for a few days in the between. Geniuses. But then old karmas kick in, and we go shopping for new bodies among moaning, groaning lovers searching to melt the boundary between themselves. And at that bell-like moment of boundarylessness, guess what pops into

288

the womb? A genius, who will be quickly dumb again. Wisdom will be sacrificed for a lower form of compassion. For primitive though the resulting infant may be, it is an incredible magnifier of love.

"Soon the parents reeducate their sprout so that it is a self, and the misery of self against the world is set into play all over again. This is the realm of the emanation body, which is the only body materialists recognize.

"The extraordinary reality known by buddhas is what you visualize in the creation stage of Unexcelled Yoga Tantra. Then in the perfection stage—when you become a buddha—you realize it. Mt. Kailash is the ever-open mandala where you get a preview, a hint, a glimpse. And here at the lake, these waters are a vase of initiation. These two—mountain and lake—unite to push us toward this extraordinary vision. The energies of great saints and sages before us have invested the ordinary with the extraordinary here, so we pilgrims can have them as training wheels of enlightenment. Here nature itself is the mandala, and our ordinary time-sense, our genetic inheritance, and our past karma all get ground up in the wheels of pilgrimage, providing this extraordinary opportunity to purify everything. That's how these two places work, I think. Now what we need to reflect upon, in the process of celebrating our achievement of being here and congratulating ourselves, is how to emulate a buddha's tolerance of cognitive dissonance.

"If we realize that even a buddha's consciousness integrates duality and unity and that's what we're striving for, we needn't feel disappointed that the big reminder is getting smaller on the horizon. The reminder is back there, but what it reminds us of is always here, right in front of us. Our challenge is to make every mountain into Kailash and every lake into Manasarovar."

"Wow!" Richard bursts out, "Look!"

Below on the beach a Tibetan woman holds a bottle to her husband's ladle. He carefully fills the bottle and splashes the water remaining in the ladle onto his face. Their child is uncapping another vessel and trading the empty for the full.

"I'll be right back," Richard barks.

We stand and watch as the Tibetans turn and smile at Richard's introduction. Jay and I move toward the dune's edge, unable to hear, quite, what Richard chants down the wind as he claps his hands before him, takes three steps closer to the family, and kneels in the sand. The moment the smile breaks loose on the three faces, Jay and I start our clumsy run. With feet banging onto the beach we see the father lift his ladle from the wave and dump the contents on Richard's head, his eyes closed rhapsodically and his mouth twisted in a barroom guffaw.

Our knees hit the sand, as Richard's laughing face takes us in, his dripping forelock transforming him in to a Seussian creature of delight. He bows to the Tibetan family in thanks, turns, and heads up the beach, as the ladle hits the lake again and drips its cargo up the sands. Black eyes dance as, behind a mustache-festooned smile, the Tibetan mumbles something low and menacingly cheerful. Jay has taken off his glasses, and I'm trying to feel the water hit his scalp and neck as if it were my throbbing arteries this ice juice assaults. I see the pouring, and black hair resisting the rivulet that bounces off and down, the shocked smile. I understand every jangling nuance. But I cannot feel it, I realize, watching the Tibetan bearing the dripping ladle up the beach like a priest bearing a smoking censer on a chain. Holy Communion. The low, chesty Tibetan chanting peppers the air, the ladle moves, I bow my head, and—hearing the throng lining up behind me—I feel something bang the bell of my skull, and burn the drum skin of my scalp. The first touch is fire, then ice, then tinglingly both. Pain gives way to pleasure and outrage wells up, overwhelmed by a laughing-in-welcome surrender. Lakelets invade my collar, tunnel through my hair, vest, shirt, thermal shirt; icy spikes leap down my back. Reflexive shaking of the head and the blinking of old eyes turned inside out, shaking like a "Good dog!"

Turning I see the rest of the platoon, including Tenzin, kneeling down, rank upon rank. Jock is taking the hit and wiping clear his bulging blue eyes. Leopoldo and Valerie, holding hands and absorbing the spill from the same ladle, crying out together as I heard them one night in their tents crying aloud. James, his mouth crumpled on the crumbs of ten thousand smiles, blinks in anticipation, until the blinking is suspended for one long, wet count, and the ten-year-old opens his left-with-aunt-who-raised-him eyes, and shivering declares, "Oh my lawd!" and starts to giggle at his over-educated mouth's spontaneous accuracy. Tenzin takes amulets out from around his neck, touches and sings to them, peering out over the lake and mumbling to the open sky, as would a Navajo or Hopi, as would an Australian Aborigine or an African Zulu. As would any and all manner of natural man awaiting his dip in the waters of the gods.

Afterward, Jay and I walk back to camp via Chiu Gompa, a three-tiered Dharma castle slouching on the hill, waving hundreds of prayer flags in wind bound for Kailash, which sits smaller on the horizon, seeming almost to settle down among the other mountains, but for its scar and luminous ice cap.

The gusts of cold air increase in strength until, having climbed the hill and gompa, Jay is not comfortable on the parapets and tries to discourage me from clambering up to a crow's-nest rooftop. From here the world is indeed charged with the grandeur of the gods. Inside, altars to Padma Sambhava praise this one who tamed the rude gods and taught them to protect Buddhism. Outside the wind would seem to carry on his work.

CHAPTER SEVENTEEN

The Border Bribe

TAD

Kailash makes the Chinese nervous. But they can't tear it down like a monastery, only to rebuild it imperfect and less magical. Instead they've tried to make a museum out of Kailash, a public relations stunt; faux historical tolerance. Like a Sturbridge Village in a Maoist Massachusetts with bare-chested men banging molten muleshoes into shape, period-dressed women churning butter, and thatching roofs in centuries-ago-outmoded tradition.

They charge a hefty tariff and tolerate the mumbling, the scraping and bowing; they keep a few old monks in caves who won't make trouble. But I can't help but wonder what wars of conscience wage unseen in their eyes. They have contempt for us wealthy Europeans and Americans, traveling great distances to partake in the mumbo jumbo at the mineral-rich lake and the spooky-shaped mountain. Now with the Dalai Lama gone and a new generation learning to disco under strobe lights and drink beer from bottles, these idiot Western Buddhists appear in ever greater numbers—to tempt the locals back to their mani stones and mumblings. Don't the Chinese secretly suspect the old magic is bubbling still and will spill out one day, like a gigantic lotus on the surface of a lake?

We stop for lunch in a village on a long, straight plateau. Well-tilled fields and neatly laid-out farms abound, with the occasional greenhouse attached. "This is China's one real contribution to Tibetan culture," Tenzin sings out from the lunch tarpaulin. "The greenhouse! Allowing a greater variety of vegetables and a longer growing season. If they all packed up and left tomorrow it's one thing we can thank them for."

"His Holiness thanks them for forcing Tibet to be more communicative with the world," Jay returns.

"Yes, yes—His Holiness sees the best in everyone. Unfortunately, unless we strongly protest Chinese atrocities, the West will sell out Tibet for Chinese business. So our responsibility as Americans is to stand up for human rights," Tenzin says. "His Holiness is a Buddhist monk, and his responsibility is to take *The Blade Wheel of Mind Reform* to heart and to accept that karma is being worked out."

I follow this up. "So if the devil himself emerges to rule the world as Yeats said in *The Second Coming,* you know, 'What rough beast, its hour come round at last, Slouches toward Bethlehem to be born?' Do we make nonviolent resistance, à la Gandhi? Or violent resistance like the Allies of the Second World War?"

Tenzin responds without hesitation, "In the long run, the Buddhist-Gandhian position of His Holiness is logically the only solution. Only peace can create peace. But sometimes, short-term, there is the exceptional use of surgical violence. Here Buddhist ethics is pragmatic and flexible in specific cases. If a monk comes upon a mass murderer who is about to kill some people, the monk cannot intervene, even if he could stop it by killing the murderer. However, a lay bodhisattva has to break the fundamental nonkilling rule and save the lives of the many people by taking the life of the murderer, if that is the only way to stop him. This kind of exceptional situation becomes almost impossible to project on a mass scale. Would killing some Chinese on the frontier in defense of the country have prevented fifty years of genocidal violence against Tibetans? The Thirteenth Dalai Lama definitely thought so. The present Dalai Lama as a youth supported his government's futile attempt to defend against the Red Army at the very beginning. Many Tibetan patriots still think the mature Dalai Lama's pacifist policy is impractical. And the Chinese and other non-Tibetans think it is laughable. They feel the warrior's contempt for those who will not fight back. This is a hard dilemma always in a specific case."

Indeed, the Chinese contempt for us seems sharper as we wend our way to the border, because we've already paid for the ticket in—this is the send off. We find a little Cold War vignette awaiting us in a place called Taklalot, where ugly cement buildings culminate in a military center that looks like a broken-down high school back home. Bored yet self-important soldiers pass in and out of the fanciest official building I've yet seen here, in this most dreary outpost of an empire. Shoes are unpolished, top buttons are undone, hats are set at rakish angles, and cigarettes are tucked behind the ear.

We are invited out of our Landcruisers and ushered inside. Lobsang talks to the Chinese first. He is polite, reserved, and for some reason of little interest to them. The drivers are who they want to talk to. My favorite is nervous and plainly miserable. The truck driver is subtly and smoothly hostile, but the handsome, wide-faced driver is docile, as if having just woken up from a nap. Clearly, the other two are using his sleepy cheerfulness as their shield. They defer to him, stand behind him whenever possible, and nod their heads in agreement with what little he does say. Whenever the quickly changing array of questioning officers gets particularly in-his-face, he takes out his papers, leans back on his heels and points to a stamp of approval, naively referring to paper authority. But the deal is not to be made on paper—certainly, he knows this.

We're led into a room filled with boxes piled against the wall, a single desk with a chair, and a Chinese flag hanging limp on a stick. We crouch by the boxes, rolling our eyes at each other, dealing with the butterflies—fits of anger and fear flare up and leave a sour smell in the room. One by one we're waved over as our passports and visas are examined. One by one we stand by the desk, as the seated kid-officer and his two cronies ask questions through the docile driver who is merely translating now, seeming to express nothing of himself at all. One by one, we talk too loudly or too softly, make too much movement or stand drooping. Each of us loses equanimity to some degree. With a morbid fascination I watch our faces tense up, while in the back of my mind I'm thinking: "What have we accomplished, after all?" Let the ordinary obstacle strut up in watered-down-pea-soup uniforms, and our anxiety rises to meet this sterile authority.

The kid in charge stews, his companions hang over his shoulders, passing our papers between each other, with the odd phrase, like cardsharps conferring with friends before making a bet. They are unimpressed with everything except themselves and the fact that several Americans are at their mercy. The kid in charge passes his fingers down the stem of a pencil standing up on the desk, grabs it at its base, flicks it around, passes his fingers down the stem, reversing it again. Over and over.

Tenzin's papers get the longest scrutiny, I think, not because he's in charge but because he's tallest and biggest, and so must be made to feel small. For the Chinese, I'm sure, his one eye is difficult to read. He's neither brash nor frightened; his vibe is one of "I will play this game as long as you like; so really there's little point in playing it so long."

Now all our papers have been scrutinized. Surely some decision must be made, and yet the officer remains seated, his lackeys remain standing, chewing over the situation glumly, prolonging our discomfort. Tenzin does not rejoin the group. Instead he stands patiently, stubbornly, expectantly. I step back up to the desk and, with trumped-up cheerfulness, engage Tenzin in some talk of making camp in Nepal tonight. I'm attempting to exude an assuredness that this small inconvenience will soon end. The Chinese watch me jabbering away, and attempt to discern whether my easiness is intended as an insult to them.

The nervous driver and the angry one get up to reapproach the desk. The docile driver says something that gets the attention of the Chinese. He burps out a phrase or two, and now the punk soldiers smile. It's an offer. Finally the sleepy, faux-naif translator of a driver has come awake. They've been waiting for this. The other drivers are called to the desk. A few questions are asked and, with eyes averted, affirmatives are heard.

The docile driver, smirking ever so slightly with disgust, steps into the hall, passports are handed back, and the rest of us are motioned back outside to have our bags checked and chalked. They give Richard some grief about his bag full of rocks. He takes out his portfolio of slides and starts to talk excitedly about his paintings. How the rocks will fit into them. How he must take home the rocks. The customs guard decides he's crazy and lets him go.

They get momentarily excited about Leopoldo's video camera, then, suddenly, lose interest. We're free to go.

The deal is this: Once we have been dropped at the border, the cars and trucks will turn around and head back to Lhasa, a journey of several days. Riding for free, and cramping everybody's style, will be several Chinese soldiers. Nastier deals have gone down, certainly.

"I thought they were going to lock us up," confesses Leopoldo.

"Paper tigers," scoffs Wolfgang, nimbly using the Chinese phrase for describing Americans.

"Very interesting, though," Tenzin says. "You see why practice is so important? We can all get very calm at the mountain and at the lake. We are spoiled with porters and cooks and teachers. We don't have to argue about who does the dishes, or what show to watch on TV, or who gets to use the bathroom first. So we can all get very cool. But add just a little hassle with some border guards and what happens to our insight? Is it useless? Maybe not totally. Did you watch yourself a little? Did you experiment with your spy-consciousness when you felt righteously innocent?"

Indeed I did. My spy is the writer, the actor, the comedian gleaning material. But unlike these craftsmen, the Buddhist spy doesn't make comment on the material. It simply observes the "I" bobbing and weaving in the world like a cork on rough water.

Fifteen miles down the road we encounter a large, fortresslike town buzzing like an overturned beehive. There's a festival in progress. The townspeople are milling about in the open square eating, drinking, smoking, flirting, laughing. Persons of importance sit on raised platforms, a motley gentility, smiling, nodding to each other from beneath battered hats, beer bottles in hand. They look pleased to see us.

Eventually, a monk in plum-colored robes enthuses with Tenzin. Indeed, our presence is most auspicious. This is the day two newly rebuilt gigantic Buddha statues are to be unveiled. The townspeople will soon be ushered in to view the new treasures. Would we like a peek?

He leads us through the darkened ruins, huge dusty rooms with blackened murals on catacomblike walls, fierce deities glaring back as we shine our insufficiently bright flashlights over their savaged features. Stuffed wolves, and even the remains of a snow leopard hang from the rafters. Interesting, that these taxidermy specimens were not wrecked, while fierce deities lie in piles of ruined plaster. Respect for nature? More likely superstition.

Finally we pass into the one hall that is dimly lit with lamps and candles, where three huge, new gold-leafed statues are enthroned, a Shakyamuni Buddha, a Maitreya, and a Manjushri. Passing by them like a line of well-wishers meeting royalty, we unfortunately get too close. The monumental sculptures have a rough-hewn feeling, the figure modeling is stiff and clumsy. Yet it is a victory of liberty over oppression, won with the hard-earned money of the commoners reveling outside. They have precious buddhas inside their temple walls again. They are refugeless no longer. We bow, make solid donations, and express our appreciation of the resurrection of these famous images. The monk is overjoyed.

Upstairs are sleeping quarters, dusty meditation rooms lit with elaborate skylights, buttressed by terraces, and a huge kitchen filled with children, families, and old monks having their teacups filled respectfully, as in days of yore. Just outside, in a half-fallen-down attic room, two young men are playing steel-stringed lutes open-tuned in a dissonant chord. From a watch pocket I pluck out a Fender guitar pick, borrow an instrument, and do my best to make music. The young men laugh. Impressed with the pick, they mimic its fast pluck. I give the amber rounded triangle of plastic to one of them and, pantomiming, insist upon his sharing it with his friend. "Fender!" I yell pointing to the pick, "Jimi Hendrix! Eric Clapton!" They nod, knowing something important is being said.

Our party is huddled in the kitchen, by the far wall, near the huge smoldering vats. Chang is offered as well as tea. I find an ancient lemon-lime soda and smile at the coolness before the nasty sweetness bubbles through. Half a cup of tea is poured for each of us and placed nearby. If we so much as sip it, a young woman leaps up to refill it. Now roasted barley powder—*tsampa*—is offered and we are invited to roll it into little balls and chew it down. Tenzin demonstrates, thanking his hosts loudly, pouring tea into the bowl of powder, rolling the moistened portion into a round ball, then popping it into his mouth. He grunts and licks his fingers with glee to the appreciation of the old monks, who are laughing, nodding, buzzing. They tell him this temple was founded by the great translator of the late tenth and early eleventh centuries, Rinchen Zangpo. The modern translator is delighted.

Against my better judgment I prepare a ball and likewise pop it into my mouth. Not bad, like a combination of undercooked matzo and raw cookie dough. The rancid taste of the tea has been overwhelmed with the oaky barley. The finish is bitter, but washed down with the sweet and sour of the soda it's more than tolerable. The hygiene, however, is dubious at best. I notice Leopoldo pawn his tsampa off to a dog who scurries away with it.

Outside, the festival is in full swing. Three clowns are stealing from each other, bopping heads but never punishing the right culprit. We are at least as amusing a sight as the clowns. I can tell that the temporary nonduality of drunkenness has achieved its effect in certain loud galleries where some of the women exude a hard but flirtatious curiosity. A beer—for purely journalistic purposes—is looking awfully good. Reading my thirst, a jolly brown wrinkle-king holds a dusty bottle out to me to the delight of his toothless brown wrinkle-queen.

"Hey, Tad," Jock calls from an alleyway, "come on guy—we're outta here."

Back outside the twisting, turning maze of the town walls, our Landcruisers languish in the wind shadow of civilization. They leap to life and we're off. In five minutes we're over a bridge and back on a steep mountain road, the driver singing to a cheesy tape of raja-rock.

Up a steep, crumbling turn the engine quits, and we start rolling backward. Brakes are applied but do not completely stop us. Unless the brakes hold, it's a thousand-foot fall to the ravine below. My heartbeat thunders in my ears. The driver deftly shifts the vehicle into reverse, jump starts the engine, then throws it into second and, flooring the engine, lets go of the clutch. With a furious noise the vehicle slows, stops, and lunges forward. He goes back to singing without so much as a sidelong glance. Jay leans forward, grabbing the driver's shoulders. "That was very good!"

Yeah. Just when I thought I was cool. Death blinks its dust-red eyes just once, and enlightened awareness panics and flees. My spy clucks its tongue in disgust.

Over the next hill the driver parks and gets out. We do the same. The other cars pull up and park. Our driver points down a steep drop and pantomimes fingers walking. Then he points at us. Suddenly—and with a wrench of remorse so strong it shocks me—I understand. This is goodbye. The emotion welling up in my throat at the thought of never seeing this man—so good and decent and kind—ever again is confusing. Everyone else seems happy to have made it here, to the next stage of the journey. Our day packs are being stuffed into our hands along with a few extra articles. Jock is consulting with Lobsang over the size of the tip. I'm rifling through belongings trying to find a gift. The last of my apricots are pressed into this sweetly smiling driver's hands.

We embrace. Turning away, the suffering of change hangs a laundry line of prose just inside my eyes: "Love is a border bribe." Down the crumbling trail I go, toward the mountain-maddened Purang River, with Nepal on the other side.

Behind us the revving vehicles turn around, honk horns, and head back to Taklalot. I hurry below in what's left of the afternoon light to the Purang, soon to be the Karnali, churning through a boulder field marking the Tibet-Nepal line. I leap quickly from rock to rock, the numbing noise of the crashing rapids massaging my mind. Wet moss and lichen are tricky, but my shoes hold well, and momentum has me over.

The golden pods of our single tents, the green two-man, the mess tent and cook's tents, all neatly pitched on a long shelf, seem even more handsome than usual. The Nepali Himalayas rise up, furrowed briefly with forests, then velveteen with juniper, then naked and pink as a newborn in the last full light. Down here the Purang twists northeast. Over the last age it has carved out the three-thousand-foot Nubuche Peak we plan to negotiate by means of the Nara La Pass tomorrow.

The Nepali side of the river is greener, as if wood sprites protected it, or perhaps the Chinese give up their cutting only at the water's edge. Full-grown cedars hang at the base of these peaks, stone fireplaces and level, litter-free campgrounds seem oasislike compared with our usual fare. However, the river's chill is caught here in the V between mountains, between countries. Even the sunny patches are cold. We throw parkas on and answer the tea bell hurriedly.

Just before zipping the mess-tent flap I hear a "halloo!" and make out figures crossing the river. Four more porters to replace the yaks we left at Kailash, two men and two young women. The smoke from our fire drifts along the river's stones and is blasted by a horizontal band of light.

TENZIN

All present and accounted for. We have left the oppressed land of Tibet. Now we must eat and rest up for tomorrow's climb. The three-thousand-foot climb! Over the hump of Nara La and down the other side! Today we were up against political paranoia, we were afraid of the soldiers and their power over us, we were frightened and possessive. Maybe they'd take our cameras or our film while looking in our bags, or confiscate some holy relics. Richard's rocks. Wolfgang's herbs. So how far have we come really? How much have we learned?

Tantric Adepts and World Artists

Tonight, I want to discuss a famous group of yogis who did accomplish exactly this freedom. Here we are, in a sort of buffer zone between the ordinary and extraordinary worlds, Nepal and Tibet, having put one foot into the extraordinary, which we've all tasted together, and now rushing home to the ordinary. The yogis who accomplished this liberation from self-preoccupation and fear, professionally so to speak, were the eighty-four great adepts, the mahasiddhas. The great sorcerers, Lama Govinda called them. I think of them more as artists, secret masters of the craft of achieving the magic body. After they master the kind of creation-stage visualization we tasted yesterday, they practice the yogas of the perfection stage wherein they simulate the death experience, train themselves to master out-of-body experiences, and finally integrate the ultimate clear-light mind with their magic body, attaining buddhahood on the subtle plane. They are the ultimate inner scientists, whom I like to call "the psychonauts."

They are supposed to be able to travel to other worlds, other dimensions with their magic body. They use that virtual reality to accelerate their evolution, gathering merit and wisdom during accelerated lifetimes, and packing it into a single life. They assume reincarnation in ordinary, coarse bodies in order to live among us coarse-bodied beings, as a way of infusing our ordinary society and history with their extraordinary perspective. They feed the whole tradition of poets, musicians, singers, artists, craftspersons; and some were kings and queens. They are all artists of life—life itself is their highest art form. The Tibetan reincarnations—tulkus, rinpoches—are a unique social manifestation of the great adepts. But the great adepts are not only Buddhists. There have been Christian mystics and Sufi fakirs, like St. Patrick, St. Francis, Ibn Arabi. There's a statement in a famous adept poem, "Vishnu and Buddha are the same to me; Shiva and Vajradhara are the same to me." They don't discriminate about labels, they've gotten beyond the symbols.

The international group of characters known as the eighty-four great adepts numbers among them the great Nagarjuna, his disciple Aryadeva, the poet Shantideva, the princess Lakshminkara, and the great Superbliss masters Luyipa, Ghantapa, Kanhapa, and Naropa. Their stories are magical and humorous, joyful and macabre. Padma Sambhava was one of them. The larger family of adepts includes Milarepa, Tsong Khapa, and the Dalai Lamas. There have been thousands in Tibet. I think many of the West's great mystics were adepts in their own right.

The great adepts are often presented as antimonastic, wild and unruly persons. But they were more, not less, highly disciplined than any monk or nun. There are three levels of vows in Buddhist teaching. First, there are individual liberation vows, both monastic and lay vows of self-restraint taken in a monastic setting. The monastic vows include celibacy, nonviolence, poverty, not lying— especially not pretending to spiritual attainments you haven't achieved. There are a couple of hundred other monastic vows, three hundred plus for nuns, two hundred plus for monks. Every adept upholds individual liberation vows, whether as a monk or as a lay person.

The second level are the bodhisattva vows expressing the spirit of enlightenment. The basic bodhisattva vow is that you will not cease in your exertions to become a perfect buddha until all beings have been transformed by you, and you've incorporated them all into your buddhaverse. Then there are many more specific vows, like not holding grudges against people, nonviolence, and so on. Bodhisattva vows are harder to keep than monastic vows because they require keeping a positive messianic outlook on the world at all times, never giving up the determination to save everybody from suffering. You're determined to help everyone—even Hitler, Stalin, Mao Zedong, or Jeffrey Dahmer—become a Buddha in some future life. Every tarantula, crocodile, scorpion, they're all going to become buddhas with you some day in the future. Every Tantric practitioner and great adept takes and keeps bodhisattva vows; the spirit of enlightenment is their motivation for practicing Tantra.

Third, there are the Tantric vows, in which you never allow yourself to assent to the perception of anything as ordinary. You see everything as a magical, poetic reality. You reenvision everything. And this involves tiny vows; for instance, you're never going to have a self-centered orgasm or waste a drop of seed. So it's a very complicated self-restraining practice at an inner, instinctual level. The Tantric vows are the hardest to keep, because they involve controlling minute unconscious urges, which is why you need to perform many rites, say many mantras, and take many retreats. You transcend billions of eons of evolution, completing the whole evolution to buddhahood in one life, or three lives, or six lives, or sixteen lives, maximum, which is really easy compared to billions of lifetimes.

TAD

We rumble in agreement. Of course! Sixteen compared to billions—very good return on your investment. You don't have to be an accountant to see this, but! Tough—very, very, very tough.

"Therefore, Tantra is sometimes called the easy path," Tenzin continues. "Unfortunately Westerners who have heard about Tantra have tended to misunderstand this easy way. We think it's some gimmick, a weekend seminar in Southern California. This is a mistake. We can understand this better when we look at Milarepa.

"What was he doing year after year hiding away in these high Himalayan caves, burning the inner fire? What was he burning, actually? He was burning karma. He was dying and being reborn hundreds and thousands, perhaps millions of times in one life-cycle.

"Sometimes, immersion in Tantra requires not living conventionally. But most adepts keep a low profile and maintain a more conventional role in societies."

"What about the clown monks?" I ask.

"Enlightened people will clown, if it's necessary to help people."

"But in festivals don't the jester monks make fun of the conventional monks as they come out of the monasteries?" I persist.

"That's not really the job of a great adept, that's more a folk-cultural thing. Like a Punch and Judy show or the commedia dell'arte. In festivals people will take on all sorts of roles, Lord of Evil, Lord of Death—different gods and goddesses. It's Mardi Gras.

"Undoubtedly, Tantra can become dangerous. The very reason it is so powerful and exhilarating is you unlock your own unconscious. You find your deep urges; you bring them out; you exorcise them. It's brain surgery of the soul, and if you do it wrong and let this amazing energy manifest a little off, this way or that—it can drive you crazy. You can become insane. You can become not only not enlightened, but really nuts. And you can screw yourself up for many lives, they say. Westerners are particularly prone to such disasters since we have grown up in a nihilistic culture with very little moral control. With our tendency to think there are no repercussions to negative actions, we have a false courage about us. So we have to be very careful about this.

"The Dalai Lama demonstrates that the extraordinary practitioner must comply with the ordinary. Within, he or she is flying from one universe to another. Without, he or she should be obeying the Ten Commandments or whatever ethical code—because that is moral behavior. This must be elaborated even more carefully in the modern cultural setting.

"We can set up one rule of thumb. The regular behavior—even of the crazy adept—is virtuous and helpful to others, and fits more or less with the conventional. So when someone becomes an alcoholic, screws everybody, even infects them with diseases, we can say, 'Whatever state has been attained, whatever you call it, is deluded. He's lost it. He's regularly harming, not helping.'

"It is important to establish this now, as we go back into usual reality, first Asian reality, and then American reality. Do not look to become subversive outwardly. Don't give anybody the excuse to put you in jail or put your picture up in the post office. Become subversive inside. It's a bloodless revolution. That's what enlightenment is, the ultimate and bloodless revolution that revolts even from the idea of revolting: thus the revolution becomes evolution.

"Therefore, with the case of Tibet we could say, 'Why fight for Tibet? They're showing nonviolence while their country is being overtaken. That's a wonderful lesson to everybody. Sooner or later the Chinese will get it. We don't have to struggle; let's just study Dharma.' And that's true. Wouldn't it be excellent if more and more people could go to Kailash? If Tibet could be a Dharma school for many people with monasteries all around Kailash filled with well-trained lamas? We could have multitudes of people from all over the world on retreat at all times. This planet needs such schools."

"The thing is," Jay sighs, seemingly exhausted by the strain of restraining his obvious enthusiasm, "the whole mother meditation. Tibet is one of the great mothers of the Dharma. And when you meditate on all the things that your mother has done for you — when I realize what the Dharma has done and is doing and will do in the future, I want to repay the Dharma mother. Which is to alleviate her suffering and set her free."

"Absolutely correct," Tenzin says, quite pleased. "As long as we remain nonviolent, as long as we refuse to hate the Chinese, it is good to stand up and speak out for Tibet. To call out against human rights violations; to stand up for anybody who's being tortured or imprisoned. We shouldn't do it in a way that hates the torturer. We should be able to love the torturer as well as the victim, while vigorously speaking against the torture and doing our best to stop it.

"Let's put it into practice. Let's pray for our drivers and the Chinese soldiers they've been forced into hosting. Let's pray that in the next few days something happens that evolves the ordinary level ever so slightly. That they inadvertantly laugh at the same thing, or are frightened by the same thing, or find something beautiful at the same moment, be it a sunset or a soaring eagle or the swaying form of a girl on the road, something that links rather than separates them. Let us pray that each walks away from the trip thinking, 'That wasn't so bad, really. They weren't so terrible.'

"Please close your eyes. Visualize six or so of them in the truck. See them all laughing, although you can't hear the joke. Lend your prayer to their laughter. Feel it growing, mysterious and mischievous, feel the laughter want to spill over into words or, better yet, deeds. Feel this oddity well up in the surprised hearts of men accustomed to anger but now unexpectedly awash with joy. Push your heart into that joy with them.

"Now open your eyes and realize you've helped create the moment when such things can and will occur!"

"The power of prayer," Richard mumbles, ambiguously, aloud.

CHAPTER EIGHTEEN

Up and Over the Pass

TAD

Breakfast is a good one with porridge and jokes. James and Tenzin set off on the trail early, in high spirits. Lobsang finally kicks us out of the mess tent. I'm still drying my hair from an early-morning river half-bath. Everyone else has saddled up packs and shuffled off. I tell Jay I'll only be a second, but delay a moment longer, watching the ritual rolling and tying and packing up of camp.

The trail teases, pulling away from the river, then rejoining it. In long underwear and khakis I zip along for warmth, catching up with no one. Hurrying by a roofless cabin made of river rock, I jog up a steep bank. After moving in and out of the river's chill, pulling away from the Purang, I'm grateful for the sunshine. A few deciduous trees dot the trail otherwise dominated with evergreens. It feels more like the Alps than the Himalayas at the moment. But this won't last long. This bluish-green hollow of pine and juniper scrub is a velvet prologue to the omnibus of rubble I glimpse, sporadically, ahead. Gravel piles and crumbling cliffs emerge, with brief infestations of brush popping up like sparse pubic hair on old, naked people.

It gets steep very quickly and I'm scrabbling along a continuous wedge cut into the side of the mountain. Shut off from the vista then opened up, then shut off again, depending on the angle of trail over terrain. The going is easy, then abruptly difficult, more difficult still, then easy again. I feel like a child being toyed with by some intelligence that refuses to step forward and identify itself.

As I teeter alongside a cliff's edge I hear Tenzin saying last night, "Tad is somewhat conspiracy-minded." Indeed, what survivor of this world isn't conspiracy-minded? A Buddhist, that's who. A Buddhist who says, "You get what you deserve. If it's your karma to fall, you'll fall. If it's not your karma to fall, you won't fall." I don't think it's my karma to fall, but I wouldn't bet my life on it. Adrenaline puts a spring in my step. I have to remind myself not to hurry, as anxiety steals over me in gentle, almost voluptuous waves; butterflies in the gut, heart palpitations, dry mouth, weak knees, tingling fingers, and dead toes. Finally, I catch up with Jay, who greets me with: "My brother would have loved this! He lived for this stuff! He was always trying to get me into the mountains more! I get a little nervous on parts of this—but I see his smiling face—I tell you, Tad, the kora was for me. This is for Michael."

We hike together for a while. I walk near the edge, about a foot away from the lip where the ground is usually quite solid—it's the secondary and tertiary trails abutting the mountain above that are shaly and give way. The edge itself does not give way, usually.

Jay is made nervous by my route. "I can walk out by the edge," I explain. "I'm afraid of heights, after all. So it's wheel-weapon stuff to walk near the edge. Take a little chance and what do you get? Far more solid a trail. Besides, I have walking shoes.

In the middle of the Himalayas you have glorified sneakers and they make me nervous."

"The way you walk on the edge makes me nervous."

"I like my stick in my right hand stabbing at solid real estate on the right, so I walk a little to the left—which is where the edge is at the moment."

He shakes a hand like a clown waving hello. "I make you nervous, you make me nervous. Maybe we should spread out a little. No, please, after you."

It gets nasty for a little while. The trail is a loop-the-loop diagonal slash across the mountain at as much as a forty-five-degree pitch. The pitch of the fall off the trail is far steeper than that, about seventy-five degrees. The steepness of the trail is fun to look back at and appraise, for we make fast, impressive progress and no trees block the view. The seventy-five degrees off the side of the trail is better off not being surveyed. Like a Doberman on a long leash, you remain constantly aware of its location without looking the beast in the eye.

The trail shifts onto an outrigger flank and the climb pulls into view. It looks steep from below, which is unsettling. Slopes do not look as steep from below as they turn out to be. I know this from skiing. I pause to take a picture. Jay stops and squints, stands on his toes and squints again: "Is it my imagination or is that very steep?"

"In either case, it's your imagination."

"Oh well, nice knowing you," Jay offers, sounding very Dharmic and forging ahead in his glorified sneakers.

No one else is visible. I'm enjoying being last and letting myself zone out down below at the landscape. I know that at drops higher than where I'm standing right now, a fall becomes deadly. With the exception of Jock, all the people on this trip are amateur mountaineers. So soon no one but he will have any business looking at the drop curling below, but no doubt we all will at one time or another. For a minute I surrender to the morbid thrill of contemplating crashing down, the edge courting me like a glamorous vampire moved in next door: "Do drop over for a drink sometime."

In the next hour concave turns are commonplace and things you can grab hold of become very important, like jewelry on a breastplate of earth. Cleavage has always been exciting, though rarely this dangerous. It's the convex turns that spook me now. The trail curves away, I can't see much. I'm just wagging my ass off the edge of the mountain, feeling like an easy target for trouble.

I'm still viewing this as a "me" against "it" world. Buddhism harasses this quickly reappearing old construct, but the construct keeps reappearing with a vengeance, saying: "This is my life you're playing with now. Not word games."

What is the meaning of life? "Don't fall off the mountain." What does the great sage say? "Don't fall off the mountain." What have I learned in the Himalayas? "Don't fall off the mountain."

For long stretches the edge consists of retaining walls back-filled with trail; these walls break in spills I can't imagine repairing without standing on air, and the trail improvises higgledy-piggledy above the spill through dried mud and rubble.

Below churns the river. Across from us is another mountain, quite like this one, but without the thin scar of trail. At this height the trees are gone. Below, lone cedars stand like majestic forest lords, teetering on the gnarled surfboard of lichened rock, at a landslide's whim. Here and there on the neighboring giant across the way, great slashes run, raw red earth dries brown with broken, dead trees scattered down the slide like a spilled box of kitchen matches. I look down at smaller pines in stubborn clumps in the wind shadows of crags, and at juniper growing beardlike over almost everything, finding some rootholds even among the ice, snow, rain, and wind-blasted walls. It's not to be seen up here, though, where there's nothing left to hold on to except rocks, which are shaly and slide easily. The trail looks like folded and refolded sections of ancient cardboard.

We're widely spaced, within calling distance perhaps, but no one's tested the line of communication for a while. I'm holding on to my sense of humor like the coiled rope we didn't pack.

The edge is interesting, the way a witchy woman is interesting. If you flat out stare at her, melodrama results. If you specifically don't look at her, other bad things transpire. So I try to sort of look but not look. Occasionally I make the mistake of obscuring the edge with the brim of my Ernest Hemingway denim cap and not worrying about it. Twice already this method has landed me in the shale at the very edge of the ledge, laughing "Holy Shit!" as I back myself into a safe position, chastising myself. "That was not good, Tad, not good at all!"

There is plenty of easier trail, too. The easy trail is three to four feet wide—a regular three-lane thoroughfare. I soon encounter Jay again, highly flustered, sitting on a rock.

"You all right?" I ask by way of introduction.

"No!" he says, looking very pissed off. "What the hell am I doing here? What am I doing this for? This has nothing to do with the Dharma. We're not even in Tibet! And where's Jock? Taking pictures somewhere! Where's Lobsang? Where is Tenzin? Mantra-ing to the void two inches to the left. This is absolute, unmitigated bullshit! Are there ropes anywhere? No! Where are the Sherpas? Carrying Valerie and Leopoldo's godforsaken video equipment. Is there any radio communication? No. Is there any communication of any kind? No. I mean what happens if one of us falls off?"

"We're not going to fall off," I say, trying to sound sure.

"How the hell do you know? You and your Irish death wish. You'd secretly love to fall off. Then you wouldn't have to worry about being a great dad, a great writer, or a great lay. You'd just be a great mess. An air-lifted coffin with lots of women crying over you."

"Yeah, but what if I only got injured? There's no fun in that. So let's get going. But there is one Dharma deal here, buddy." I try this lightly. "If one of us falls, we shouldn't take the other along."

"Oh great!" Jay flops his hands to his thighs. "A buddy system with no buddy—is that it? Great! Just what I always wanted in life. A friend I really could not depend on!"

"Just walk where I walk for a ways. And don't look you-know-where."

"This is absurd. This is peak season! I could be selling apartments like crazy on the Upper East Side. Flirting with long-legged divorcees, telling them—"

I break in: "I'm a Buddhist! I've been to Tibet! I know Tantric secrets that'll send you into orgasmic fits for fifteen hours on end!"

I keep my mouth shut until I've climbed to the top of the next rise, where Valerie is congratulating James on his progress thus far, while Leopoldo is being admirably candid about his fear of the precipice and the snow ahead. Above, the trail is like a lengthy clothesline progressing toward an unseen anchor. It sags between props, then steepens again. We're in a sag spot, from which I see Tenzin's red parka ahead sprawled over a rock just before a long, steep stretch twisting sideways where a wind-shadow preserves a hundred-foot patch of snow. Wolfgang is pushing up to Tenzin with his two sticks, with Jock in the lead and Richard plodding right behind him, straight into the snowy stretch. With Lobsang— Where did he come from?—standing in the middle of the whiteness.

Furtively and cowardly, I abandon Jay and the others to the rear guard. Not wanting to hear about fear right now, I press on, hurrying past Wolfgang to catch up with Tenzin, who is surveying the slope, looking very much the commanding officer. As I arrive, a cry comes up from below. We stare back down the trail and at one another, horrified. Could this be what we've all feared? Is someone hurt? Did someone fall?

"Where's James?" Tenzin demands.

"Down the trail . . ."

"Shit! Jock! Lobsang!" he cries out. "James! Down there!"

"Should I—"

"No—let them," Tenzin says, as Lobsang, moving very quickly, his face set in absolute neutral, passes without acknowledging us. Jock clocks in right behind him. But for the sound of their rapid descent, the mountain is absolutely still. We're holding our breath. The seconds tick by and dread builds. It's been quiet too long. The news is going to be bad. I steel myself against tragedy, clenching my teeth.

"Is all-ri . . . ight!" Lobsang's two-tone call announces happily.

"*Om mani padme hum!*" Tenzin sighs aloud, immediately admitting fault. "We're too spread out. We must have a Sherpa here for anyone who wants one. This is getting a little more serious than I anticipated. We have to regroup. Snow and ice—now, Jesus! It's a good thing Nena isn't here for this," he laughs. "Damn. If James had fallen badly we'd really be—Hey! Jock! What's happening?" he booms.

"James wants a Sherpa for this—" Jock pants, "he's a bit upset."

"Of course, he is! Perfectly sensible! We got strung out too far."

Richard, halted halfway up the snowed-in section, is reassured of no accident and resumes his ascent. He's picking along from one frozen foot and hoof print to another, gingerly working through muddy snow and ice to a boulder at which he stops and rests, rubbing his knee thoughtfully and waving me on.

"Be careful of the snow, Tad!" Tenzin drones behind me. "It could give way. Maybe do as Richard did—nearer the edge. It's more solid there!"

It's strange for Tenzin to get nervous over this. Hearing that cry from below must have really rattled him. The deep snow has been wind-packed more solidly than Styrofoam. Jabbing the edges of my boots into the whiteness, I cut and lift, and cut and lift, side-stepping up the hill as with my first skis at eight. Far from being difficult, this turns out to be the easiest steep section of the climb. Others don't like the Styrofoam, or don't trust the technique. True, you need a heavy sole on a heavy shoe to really bite in.

Leopoldo's climbing with herky-jerky movements, ashenfaced. James is calm, but tired-looking and slow. Jay's glorified sneakers are a disgrace. I put my camera away after one quick shot of Tenzin on the Styrofoam. It's a moonscape of badlands, gravel falls, and sand slides, dotted with one pocket of snow, all the way down to an ancient mirror of a river.

To take pictures in such a situation is not polite, it makes people superstitious and even more nervous. What if something bad did happen right after I took a picture? Who's to say it wasn't my camera that distracted them? And even when everything turns out OK, why capture people at their most nervous? *Schadenfreude* is a German word meaning happiness at the expense of others. Because I do not want to exhibit *schadenfreude,* I refrain from taking pictures of bad spots.

Following Richard up the last of the notches, we rest at the top, surprised that a more dramatic view doesn't reward us. The reason is simple, this is only the first of three steep hikes strung together with long sloping cuts across an undulating mountain. The middle undulation is in shadow—one long walk along a trail whose width we have no way of knowing.

First we go down again, then over, then up, then up some more. Then, just when we think we've got a clear shot, a yak appears, with several hundred pounds of timber tied lengthwise to its body. We stop for a long lunch, and, wouldn't you know it, Tenzin starts to talk about death.

TENZIN

Facing Death

Just as every lifeguard must know CPR in order to protect swimmers at the beach, similarly every lama and—until recently—most Tibetans knew the basics of dying mindfully. Not only because we might die today, but because one day or another we will die. We must die. When we do, if we can recognize the normal phases we can expect to go through, we can relax a tiny bit and die with some skill and grace. I know several of you are familiar with my translation of *The Tibetan Book of the Dead.* Still, I thought a good topic for today would be: everything you always wanted to know about death.

There are eight stages of dissolution. Whether death comes peacefully at home or happens due to an accident in your car or an airplane crash, or even a fall from a high place, the same experiences can be expected to occur as you die.

First you will note a buzzing all around; some call it a ringing in the ears. Hallucinations set in. You go into a dreamlike state where the things of this life are swirling around you. Let them go.

Then you'll encounter a smokiness. Let it go.

Then you'll see sparks, fireflies, roman candles. Don't be afraid of this. Relax. Let it go.

Then you'll see a clear candle flame. Try to stay still with that, then let it go.

Then you'll see the open sky full of luminescent moonlight.

Then the sky full of radiant sunlight.

Then the sky full of darkness—which you mustn't be afraid of. Darkness at noon, so to speak. An eclipse-like phase.

The eighth and final stage of the death experience is the clear light, pure transparency, like the open sky filled with the predawn grayish twilight, where the light seems as much within the objects as shining on them from outside. Stay alert, even as you fall asleep during the moment of darkness, to be ready for this clear light. For when you concentrate on it you're becoming aware that you, yourself, are a clear light, that this light is you as one with the infinite buddha-mind, Shiva-mind, Godhead, Trinity, Great Mother. Guided by that awareness and that transparency, you won't feel driven to arise again immediately, you won't be attracted to this or that form so easily, and you'll have more choices about where you go, how you move, and to what imagery you're attracted, which dictates in whose womb you reincarnate.

Om mani padme hum, which you've seen inscribed everywhere on rocks, prayer wheels, giant prayer wheels—though it calls upon Avalokiteshvara, the bodhisattva of compassion, as the holder of the jewel and the lotus, its deeper meaning is the cosmic vision of male-female union. *Om mani padme hum* declares that everything is perfect in every atom in every instant, that compassion and wisdom are present everywhere, that love is present everywhere. Bliss emerges from everything everywhere. There is nothing to fear. Even when it looks like hell in front of me, I can just embrace it and it will turn into a bed of roses.

So *Om mani padme hum* is the safeguarding vision of the compassion of Avalokiteshvara extending around us. It's like the All-
state commercial, but with Avalokiteshvara's thousands of hands
holding us up in moments of death and rebirth. *Om* is the god
realm, *ma* is the titan realm, *ni* is the pretan realm, *pad* is the hell
realm, *me* is the animal realm, *hum* is the human realm.

Each syllable goes to a different realm of the universe. Reciting
this mantra, you join the pulsing heart energy of Avalokiteshvara,
who is constantly beaming emanations to different parts of the
universe. It's beautifully expressed in *The Jewel Case Array Sutra,* in
which Avalokiteshvara travels to hell in his multiarmed form and
releases tears from the eyes in the palms of each of his thousand
hands, and these tears flood the red-hot griddle land of hell. It
cools down and then he creates an energy beam, a laser or tractor
beam, and sucks all the souls out of hell and installs them in different buddhalands so that the beings get relief and are torture-free
for a lifetime or two.

Wolfgang came up with a wonderful parallel for this image of
salvific power, aligning it with an image he remembers of Christ
on the Cross. Christ dies and then flies straight to hell, where he
cannot be held, but blasts straight to heaven with all the sinners of
hell riding the powerful wave of his virtue. It's a lovely vision. Hell
freezing over, hell flooding over, the lair of the dark one bathed
in sunlight—whatever! Here, it is the compassion of Avalokiteshvara.

Tibetans wrap their minds around *Om mani padme hum,* instead
of ruminating on some alienating personal thought like, "What do
I do? Where do I go? What do I fear? What do I want?" They
trance out on the mantra, which is like saying, "All is well. All is
well. All is well. Everything is perfect. Wisdom and compassion
uphold every atom!" And the prayer wheel goes around reinforc-
ing that energy.

You can visualize a six-sectored wheel, with *Om mani padme
hum* written on the six spokes, spinning in your heart. Its rainbow
light radiates from a spiritual dynamo that sends it out everywhere
in the universe in a flood of heart pumpings, and their karmic

echoes come back to you in the relieved prayers of rescued living beings, which only increases the power of the circuit.

Indeed, this is what all Tibetans are doing! So when a porter carries a one-hundred-kilo load up the mountain, mantra-ing out on *Om mani padme hum, Om mani padme hum, Om mani padme hum,* if he falls off the cliff, he's carried off by the mantra. Even if his body is smashed, his mind is cushioned by a never-ending mantra that fuses with the heart of Avalokiteshvara, and—bingo—inside of so many days there is a positive rebirth. Nothing is lost. More than likely he's traded up out of being a porter. More than likely he'll be a more learned Buddhist; if not a high lama, then a high layperson, on the strength of his faith and focus on *Om mani padme hum.*

Think of the thief crucified to the right of Jesus, who with his last strength bears witness to the true Son of God. So certain is he of Christ's divine destiny that Jesus, mid-agony, smiles on him, saying: "For your faith in me you will be exalted at my right side in heaven this very day."

Anyway, one thing to remember, if we want to enter into this extraordinary reality to insure our evolutionary progress, is that we don't want death to become an obstacle or an interference. So in case we do die sooner than later—the car goes the wrong way, or a madman with a gun gets us—we hold on to this life as long as is sensible, but when the inevitable suddenly comes, at a certain point the thing to do is not to fight it. Sure, we should fight to stay alive whenever possible; but when death is clearly happening, it becomes extremely important to stop fighting and be very calm. Use your intelligence to die well. You can be prepared for this from now on if you take care to live well.

We want to have the mind always in a positive flow. Here is where mantras are unbelievably helpful. If you develop an inner murmuring like water flowing, your mantra will bring grace and gracefulness to your last stand. A death where the mind easily leaves the failing body and rolls on with the mantra unimpaired, even released, for you have tuned your little wheel of a life to the greater wheel of the Dharma.

Tibetans knew how to live beyond death in a multilife understanding, and that's how we have to learn to live. Instead we split the atom, and in splitting wisdom from compassion, we manufactured a nothingness maker. The ultimate killer. Suddenly wisdom became the enemy rather than the protector of life. "Behold Vishnu, lord of destruction!" is what Oppenheimer said, referring to a fierce vision in the *Bhagavad Gita,* upon seeing the first mushroom cloud. But by setting *Om mani padme hum* free, Tibetans performed the nuclear fusion of Tantra. They did not set matter against itself, they freed matter within itself. They chose to explore the inner technology and not to play around with atoms. They went within the atom into mind and mantra.

TAD

Suddenly I stand up, waving my hand idiotically like someone in a crowd when a television news crew points a camera at them.

"Yes, Tad," he says.

"What if I don't know the visualization of *Om mani padme hum* that you just described, say I've never heard what you've just told me."

"Yes?"

"But anyway I recite, '*Om mani padme hum,*' because I've heard it brings good luck."

"Right."

"By saying these otherwise meaningless syllables am I included in an extraordinary equation?"

"Yes. You are getting close."

"Even if I am ignorant of any of these more profound implications?"

"Absolutely right. Anyone who begins to say it starts to familiarize themselves. Early visualization practice of the creation stage is called familiarization, like a baby listening for the particular heartbeat of its mother. *Om mani padme hum* is the heartbeat of the archangel of universal compassion, the heartbeat of God, Buddhist theism if there ever was any. It is the heartbeat of the strong love force of the universe."

"Perfectly clear, Professor, thank you."

"Then once you get familiar with the heartbeat, eventually you'll meet someone like me or even a real lama, whom you can ask for the *Om mani padme hum* initiation. Then you get into another magical level: the holographic vision that is transmitted. Some people will meet Avalokiteshvara in a dream, or Tara. The technology becomes more refined, more developed. Saying the mantra more with deeper insight, your familiarization is enhanced and your life merges with the mantra."

I envision a singer finding the voice of the earth and singing a note in harmony with it, resonating with the earth, and becoming, thereby, an adjunct to the earth. This is Hopi thought; the singer becomes one with the world, instead of compartmentalized off somewhere mumbling Hamlet's soliloquies.

"So stop with the long face!" Tenzin yells, tapping the brim of Jay's Geographic Expeditions baseball cap. "You're worried about a dead brother, your mother, yourself—falling down the cliff. Get with it, Jay! There are no dead people! Your long lost, dearly departed, most beloved is the baby in the pram going goo-goo, gah-gah. There's no longer anything to mope about. Find your lost loved ones in your neighbor and be kind to your neighbor. For all beings," he yells, looking at each of us, "are. They never are not. They are either alive or between. There is, hypothetically, a split second between life and the between that is properly called death. A boundary, a line with no width, something ultimately not there except as an arbitrary border. We are all this long, never-ending story. We can either keep going on and on addictively—a daytime soap opera running not forty years but forty trillion years—or we can find freedom from that bondage and then carry on a cosmic play at will.

"So don't fear to die. Death is a natural liberation. Of course, avoid and postpone it as long as possible, since your human life is so precious for the opportunity of full liberation. Free yourself from unconsciousness so you'll be sure to face death fearlessly."

Silence. I observe that Tenzin looks happily at each one of us, appreciating his own attunement to the deep potential of peace and freedom. No one seems to feel the urge for more "buts" and "ands." The silence is nourishing, easy. Only I am wondering, still, "what if" and "if so." But the force of the group's shared sufficiency somehow keeps me quiet this one time.

After lunch and a rest, people arise with sighs and groans and carry on much farther up, to the top of this most difficult pass. Then swiftly we come down to a lush camp by a rushing, icy, milky, glacial river.

CHAPTER NINETEEN

The Eclipse

TAD

The next morning, freshly invig-
orated by sleep, Dharma, and instant coffee, we cross a narrow,
picturesque footbridge. The planking is sixteen or so inches wide,
four feet above the water, and without handrails. Those of us with
walking sticks hold them horizontal as we move stealthily over the
churning rapids. Tenzin starts off. I'm right behind when I recognize a mischievous glow lighting his face. The crashing water
brings out the boy in us. Suddenly he wheels with an upturned
stick, but I'm ready for him. I choke mine at either end, thrust it
forward sideways, and demand the strike. "Hah!" Then, whirling
my stick around in slo-mo time-honored choreography, I whack

back with "Take that!" and strike his sideheld sword. A smile of satisfaction smears both our faces.

"Back!" he yells over the crashing water, "I was fencing champion of my class at thirteen!"

"Back!" I return, undaunted, "I was fencing champion at fifteen!" Leaving out that most of the class were girls.

It's Little John and Robin Hood. What fun it would be to play the whole game through and one of us end up in the brook, but I know better. You can't win, fighting a superior. Police put you in jail. Professors give bad grades. Gurus make you the laughing stock. I take a step back, bowing my head. "After you, royal sir."

Tenzin swells his chest, and proudly accepting the accolade, he proceeds—then me, then Lobsang, quietly amused with our antics.

Now Lobsang makes silent miles with me for a few hours, and I need every bit of breath to keep pace with him. My stomach is bothering me. In the early afternoon we hit the river again and I check out of our quick march. I step out on river rocks and *Om mani padme hum* on the sun-bleached boulders. Hat and glasses off, eyes closed, the mantra and the river together drill a hole beneath me, like a stone whirling round a rapid's crater, excavating without an engine.

With my eyes closed and ears effectively deafened by the river, someone could steal up to me and push me into the water. I feel vulnerable. Maybe that's why Tibetans meditate with their eyes open. To not close your eyes on this world, but to see through it. This is the view, so I try it. I open my eyes and let the river and mantra drill through the world.

When I get back on the trail, I don't know if I'm ahead of or behind the platoon. Ahead and behind seem to be my preferred positions. I'm pushing my luck a bit, playing around with getting lost, but I soon catch up with Jock, who is the caboose, and we hustle up to the rest.

Now Tenzin, Jay, Jock, a new young Sherpa, and I take an alternate route, to visit Toothpaling Gompa, overlooking the junction of the Purang's meeting with the Karnali. This proves to be the steepest drop on the narrowest trail yet.

Tenzin is a buzzing beehive of mantras, neither arrogant nor afraid, just moving and mantra-ing and not falling off. Next is the Sherpa, then me, then Jay, and finally Jock. Jay is doing much better with the edge until the new Sherpa stops in the middle of a nasty section and starts preening on one leg, shouting and shaking his sinewy torso for the heavens to behold just what a cool Sherpa boy he really is. He picks up a rock and throws it below, causing a wisp of smokelike dust, and a far-off watery crash. Jay and I look at one another.

Number one, breaking momentum on a bad spot is not cool. It becomes difficult to begin again. Panic creeps over a still body faster and more swiftly than over a moving one. Number two, never throw stones. Landslides are bad enough under the best of conditions. Jock pulls into sight and can see from our eyes we are not happy. Nor are we the least bit shy in saying why.

It turns out the gompa is locked. A novice shows up with two younger boys, both in robes. They know where the key is hidden. We unlock the gate and peruse the interior. The children irreverently blow into the monk's trumpet, making a feeble, fartlike sound. Tenzin scolds these offending sorcerer's apprentices, hissing happily at them in Tibetan. The late afternoon sun darts over a fenced-in courtyard, invading the main altar and chapel; meditation chambers twinkle in shadow. Dust motes kicked up by our intrusion sparkle in the dim chambers' light with the intensity of snow at the topmost channel of Kailash. Tenzin borrows a hefty offering from me for the altar and relocks the monastery.

The now-less-challenging route skirts the knob where the gompa sits. Below is a dust-bowl valley popping with baby Christmas trees bathed in a lavender light. Over the eastern side of the gap we can see the lower trail cutting in and out of the shadow thrown by Toothpaling's high ridge. Trekkers, probably our party, are studded all along this steeply descending brown seam. Their low road looks no less perilous than was our high road. The brash Sherpa has been ordered to the rear. We hike quietly, knowing an emergency cry could be heard across the notch. Though our two parties are helpless to assist each other, a wariness, coupled with a guarded optimism, bounces along with us, a feeling that the worst is surely over.

Coming up there's a wide delta where the rivers meet; sandy flats with boulders sticking up like raw vegetables in a dip. What a relief to be on ledgeless terrain! A yak train clambers along the river. How good to be down! We fall out and wait for our other half. Tenzin finds a comfortable spot on the cobbled terrain. Beneath a gnarled Japanese-looking pine, he crosses his legs and holding his turbaned head high, zones out. The picture is archetypal. All soft, dusty, pastel tones. Man and lone tree in desolate wilderness. I find myself wondering, "Is it my guru I see meditating under a tree?"

Lobsang marches into sight. I put a finger to my lips to protect the quiet. "How was your climb?" I ask him softly.

"Not too easy," he answers, smiling cryptically. "How was yours?"

"Not too easy," I return, suddenly enjoying, the understatement of the East.

Reunited, we hike up a ravine in the cooling shadows. Behind us, glowing from a final pool of daylight, Toothpaling Gompa reigns on a dais of rubble, our scar of descending trail the only section of the hill not dotted with brush. Flanks of gauzy mountains appear and disappear in the distant haze, all spotted with growing things that fail to obscure the sand from which they grow.

In near darkness we arrive at a government outpost. We show passports and visas; the extra photo we were instructed to bring becomes a trekking pass. We'll have a plainclothesman accompanying our party from here on. All this officialdom performed in a rustic cabin absolutely surrounded by huge marijuana plants—yaks going nuts gobbling the buds just as fast as they can munch them down.

I keep meeting up with the Karnali. Each time it's bigger, more boisterous. This afternoon Jock strips down, dives in, screams, leaps out, covers himself with a towel, and races back to his tent. We're camped, quite militarily, overlooking the river. Each tent has its own few feet of beach front. I make a bonfire a hundred yards away and smoke my socks dry.

The next day I take off on my own again, until I meet up with a train of porters. There's talk of a hot spring in the vicinity, and the thought of a steaming pool somewhere entertains me until, as quickly as booze appeared on Kailash, beauty steals up the hill-side. Escorting younger brothers, she is coltish, but unquestion-ably myth made flesh.

Skin dark and smooth as Aladdin's lamp, earth-eyed, with brown hair, her eyelids, nostrils, ears, and lips all seem to be made of a hot-poured metal, shadowed gold lurking beneath the filth of a girl in a work skirt and sweater-coat. Slightly close-set eyes, beaded, wary, yet hungry too; perfect small, dark brows flowing doelike down onto that straight, long nose all but invisible when she looks right at you. The terse, watchful mouth, curled in; the poised chin, high cheekbones. Turquoise hoops at small ears; coral beads at sweet throat. Small, nimble, standing against the hillside where I ask, with tremendous dignity. This is not the first camera lens she has looked down, as a voice in my head states: "Two hundred dollars to her parents and she's yours. For life."

That's what the white slavers pay. That's why there are entire Nepali villages with no young women in them. They're taken to Bombay and Calcutta. Because there is a whoremaster in men who must be dissolved on a daily basis.

I think this while meditating on my daughter, who is eleven. This bronze beauty is fifteen. Would I want someone buying my daughter? But it's there in my mind, even as I meet two American anthropologists hungry to speak English and barter a few supplies. I succeed in finding a way of asking about her.

Oh yes, she'll marry a family of brothers, I'm told. And have her pick of them. All children of this polyandrous family will be attributed to the eldest brother, who does the actual marrying. If she doesn't like a brother, she can refuse him. If she particularly likes a brother, she may spend a majority of time with him. But unless she wants to become a nun, this is the way it is for her.

Her brothers and she play about the field. Now she lounges like an unbrushed thoroughbred, laughing and teasing them, wait-ing for her father or my proposal of marriage. Or both.

"And where is the hot spring?"

"About three-quarters of a mile back the way you came."

"That's probably where the rest of my party is," I say, knowing I should hike back and join them. But while she's making an excuse to stay near me, I can't leave her or leave off lusting after her, this unwashed Nepali mountain girl, or lashing myself with thoughts like: "One midnight in the hot spring? I could make her parents rich!—and she could still marry a batch of brothers as they do around here."

And my selflessness? My give-and-take meditation? Transcendence of self and other? Understanding of emptiness? Where's the blade wheel? Gone! Vanished into short, longing looks thrown across a meadow of marijuana brush stinking up the sticky Himalayan air.

I don't make it to the spring that afternoon. But the following morning, right around dawn, I scamper up for a sunrise soak, and following a path through thigh-high hay, I find a hot pool nestled, womblike, among rocks. Stripping down and holding on to something quite like an olive bush, I ease myself into the blessedly steaming water, sure that there has never been such voluptuous joy.

Tantra states that a human self is a male-female in union. Strange as this sounds, it's always made sense to me. I grew up with sisters everywhere and I've always surrounded myself with women. Could Tantra be right? I wonder, happily splashing away. Might I have a visionary consort—some perfect, secret love hidden in my subconscious? My noisy appreciations surprise some local boys on their way to the fields. Waving at them, giggling to myself, I yell: "You'll hold on to beauty, won't you boys, and never let her near this gringo? Yes! Hello! Lovely hot river you have here!"

Merely a man again, delightedly scrubbing, enduring a fit of infatuation, desire separates me from my visionary consort. It's nothing new, mind you. Like a twenty-four-hour flu. If I can stay away from the source of infatuation for an entire day, I'm all right. In my mind this morning she's a cat more than a colt, my roughshod princess. Her eyes, nostrils, and lips meld into a thirty-two-petal lotus in my mind.

Lean and clean, I return to camp in fresh, cardboard-hard clothes. I will stay with the platoon today, I think. Remembering my moment closest to the north face of Kailash: being less unique and more magical!

In fact, I will almost instantly change my mind.

We plod past a flour mill on the way out of town, where the hot brook meets a cold one. The larger stream turns paddle wheels inside the shed and grinds the flour for the town. All in all the river passes through three separate sheds. The ground is strewn with white spills. Perambulating haystacks turn out to be women and children carrying grist for the mill. The women carry astounding loads. There is to be a festival today; animals will be traded and sold; races and contests, food and chang. A good thing . . . to miss. We keep walking to the high falls.

After a month on rubble, a true waterfall proves a most welcome sight. It's an actual frothing cataract, complete with spume exploding off rocks, throwing rainbows, and breeze-buffeted spray. Reluctantly marching past we hike relatively close to each other, which should be OK, but seems to combine the negatives. No substantive communication is possible, yet meditative isolation is not maintained either. Really, it is best to hike totally alone, I think. But, alone, one runs the risk of losing value in the group's eyes. The pack talks about the loner. His portfolio gets a bit shredded. It's human nature. We all do it.

We've stopped and are waiting for James. Much manure ripens fragrantly in the midday sun, and many flies light on the manure. But for these flies, suddenly sweeter still are the white arms and necks and ears of these sweet human beings flopped onto a blue tarp, covering their faces and arms and swatting.

A Sherpa runs up with news: Travelers from Simikot say all flights are canceled due to the eclipse. "Probably all of India. Maybe all Buddhist-Hindu countries." Lobsang estimates, "Maybe sound like a half day to me — eeee."

This logic is cheered. James ambles into camp and we stuff ourselves, as usual. After lunch no one can move. I'm thinking about rousing the energy to find some breeze by the stream, add a few pages to the scribbles, maybe even take a dip. Jay is stolidly carrying on conversation with Tenzin about Joe McCarthy.

"Now my mother," Tenzin remembers, happily, "had unswerving confidence in the power of the stage and felt certain that television would be the end of McCarthy. That the camera would catch him in the act—whispering with Nixon, an evil grin flickering on his face—and that the truly horrible character of the man would be conveyed to the American people, at last. That this triumph of his—this awful witch hunt—would be his undoing. In fact, she was right."

All around us children bicker with each other. Every few minutes a Sherpa will run up to them, hissing. They retreat, but no sooner does the Sherpa leave than they commence creeping back, mumbling among themselves, like jackals, drawing closer to what they want.

Leopoldo and Valerie were accosted for candy, pens, money. They did as they'd been told to do and flatly refused. Rocks were thrown at them. Leopoldo says he saw a child offering her sexual parts to him. Everywhere children beg. Nor am I in the least satisfied with our position of grimly withholding alms on the grounds that this will only encourage them to beg.

"Hungry children will always beg!" I argue, "They should beg!"

"Feed them and they'll be no getting rid of them."

"There's no getting rid of them anyway," James observes, drolly.

Richard gets up, saying something about the river. With what seems the energy it took to climb Drolma La I pull myself into a standing position and follow with notebook and pen. I aim toward the pasture wall and the river roaring enticingly beyond. Richard, despite his bum knee, is already over.

Avoiding cannabis and thistle, I climb to the top of the wall and amble along it, looking for the ideal stone upon which to descend. Now I realize how high and narrow it is, how dazed I am, how my feet have forgotten how to dance. I've strung my gambit out a step too far—and failing to rescue myself, I tumble into the road.

Two locals help me up. Where did they come from? Making unhappy sounds, they pull away the boot cuff of my leg. Yes, we see it sweating blood, not dripping, just oozing. I thank them and stand up, grateful for the tetanus shot I got in Kathmandu. Animal shit and flies are everywhere. I hobble to the river and plunge my leg into the water.

One by one we struggle to the river. With only a bad bump on the ankle, I bushwhack upstream, in need of white noise and solitude. Snaking between roots and huge boulders, around a twisting turn, I emerge into a steep tree-shadowed canyon. At the base of the canyon is the widest, fattest, most scarred tree I've ever seen, growing off a boulder the size of two buses side by side. Closer to a thousand years old than a hundred, the exposed roots are each as wide as a fifty-year oak back home. I nestle into the shadow of this colossus, like a kitten cozying up to a dinosaur. It's cool, quiet. I'm alone and happily scribbling when Jock appears, doggedly doing the explorer bit, with Richard and Jay not far behind. I feel invaded, perhaps I should move again. Then I hear the trumpet blast of Tenzin's two-tone tenor. He's traveled the easy way upstream, on the bank above, and is obviously in the process of coming down.

It's going to be a group scene, maybe even a Dharma teaching by the river. Unhappily trying to finish a page, I tunnel a little deeper into my notebook, then glance up to see Tenzin sprawled on his back with his head two inches from a boulder, a shoe under his armpit, his EMS walking stick in his hand, bent more than in half. He's shaking it—furiously delighted.

Richard is screaming, "Jesus Christ, did you see that?"

I look at Jock, who is one silent, bug-eyed dude staring at Tenzin. "I'm all right!" Tenzin blurts out, glancing up at the cliff, in shock. "If that's possible."

"What the hell was that?" Jay is demanding. "Did he just fall the whole way from up there?"

"No," Tenzin yells, rubbing his knees and shoulders. "I didn't just fall. I flipped. Then I landed on my stick and it broke my fall. Luckily. Amazingly."

I offer him some arnica from my fanny pack.

"I wouldn't know where to put it, Tad," he laughs. "I honestly don't feel hurt anywhere—maybe later, thanks," he says, accepting his other shoe and the package of Tibetan prayers he dropped during his fifteen-foot free-form fall onto a boulder-strewn riverbank. He found the one half-sandy nook in the entire canyon front.

The resilience, the luck, pluck, and unconquerable energy of this man are inexplicable. I take his stick from him, staring at it, aghast. Richard's shaking his grin back and forth in disbelief. Together we try to bend the metal back against the fulcrum of a boulder. It's getting straighter.

"Looks better!" Tenzin encourages, "More character."

Abruptly the stick breaks in half. "A little duct tape, perhaps?" Jock offers as Tenzin leads the laughter.

Unbeknownst to us, Wolfgang has turned his ankle two hundred yards downstream. More injury has happened in this last hour than in the previous twenty-five days. We're looking at one another in slight shock, trading stories, blinking our eyes, and shaking our heads.

"You see?" Tenzin muses aloud. "At the time of an eclipse everything is amplified. Tibetans say the eclipse magnifies whatever you do, good or bad, one hundred thousand times. So if you are doing mantras, they are incredibly effective, and if you are losing your balance, you are going to fall. Whereas at other moments in our life we lose our balance and catch ourselves again. So, we must be more respectful of this law of nature. In particular, I must observe it better or sacrifice this neck that I find so extremely useful." He giggles at his own mortality; I can't help but giggle with him.

Lobsang walks up, looking sheepish. "Porters not so happy," he reports. "They say we should not climb mountain during eclipse. They say we should make camp and do nothing for eclipse."

Our worn-out troop cast hopeful looks at each other's faces. "Tell them we think they are absolutely correct," Tenzin summarizes. "Let us simply get away from the stinging flies of these fields and make camp at the next decent spot. We'll mantra the whole way there, and do nothing but meditate and chant through the whole eclipse." Then, not satisfied to have a messenger impart such news, Tenzin throws a hand in the air, happily haranguing the porters. He wanders over, congratulating them in raucous tones, fist on hip, and limping slightly.

Minutes later we're mantra-ing across the stone bridge over the tumultuous river. I feel the cool, invisible bath of the river's ozone-laden spray, and nod my head in respect for the lessons imparted in its shadow. I look up the frothing, surging river to the gigantic, scarred tree at the roots of which Tenzin was thrown by the local gods of this grove in collusion with the sun and moon of this earth.

Up a short rise we spread out in a god's garden of gigantic rocks. Trees and brush with small goats bleating among huge boulders, some of which function as court and castle for flocks of birds. These squawk and flap, wondering, perhaps, if they should move their raucous celebration of the strangling of the sunlight. In the hills above and below us we can hear the banging of pans, and the ululations that will build in frequency over the next hour.

The porters have cut pinholes in cardboard. Usual chores forgotten, they're peering at the sky and chattering together more loudly than the birds. Tenzin leads us on another twenty-five yards to a large, flat rock, abutting a smaller, bridgelike arch. Taking off his day pack and unwrapping his prayer beads, he mantra-melts into a half lotus, as we, with monotone musical accompaniment, throw down our bundles and lower ourselves to the warm, bright boulder with him.

TENZIN

Slipping Free Between Realities

For the next half-hour during this eclipse, we should try to put ourselves into the most totally positive frame of mind we can, since the eclipse has this tremendous power to amplify our deeds, they say. An eclipse is a moment when the world slips between dimensions, when everything becomes possible — a quantum leap in positive evolution or a precipitous fall. The traditional Indian image for the eclipse has the sun being swallowed by the dark planet, Rahu, the all-head demon whose body was cut off by Vishnu's discus the first time he tried to swallow the sun. Again and again he gulps it down, only to have it reemerge in the sky. In the Tantric subtle physiology, the sun stands for the right channel, the moon the left, and Rahu stands for the central channel, the channel of union. So on the subtle level an eclipse is a time that evokes the entry of neural winds and spiritual drops into the central channel, enables the Tantric yogi to consciously enter the realms between death and life, to master the subtlest processes of existence.

This is an apocalyptic moment, a perfect moment to contemplate one last time the apocalyptic vehicle, the vehicle of the diamond thunderbolt, where buddhahood is achieved by quantum leap in an infinite split second of bliss-void indivisible.

The Chakrasamvara Superbliss Unexcelled Yoga Tantra mandalas, of which there are thousands of forms, are maybe the most amazing things that exist in the buddhaverse. Once you realize voidness or selflessness, what you realize is that your world is what you imagine it to be, maintained by the shared imaginative patterns of all beings. Your mind is completely intertwined with other beings' minds, so we must focus our minds all together to create a better reality. Though it is fluid and subtle, there's still an objective reality, because there are so many subjectivities other than our own.

Once you recognize that the ordinary world you habitually imagine is a mandala of inadequacy, which we are all mutually creating, you can begin to practice systematic visualizations and behaviors to create enlightened forms of self and world. So you create yourself as a buddha, as an enlightened, compassionate, and wise being. You simulate what it would feel like to feel that secure and confident and loving, in order to approach that condition for real. And you visualize others as deities with whom you interact in a perfectly ecstatic and blissful way, such that the world is made of living jewels.

We are so fortunate to have been here, to have gone around this wonderful mandala mountain, here where the mandala is always wide open. Everyone was invited in. Beings are spiritually streaming in and out all the time, particularly those who are drawn to come and go round. And of course the ultimate thing is to become Chakrasamvara Superbliss Buddha yourself, using this methodology to accelerate your own progress to buddhahood. Rather than saying, "I'm going to be bodhisattva, to become a buddha and save all beings millions of lifetimes and eons in the future," you go into another dimension, a virtual reality wherein you can accelerate the evolutionary process. And then you bring back what you realize about what it's like to be an enlightened being in an enlightened environment and you try to accelerate the development of others along with you.

As we have tasted, in Tantric visualization you dissolve your body and environment into voidness and then visualize systematically that everything around you is the measureless-mansion crystal-jewel royal palace, with offering deity attendants, and that you are the king or queen within. You develop that feeling, and then within your own body, you feel your energy currents and subtle male and female spirit-essences as if they were living, microcosmic gods and goddesses—so that there is a mandala within your body, and even your bodily processes are these miraculous great bliss exchanges between gods and goddesses.

You create these inner blissful realms by developing a stable ability to revisualize your whole embodiment and to restructure your central nervous system, condensing it down to the central channel of union. It is interesting the way mammalian biology is set up. The human mammal is so incredibly close to the realization of the blissfulness of empathy and altruism by transcending the self-centered perspective. The one moment available to all when you can open the doorway of selfless merging and melting—when even a third being can enter into the equation and conception can occur—is orgasm. The two beings temporarily have their boundaries open spiritually as well as physically, and therefore they are receptive to the entry of another soul. And that other soul comes in and rides that gene-union, bringing along its individual spiritual gene and creating itself as the third being.

What we usually don't realize is that orgasm can go much deeper than the ejaculative process. The ejaculative explosion is not the real melting bliss, it is the termination of the bliss, a kind of instinctual self-assertion that reaffirms the individual boundaries of the partners. The bliss part of it is the melting together, when the window is opened for the new being and the seeds of the melters can mingle. If there were no fear of dissolving, if the dissolving were not subconsciously experienced as a frightening death, then the bliss of merging should theoretically know no limit, there should be orgasm in navel, heart, throat, and even brain, and finally, infinite centering expansion.

But when the individual is still habituated to its sense of alienated identity, then its whole being focuses on asserting its separate self by recoiling from the event horizon of orgasmic dissolution. Then the surge of passionate bliss toward union turns to unconscious grasping, the automatic recoil into separation. That's why self-centered passion is addictive, because it isn't satisfying enough, it's always ultimately disappointing. Full satisfaction isn't addictive, because it opens out into endlessness, leaving you free of craving. Things that hint at satisfaction and then frustrate you become addictive, because you have to keep going back, hoping for better luck next time. So the Superbliss Wheel Mandala Palace of our sacred mountain is not something we have to come back to again and again, if we understand it rightly. It is a doorway to seeing the entire universe with axial centrality in every atom, feeling the bliss of male-female union in every cell, on the subtle plane of deepest reality experience.

That channel down the center of Kailash is like the yogic central channel to the crown of the phallus, one of the experience centers that can become great bliss wheels, when you can focus orgasmic energies without the dissipation of emission. When you learn to control that, then you can create the virtual body of Superbliss Buddha male-female union, in which subtle body you can go to other universes, live whole lifetimes, do five hundred lifetimes in a session of contemplation. And each time you gain the same merit and wisdom, love and compassion that normally, in coarse reality, would take a whole lifetime of achievement.

You use this virtual reality to accelerate your evolution. For the bodhisattva the motive for doing so, of course, is not that he or she is impatient personally, unwilling to spend a million lifetimes helping beings to become perfect buddhas. Rather, when bodhisattvas meditate on mother recognition and see all beings as their mother, they can't stand to make all those mother-beings wait for help. They want to accelerate all their evolutionary lifetimes into as short a span as possible, to compress them, as in a computer's compression algorithm. What the Tantras are all about is this acceleration of evolution in order to bring help to beings more effectively and more rapidly. Tantra makes evolution itself into an art form.

In all his caves, Milarepa was accelerating his evolution, experiencing millions of lives and deaths in a single lifetime. Say you have certain flaws in this life, and you figure out how they came about karmically and what merit you have to accumulate to lose that flaw. In the subtle virtual reality of Tantric practice, you can virtually die and then be reborn without that flaw. The dying dissolution process becomes the way of reshaping the qualities of your existence.

That's why Milarepa was in those caves, he wasn't just in there hiding out from humanity. He didn't want to be distracted by people interacting with his ordinary form all the time; having to go get tea and pack his bag and run around. He needed to be in the least distracting situation so that he could travel in virtual reality and experience many lives and perform good deeds all over the planet and on all planes of existence.

When we sat together at the Holy Lake, I gave you a taste of the visualization practice of the Superbliss Buddha. Normally this is esoteric, not for the uninitiated. But our circling of this sacred mountain, where the glorious Superbliss Mandala is always open, has been a kind of initiation directly from the nature buddha. And my teacher and spiritual friend His Holiness has set an example by opening up so many secrets in order to clear away suspicions and inspire the world. We are in extraordinary times, times of apocalyptic danger and revelatory opportunity. We humans hear much about the former, but all too little about the latter. Sometimes it is hard to accept how blessed and lucky we really are, how beautiful the universe can really be. Sometimes it is as necessary to liberate the imagination as it is to hone the realistic wisdom. So I have shared with you some hints of the sublime potentials you can realize in your lives.

I am going to give you one more kind of encouragement, since it did seal my own delight in this sacred journey: Something really amazing happened to me yesterday when I was meditating up in the hot sulfur spring. I was doing my usual rehearsal of the death dissolution process, letting go of the sense of subjective grasp over the experiential situation, ignoring all thoughts, imagining the eight stages of dissolution at death, mirage, smoke, fireflies, and so on. You're supposed to practice that several times a day during a retreat or if you're really serious. It's a good reminder. Suddenly the process took me over for a timeless moment, way beyond my own abilities, just probably to encourage us. At last I really felt the fire of this sacred mountain. Something, maybe the mountain, maybe the eclipse, or just the intensity of exertion, pushed me to the fire point within.

I was alone. I stripped down and rolled in the black mud, immersing myself in the hot water. I lay as if in a trance, feeling almost faint. After a while I had the urge to sit and meditate, so I gingerly clambered over the rocks to the small waterfall. I found a tolerable position on the rocks under the hot flow, entered the lotus posture, prayed to my lama, and focused my thought and breath on the central channel. My mind was empty of worries for the moment, as if on holiday. The hot water made a streaming sensation down my skull and neck and torso.

Going through the dissolving process is a sequence of experiences I go through often in imagination. This time, suddenly, I felt surrounded by a buzzing, sizzling, roaring sound, as if a gigantic rush of molten energy like a volcano was erupting within and all around. There was searing heat and yet I seemed to be in the perspective of the sacred mountain itself, neither Shiva nor Buddha, but a giant living crystal rock, aware of all of this within, yet completely free and still and cool. I felt an overwhelming surge of joyful giving toward all beings. It encompassed especially a very detailed vision of all the activities of the many beings in great mother India to the south. I had been reading Jay's copies of the

Far Eastern Economic Review in my tent at night at the end of each day, marveling at the enormous economic activity of the Asian countries. Somehow all that tremendous industry, like the buzzing of huge hives of fire bees, seemed completely connected to my flow of goodwill toward all beings. Honey of life and happiness was flowing out from my crystal mountain's flaming void. Thunderbolt energy was crackling in all directions. A roaring, seething, hissing sound exploded all around.

I felt an overwhelming appreciative love of all beings, of their indomitable energy and relentless creativity. I did not feel my usual frustrated longing for them to have success and welfare, pleasure and freedom, as I usually do when I witness the poverty and want, the suffering and servitude. It was not that I was giving anything to them. It was that I felt connected to their own deepest heart's energy that would not be denied. From the long perspective of my mountain vantage, the time required for their struggle seemed insignificant, their satisfaction already clearly inevitable. The release was feeling the fire of manifest accomplishment erupting spontaneously without my worrying or conscious effort.

Your voices, my friends, calling for me, brought me back to my precarious perch on sharp rocks in the funky, heated, steaming cave. I felt exposed, shy, as if discovered being something nonordinary, some odd natural manifestation. "Isn't it fabulous?" someone called, and my usual voice came out of the vanishing volcano. "It is really, really great! The mountain trickles forth its teaching, way down here! Such bliss!"

Now we all have the problem of returning to the world. Tomorrow we will fly to Kathmandu and then onward, home, to our beloved land of the free and home of the brave. If we have had a glimpse of the majesty of our mountain, we will not miss it in some addictive way. We will bring its blessings along with us and share them freely around the loving world. We will work within the nonduality of the extraordinary and the ordinary.

Remember the ox-herding pictures of Zen, in which the saint returns to the marketplace with open hands. The deep meditation that she perfected in solitude is now brought back into the ordinary world, the very world previously seen as the enemy of extraordinary vision, as a threat to the deep mind-well of the extraordinary. But the magic body has been attained, time and space are overcome. Now the saint returns to the marketplace, so focused in her transcendent magic that it persists, unencumbered by the unmagical world because she knows that the ordinary nests perfectly within the extraordinary.

Even though we are not Milarepa, we haven't developed the inner-heat yoga or the power of flying through the air, still we can take the word of the accomplished ones and try to simulate their goodness. We go back to New York or Chicago and find subway cars filled with nervous city dwellers. Now we can see them as a Noah's ark filled with beings who have had dealings with each other for eons and eons, always trying to escape the flood, get to their station, escape from plague, poverty, AIDS, drugs, loneliness. We've been in this subway car with them forever. Even if we're successful financially and start taking cabs, we must think about who's under the street in that subway car. We mustn't forget about them. We were with them and will be again and again, forever. Let us try to live poetically, openly, finding the amazing in the ordinary. Let's take our Kailash energy with us for the blessings of the world of beings.

Now we are entering the complete eclipse of the sun. Listen to the villagers along this ridge; they are banging on pots and pans and shouting to ward off evil spirits. Suddenly it's night and day at the same time. Let's be silent and open to nonduality as the ultimate loving tolerance of extreme cognitive dissonance. *Om mani padme hum. Om shri vajra he he ru ru kam hum phat phat, dakini jala shamvaram svaha. Om om om sarvabuddhadakiniye vajravarnaniye vajravairochaniye hum hum hum pat pat pat svaha.*

I am so happy we have succeeded in our mission. This is a wondrously auspicious event. I cannot really tell what it means, even now, though I do know we all have changed. My world is indelibly marked by this blessed mountain. There is something cataclysmic yet gentle, preserving yet transformative in the mountain and in our contact with it. I am confident that all is for the good in this world where living-jewel mountains erupt with love and joy, where they can flip us totally around and catch us gently.

As my mother used to say, in almost every conceivable situation, as a final word: "All is well!"

TAD

We fall silent as the light goes out of the day. Tenzin's talk seems like songs from a much-loved album of the mind. But this isn't a record—it's a concert. Though I wasn't even at the hot spring, still I get to hear the song that was realized there. For me this talk is "Bob Thurman's Greatest Hits" but performed live. Ruefully, I wonder if Tenzin could even have had this vision if I'd been at the spring, emoting as I usually do, talking, jangling, laughing—filling up my share of the world and then some. For once, I'm glad I wasn't where the action was; I'm glad not to have interfered.

Suddenly, I'm happy to have no question. To make no point. In this twilight that I dare not even look into, in this night-day that is the hyphen between my own death-life, I take a breath between worlds and say nothing with it. Not even a mantra. Just a full, gorgeous, empty breath. Yes, pans are clattering. Birds are preening and yakking, flapping their wings, defecating on the huge rock they've gathered on.

Neither crows nor peacocks, what are they? They're me! So full of themselves, so self-righteous and loud and proud. Recognizing them as such, I quiet myself, finally. This is what Tenzin has hoped for, I know, that I hush the storm of words. But he couldn't throttle me or argue me into silence. I had to come to it myself. At a place where there is no contest, when sun and moon are one.

Tenzin sits tight, quietly reciting mantras as the eclipse reaches full darkness. The mountain people bang and shout in the distance. Some of our group get up and look through pinholes in the cardboard. I stay put, sending out waves of new resolve through the dark silver gap between the dimensions.

CHAPTER TWENTY

Kathmandu

TAD

At the domestic airport in Kathmandu, we say good-bye to our Sherpa friends. A farewell with a hired servant who has become a friend is tricky. The handshake with Lobsang cannot say what needs to be said. As with the good-bye to my favorite driver, I'm frustrated with the linear nature of time and space separating us. Something simple and profound could be, but is not, accomplished in this farewell. The spy in me recognizes a spy in him; we've witnessed the borders of self falter and all but give way. But now—down the mountain, after the job—what can be said? It's there in Lobsang's brown-stained eyes, that slightly inhuman glance—half animal, half saint—eyes that have looked upon high-altitude life and high-altitude death, and all that's hung between. Windows on a mind that knows: "We are more than we think we are, and less."

Back in the temple-town neighborhood of Boudhanath, where we are attending an afternoon teaching by a local rinpoche, we're strolling through the dozens of Dharma-relic shops around the vast stupa. Behind us is a disappointed shopkeeper who was certain the pictogram upon which I lavished such attention was about to be purchased. We wander to the prayer wheels that line the outer walls and amble along, spinning the wheels, chipping away at what separates us, dancing the same dance.

This is an ancient Buddhist village inside an ancient city sprawling with everything, excluding nothing. Hindus are a majority in Kathmandu, but a minority here in Boudhanath. High on a ledge a monkey watches us make our way around the stupa. I make brief eye contact, becoming aware that a high being disguised as my inferior is enjoying the comedy of our situation. I make salutation to the monkey. I look at the street before me. Here, too, the Dharma dances.

At my feet brickworkers lay ancient blocks in fresh yellow sand. A couple of wrens bathe in dust. Tenzin can't resist. "We must deal with postenlightenment reality even before we're enlightened. Look at these birds bathing in dirt! What a reconciliation of dichotomies. That is exactly what bodhisattvas do when taking a bath. They can bathe in what would make others sick. The great adepts include poets like Blake, Whitman, Emily Dickinson, and the Beats. Shelley said all poets write a different part of just one poem."

The bricklayers look up, feeling our appreciation. One looks quite familiar to me, his mouth moving on an all but silent mantra. I greet him, *"Namaste,"* the commonest of Nepali greetings. He brightens but still holds to his mantra. Ten yards ahead a restaurant door opens and a grandmother shoos her children into the street happily. Tenzin remarks, "When you open the door for someone, imagine you are opening the door of liberation for them, introducing them to transcendent wisdom." Passing a street sweeper performing the universal ritual, Tenzin continues, "When we sweep, we are cleansing the environment and all our minds, purifying the whole world of its ordinary imperfection. Let's follow the example of the ancient masters of the Kadampa order, and turn all ordinary things around us in our daily lives into occasions to increase enlightenment, wisdom and compassion, freedom and happiness."

Rounding a corner, we come upon a minibazaar occupying a barren lot. Bicycles that are never ridden, but rolled hung with merchandise, stand at slight angles to the street. Pit fires smolder beneath grease-spitting meats. Incense from Dharma stores blends with the aroma of roasted goat and lamb. A butcher does his butchering on a block beside which offal lies, prey to flies and fast dogs.

That night we hold a farewell dinner in an Indian restaurant near the Yak and Yeti. We have all become good friends, yet no one seems to feel the need to affirm it overly much. We toast Kailash, Tenzin, Jock, and each other. Everyone toasts everyone. Richard reminds us of Lama Govinda's beautiful statement about the brotherhood and sisterhood of those who have circled the sacred mountain. He then shares as a final toast his grandmother's greatest saying, as his special gift to us all, her own great teaching of the Dharma, about how to live in the immediacy of the infinite moment. "If you ever get to it, and then don't do it, may you never get to it to do it again!" The next morning I see everyone off, one by one, cherishing the one more week I have alone in this, my first Asian city—all by myself—to test run the new Tad Wise.

I return to the Kailash guest house and enroll in what remains of Chokyi Nyima's seminar. Toward the end of the week a catlike character, who will lead me through the very last maze of my journey, catches my attention.

I first see Damon arrive at class late one afternoon in the large lecture hall of Chokyi Nyima's monastery, hurriedly do his prostrations, and settle against the wall. The next morning after my walking meditation around the stupa I stop into the Pilgrim's Tour for coffee and curds and encounter him holding forth, effortlessly filling the room. Of medium height, dark-haired, with thick brows beneath which brown lynx-eyes flash, he is disconcertingly familiar until I realize—of course—he reminds me of myself! A long-lost little brother from some Shakespearean comedy set in the Far East.

His name is the word Yeats used to describe the higher self, who looks upon our daily doings with compassion mixed with not a small measure of impatience. Damon is the local monastery rat. He's been here nine months and has studied with most of the teachers. I've been romantically reunited with my guitar. He's impressed with me as a troubadour. I am impressed with his grabbing monks by the shoulders and smashing their foreheads into mine. This beats shaking hands by a lightyear or two.

Damon encourages me to take refuge with Chokyi Nyima. After the lecture that afternoon, the rinpoche invites "anyone who wishes to take refuge to remain afterwards." Damon and I exchange glances. He leaves, I stay.

Chokyi Nyima sits on his ornate throne and assures a dozen or so of us: "If you don't study the Dharma in this life you will study it in another." I repeat the rinpoche's chant of devotion to the three jewels. The Buddha, the Dharma, and the Sangha. I make prostrations. This is good, a raft in a swirling sea. He ties a thick red thread around my neck, muttering a prayer with an infectious smile. Next I register with the Swiss secretary, who fills in a Sanskrit name meaning "seeker of wisdom" on a certificate bearing the monastery's seal. Though he doesn't know my name means "a bit wise," a continuity runs through West to East. I ask him if I might have a private word with Chokyi Nyima.

At the sight of the rinpoche, I put my hands together and bow my head. He happily waves me forward. I explain that I came to walk around Mt. Kailash with a famous teacher, Robert Thurman. "We have some of this on trip." I gesture fist against fist. "Now I must write about it. Should I say what happened, should I criticize him? Today I am a member of the Sangha, and Robert Thurman is my teacher—I must honor and thank him. My problem was: how to do both."

"You may criticize him," Chokyi Nyima says, pleased and nodding, "but you must do it with love."

I fast all day after taking refuge, and that night I awake ravenous in blackness. I find a light and tear my pack apart, finding nothing to eat but some beef jerky Jock gave me ten days before. "Can't eat meat on the day you take refuge," I say aloud, while ransacking the desk, checking the bureau top and the closet shelf, even checking under the bed to make sure some provisions haven't slid there. Nothing. In the end I eat the jerky, all of it. A Westerner would say the meat was spoiled. An Easterner would say I should have been fasting. They're both right. Result? By dawn I'm croaking at the toilet bowl.

Forty-eight hours of isolation later I take the cushion from my room's one chair and sit cross-legged on the dawnlit rooftop of Kailash Guest House as off-tune trumpets flatly drone the "come to order" and "clear the mind" signals from half a dozen monasteries. Through dimmed eyes I see the oily crows sliding past like feathered puppets on monofilament lines. I hear the monks chanting in yards in front and behind me, and the pretty young girl who cleans my room giggling at me while hanging out the laundry in her dirty pink dress. Through it all my eyes remain half dimmed. All else springs from this dimmed view. On Yeats's tomb is carved, "Cast a cold eye, on life, on death."

I concentrate on a terra-cotta tile at the lip of the barrier skirting the roof. Crows land near it, the cleaning girl saunters past it, cows being led to pasture moo below it, the green hills dance over it, a jet plane etches the sky above it. A burro hee-haws in angry protest unseen on the road, its master shouts bitterly back, a dog barks at the shouting, a child shouts at the dog. The sky lightens from pink-gray to pink-blue as an all-but-choked fire sputters again to flame. All this is not the terra-cotta tile at the roof edge, but all this impinges on the tile, or my view of it. So I let it impinge and then I let it all go. Clear the view!

I succeed and fall off, and succeed and fall off, like manning the rudder in high seas. For entire seconds on end clarity is attained. Between thoughts of seducing the cleaning girl and throwing rocks at the burro, shaving my head and joining the monks, renewing my ticket and getting on the jet-plane. For entire seconds on end I view the terra-cotta tile stripped of these impingements.

Envisioning His Holiness the Dalai Lama smiling on this brave beginning, I pick myself and my cushion up and prepare for rounding the stupa with 108 mantras on this already well-begun, meritorious day.

I find Damon at the Pilgrim's Tour but forgo the usual litany of caffeine, sugar, starch, Dharma-chat, girl-watching, stupa-life for Dharma bums. A sweet retarded girl who is often nearby visits our table. Damon motions the boy at the counter to bring her a hard roll and coffee. She tries to thank Damon by draping him with a necklace of marigold blossoms sewn together. He stops her, saying, "No, Tad is buying you breakfast. He needs the flowers." So she garlands me with the marigold necklace and a full loving smile. As we leave we meet the sandal-handed man, who prostrates round the stupa every day of every year. Damon makes a loud noise and kneels before the leather-clad one.

"Dalai Lama make big fuss over sandal man when His Holiness visit," Damon says in the pidgin English we all speak eventually. "Makes big kiss on his head. We all cry for joy!" At these words tears leap to my eyes and I find myself hanging the marigold blossoms on the sandal man. We purr around each other like happy lions.

Later in the morning I give a huge hunk of stained Tibetan turquoise to the abbot of Dilgo Khyentse Rinpoche's monastery. Damon said the tainted stone might be dangerous to a layperson. Dilgo Khyentse was the main Nyingma tutor of the present Dalai Lama—and was informally recognized as a living buddha.

The abbot hefts the stone, smiling at me and smirking at Damon, making up his mind. Next thing I know we're summoned into a shrine room in which the skull of Dilgo Khyentse resides in a large thronelike box. Although the much-loved leader died less than a decade ago, legends concerning this skull are many. Some say it wouldn't burn in the funeral pyre. His Holiness writes in his autobiography of viewing the skull of his teacher and recognizing the marks of a buddha on it. Also in this room is a guru rinpoche statue, the contents of which were revealed from behind a wall at Samyey. We prostrate before these and then mantra and meditate before them.

The abbot roots through a drawer and removes two tiny packages of folded newspaper that look like grams of coke, circa 1979. He gives each of us one. Damon places it to his third eye; I do the same. "This is salt that cured the body of Dilgo Khyentse," he whispers. "Put it on your altar." I neglect to tell him I have no altar. Next a grubby bottle is found, some drops splashed in Damon's hand. He levers the brown mess into his mouth and licks his unwashed hand. "No booze," he assures me. It's called *mindrip* and it's a blessed medicinal drink. I repeat the procedure exactly, which is a desperate act of faith, having just been deliriously ill.

Damon helped me set up an appointment with Boudha's fortune-telling mirror man, who is a son of the famous magician Lhawa Wangchuk. The son has inherited his father's three circular mirrors, through which he maintains a Tantric oracle. Appropriately enough, the inheritor is given to drink, which is why appointments are made in advance through his wife. Reputedly the shaman stops drinking, does purifications, and then consults the oracle.

A drunken magician! Perfect. I've contributed a few days of sobriety to a Tantric master—which is a contradiction in terms, I know. Tantra does not recognize the word "sober." Everything is beyond belief always.

Damon explains my presence to the mirror man as I prostrate myself before his altar. We hum our languages, I say the Tibetan *"Tashe dela,"* as well as "Namaste," meaning literally: "The divine being in me recognizes the divine being in you." His wife enters the room, we bow and smile before she kneels beside a low writing table. Damon and I are invited to sit in chairs as the oracle-keeper settles into a half lotus on a minithrone before the mirrors.

The wife asks, "What are your questions?"

I ask one. The wife translates. The shaman starts mumbling at the mirrors and throws rice in the air as an offering. He sits in silence half a minute, then in low gravelly tones barks out three- and four-word clumps of Tibetan. She transcribes.

I am asked for another question. Same deal.

I ask about the other woman.

I ask about Cynthia.

I ask about my children.

Finally the seated scribe translates the answers.

The other woman? "They say, you and she were dancers in Shoba heaven. Pure land. But no—you don't marry in this life. Sometimes dance is sexy. But more you should do together—" and she describes a theatrical tradition that reenacts teachings of the Buddha.

And Cynthia? The Christian mother to my newborn? Do we marry or break? "You marry, for Christian and Buddhist go same place. End same place. You stay with her, make family."

One by one my questions are answered. I place a donation on the altar, which the mirror man doesn't look at. Then I approach him with a ceremonial scarf, I bow and place it around his shoulders, slightly embarrassed. He laughs, looks at it, adjusts it once, then takes it off and puts it on my shoulders, laughing and bowing to me. He tells his wife something.

"He says you come back in an hour and he will have something for you and your daughter. He says you should stay close to Milarepa and find a yogi to study with—a Tantra master like my husband."

"Not a monk?"

Damon translates. Master answers. Wife laughs, interpreting:

"He says better to have woman in your practice. Hand cannot clap against air; needs other hand. Therefore better you study with yogi than monk."

All in all it's strange, bittersweet news. After goodbyes we head back down the weaving alleyways, past Chokyi Nyima's monastery. At the corner a beggar accosts me.

"Yes, yes! This is a good day for you!" Damon laughs, greeting the thin, darkly bearded beggar like an old friend. "Give him money, Tad." Shaking my head at the arrogance of this brash boy, I dig in my khakis and put change in the beggar's hand. The beggar starts bowing and nodding.

"No, no! Give him more than that! Twice that."

I flinch a little, but a bill appears in my hand and is transferred into the beggar's hand. The beggar has started singing to the heavens in gratitude, waving his stick like a sorcerer's wand.

"Now give him the shawl."

"What?"

"You heard me."

"Are you crazy? The mirror man gave it back to me after I blessed him with it—this is a very special shawl."

"Exactly why you must give it to the beggar," Damon explains, smiling hard and having much fun at my expense.

"Damon!" I hiss, pressing my lips together, and cocking my head diagonally. "I don't want to give him my shawl."

At this he stands close enough to kiss me and whispers: "Yes, you do, Tad."

I heave a great pissed-off sigh and then I give the beggar the shawl. In fact, I drape it ceremoniously over his shoulders, straightening it, carefully, as a small section of the street goes still, everyone silently watching.

The beggar is casting amazed looks at his shoulders, he doesn't seem to understand totally. He peers at me, unsure if I'm a ghost. He smiles, deciding I'm not. His hands adjust the scarf, his shoulders rise up tall, a proud stick marking time, as off he strides, deep in conversation with the new regal being he has awoken within.

"One lucky beggar," I remark as he turns and shakes his stick at me, happily apologizing for the drunkenness my generosity has caused him.

"Come on, Tad—you've got to pack. And there's something I've got back for you in my room. I'll meet you at your place in fifteen minutes."

Packing is easy. Damon returns with a printed teaching he's having an amulet case made for across the street. He's brought a small corked bottle and accepts Manasarovar water in it. I give him my spare tape recorder. He's ecstatic and promises to be my pack animal all the way to the gates of Boudhanath. Hurrying down the steps to retrieve the amulet from a neighboring shop, Damon bellows my name from the bottom of the stairs.

"Tad, get down here quick!"

I take the stairs two leaps to each landing, in eight steps I'm at the bottom, where the maid and landlady stand with laundry baskets in their hands and curious looks on their faces. I follow Damon's eyes into the shadow of the courtyard, and there, in a pool of darkness, kneels the beggar, bowing forward at the sight of me, mumbling praise with the sweetest, shyest, most loving eyes I have ever seen. As I step forward his humming becomes louder. He takes the shawl from off his shoulders and, holding it aloft, chants reverently.

Unable to speak, I kneel, and he ladles the silk over my neck, arranging it on my shoulders, mumbling honeyed words of praise. My hands still his hands, our eyes meet and melt. I put my forehead to his forehead and buzz a word, laughing and crying, which he buzzes back. *"Nam-as-teeeee . . ."* I drone. *"Na-ma-steeeee . . ."* he drones.

Never happier.

About the Authors

Robert "Tenzin" Thurman is the acclaimed translator of many Tibetan texts, such as the *Essence of Eloquence* and *The Tibetan Book of the Dead*, and the author of many books, such as *The Central Philosophy of Tibet*, *Wisdom and Compassion: The Sacred Art of Tibet*, and *Inner Revolution*. He is the Jey Tsong Khapa Professor of Indo-Tibetan Buddhist Studies in the Department of Religion of Columbia University and director of its Center for Buddhist Studies, and cofounder and President of Tibet House New York. He is a close friend of H. H. The Dalai Lama, and one of the most visible and respected Buddhist scholars and thinkers in the world.

Tad Wise is the author of the novel *Tesla*. He is also an actor, singer/songwriter, English teacher, journalist, stone mason, and father of three.

Refuge Visualization -- P. 59, 72

Milarepas Tummo - 77

Another Viz - Good but Long P. 277